DEINSTITUTIONALIZATION
and the Welfare State

DEINSTITUTIONALIZATION
and the Welfare State

PAUL LERMAN

RUTGERS UNIVERSITY PRESS

NEW BRUNSWICK

NEW JERSEY

Library of Congress Cataloging in Publication Data

Lerman, Paul, 1926–
    Deinstitutionalization and the welfare state.

    Bibliography: p.
    Includes index.
    1. United States—Social policy.
2. Institutional care—United States.
I. Title.
HV95.L46   361.6′8   81–5909
ISBN 0–8135–0934–3   AACR2

To Morgan's People

Contents

Tables

Preface

In September 1976, I began work on an eighteen-month research contract for the Division of Special Mental Health Programs of the National Institute of Mental Health (Contract no. 278–76–0087 [SM]). The purpose of the research was to review and analyze documentary and published materials on social control and treatment issues involved in deinstitutionalization. Even though I initially knew very little about the fields of mental health, retardation, aging, and child welfare, responsible officials reasoned that I might offer fresh insights gained from my previous work in juvenile corrections. Because I seriously underestimated the time needed to discover, digest, and assess published and documentary materials, my final report was not completed until September 1978. A sharply reduced version of this final report was prepared in 1979 and published as a government monograph in 1981. This book constitutes a substantial expansion and rewriting of the monograph.

The interested reader will readily discover that the government monograph contains only about one-third of the information and analyses found in the present work. The most substantial additions include: a historical perspective of the multiple societal welfare functions provided by specific institutions and the total institutional system, within and across time periods (Chapter 2); a new section describing and explaining the utilization of institutions by juveniles in the fields of child welfare, corrections, and mental health, including a fifty-year trend analysis (Chapters 7 and 8); a major analysis of the welfare policies associated with the promotion and impedance of deinstitutionalization efforts (Chapters 9 and 10); and a more reflective final chapter, offering greater breadth and scope to the summary and conclusion.

Besides these distinct and extensive additions, I thoroughly revised the provisional explanation of the origins of deinstitutionalization in mental health (Chapter 6). This was done to take advantage of research undertaken after completion of the government monograph. In summary, the content of six of the present eleven chapters is different from that of the government publications. Rather than a padded expansion of the monograph, the book offers a more complete and uninhibited analysis of materials and documents I deemed pertinent.

This work is organized around a different conception of the societal and historical meaning of deinstitutionalization trends and issues. As a result, it encompasses a much broader perspective than the mandate associated with the original research contract and government monograph. In preparing the book I felt much freer to speculate intellectually about and connect historical patterns of institutional utilization with the emergence and expansion of the American version of the welfare state.

In the United States, public welfare—broadly conceived—has always been associated with both "indoor" and "outdoor" relief. As a matter of historical fact, outdoor relief (or its modern counterpart, income-maintenance programs) cannot be understood as a policy concept without reference to the various institutions associated with indoor relief (i.e., almshouses, insane asylums, dependent and neglected facilities, workhouses, etc.). Because the benefits of food, shelter, care, or treatment can be delivered indoors or out, public welfare has always had the potential to provide a varied and changing balance of subsidized benefits and social controls. This fact was understood by nineteenth-century reformers and officials, and even by the pre-1930 elite leadership of charities and corrections. The privately based, dominant leadership of charities and corrections in the pre-Depression era consistently favored indoor relief, and, therefore, institutionalization, over publicly subsidized outdoor relief. Only private organizations could be trusted to provide temporary relief assistance in the home.

Besides an antipathy to providing the "dependent classes" with relief and care in their own homes (or in those of relatives), many of these elite leaders (from about 1880 to 1930) also shared a conviction that institutional "inmates" were representatives of the "defective classes," and, therefore, constituted a danger to the genetic "stock" of America. America's proinstitutional policies were buttressed by the belief that the "dangerous classes" consisted of not only criminals and delinquents, but also the "dependent and defective" classes.

Deinstitutionalization policies required, therefore, changes in the beliefs undergirding public welfare policies. Whereas these beliefs were under attack prior to the 1930s, America's Great Depression helped undermine the beliefs about the dependent and defective classes, and fostered a home-based relief and care policy. These changes in belief alone cannot account for the onset of deinstitutionalization, but the depopulation of mental hospitals cannot be fully comprehended without linking this policy change to the emergence and expansion of the Social Security Act of 1935. By expanding on these insights, this book helps explain why welfare funds—not mental health, retardation, and other targeted resources—provided the fiscal foundation for diminished reliance on traditional institutions.

Although some readers may believe that a professor of social work has a vested interest in emphasizing a welfare perspective, I believe that the empirical data and analyses will obviate a premature categorization of my beliefs and assumptions. As a matter of record, I did not begin with this welfare perspective. Rather, many analysts of trends and issues persistently referred to the importance of federal welfare funds; some even insisted that these funds provided an incentive to shift state welfare costs onto the federal budget. As a result, I had to reeducate myself about the various titles in the Social Security Act, including the timing and wording of amendments and regulatory shifts. To assist my readers, I have tried to be detailed and precise about the exact titles and sections of the

Social Security Act (as amended) used by state leaders interested in promoting the depopulation of traditional state institutions. If I seem repetitious at times, it is because I know how easy it is to forget the welfare titles discussed in Chapters 6 and 8 when assessing impediments to deinstitutionalization in Chapters 10 and 11.

Whereas other authors have noted the reliance on welfare programs for former and potential institutional residents, none has explicitly analyzed the intimate historical relationship between indoor and outdoor public welfare policies. This work differs from earlier analyses in other ways, such as the interpretations it presents of institutional trends and policy debates. But the most novel difference is probably its study of how the emergence and expansion of the welfare state is linked to accompanying changes in conceptions about the dangerousness of mentally ill or retarded persons, shifts in treatment modalities and technologies, and the growing preference for proprietary medical and welfare organizations. These post-1930 welfare and nonwelfare developments are assessed for their relative ability to make sense out of the descriptive trend data referring to the onset of deinstitutionalization, acceleration of depopulation trends, interstate differences, and age variations.

To understand and interpret trends and issues in diverse social problem fields, I had to locate and master the facts in a great number of disparate documents. My research assistant for the contract period of eighteen months was enormously helpful. Dr. Norma Weiss not only assisted in finding obscure and fugitive documents, but also helped make intellectual sense out of the vast array of historical and current materials.

State officials in Pennsylvania, Massachusetts, Minnesota, and California were very helpful in sharing many informative reports prepared by, or on behalf of, their state agencies. They were also quite gracious in arranging site visits to traditional and nontraditional institutions and programs. Although I cite few personal observations in the text, these contacts with actual places, persons, and local officials and administrators sensitized me to concerns peculiar to each problem area. A variety of federal officials were also cooperative in providing information or recent reports. Of course, none of the helpful state or federal officials bears any responsibility for the manner in which I understood and interpreted data or documents.

Any implicit or explicit judgments or criticisms of policies are not designed to embarrass specific persons. I am interested in emphasizing differences of ideas, interpretations, and value judgments rather than personal disagreements. I hope that the organization, content, and style of the ensuing chapters support this type of analytical intellectual discourse.

I am particularly pleased to acknowledge the amazing accuracy of my secretary, Barbara Molnar, in decoding hundreds of written pages and transforming them into a legible manuscript. In addition to scoring high marks for fidelity of linguistic translation, Barbara also typed quickly and handled numerous changes with equanimity. There are others who also helped, although their role was less direct. Three retarded adolescents, recently released from an institution, revealed a spontaneous appreciation of living in a freer environment. Their reactions demonstrated the personal, human meaning of the least restrictive doctrine. It is also difficult to forget a mother nursing her cephalic baby in a suburban community residence for developmentally disabled children, and sharing a portion of her pleasure of being with her child when she—rather than an institution—directed. Besides these personalized expressions of new and nontraditional modes of offering help, I also recall the stark contrast between drugged and undrugged former mental hospital patients—the former moving about their community residence like zombies, and the latter eating and behaving as if they were free-moving residents of a local hotel. Such varied images are certainly not representative of de-institutionalization alternatives; however, these vivid cases of ex-inmates reminded me that shifts in policies did indeed have human consequences. It is not necessarily sentimental to believe that living under the least restrictive physical, social, environmental, and chemical conditions can be valued for reasons other than fiscal or treatment efficacy.

During the writing stage, when intellectual sparks and apt words were not readily forthcoming, I also benefited from the good humor and companionship of family and friends. Because my dog, Morgan, is also part of this expressive network, I often refer to this loose collectivity as "Morgan's people." I could always count on one of Morgan's people to help restore my intellectual energy by enticing me into a game of ping-pong, a discussion about ERA, an evening cocktail, or a ski holiday. If none of his people were around, I could always count on Morgan to take me for a much-needed walk around the block.

DEINSTITUTIONALIZATION
and the Welfare State

1 Introduction

During the past decade a great deal of attention has been devoted to analyzing and discussing problems associated with the deinstitutionalization of residents of state-administered facilities. The diverse body of literature represented by the key term *deinstitutionalization* (hereafter referred to as "DE"), is now quite large and continues to grow. Among the authors cited in a bibliographic list are federal and state legislators and investigative staff, state and federal judges, government officials, researchers and consultants, union-sponsored writers, human-service professionals, university professors, and journalists. Getting "on top" of such a literature is a complex task, not only because of the array of bibliographic sources, viewpoints, and idiosyncratic styles of reporting, but also because the literature tends to be sharply compartmentalized by each author's concentration on only one social field. Authors of mental illness trends and issues tend to be unaware of the phenomena occurring in the field of the retarded, just as writers about juvenile status offenders tend to be ignorant of the trends and issues involved in caring for the aged outside of their own homes.

This study deliberately pursues a multiproblem, rather than a unitary, line of inquiry. This broad focus is the major difference between this and previous studies. The purposes of this approach are twofold. First, it can provide fresh insights into trends often perceived as pertaining to only one social problem area. Second, it can provide the breadth necessary to understand general social-policy issues—issues that cut across particular fields or interests.

In order to delimit this dual set of purposes, the following chapters deal primarily with trends and issues associated with reducing the use of traditional institutions and with the emergence of residential alternatives. Chapters 8 and 9 are devoted to juveniles. Otherwise, the data analysis and discussion tend to center on adults and the fields of mental illness, mental retardation, and aging.

Operational, Normative, and Analytic Meanings of Deinstitutionalization

Any serious analysis must first define the focus and boundaries of the study. This is particularly necessary in understanding DE. Although it is difficult to find many definitions in the vast literature, an operational definition can be inferred by observing the way the term has actually been used in the literature. In addition

1

to the operational meaning, one can find the normative meaning—explicit definitions that stress the strivings, intentions, ideal goals, and desirable outcomes
sought by authors of reports and articles. Ideal goals can also be found in recent
judicial decisions and statutes. A third definition can be framed from a more historically reliable and valid understanding of the meaning of "institutions"; we
can then create an analytic definition that is less reliant on institutional usage.

To highlight the importance of making these distinctions among meanings of
DE, we can review the normative meaning offered by the General Accounting
Office in a recent survey of DE problems and issues. According to the GAO
report, DE

> can be defined as the process of 1) preventing both unnecessary admission to and
> retention in institutions; 2) finding and developing appropriate alternatives in the
> community for housing, treatment, training, education, and rehabilitation of the
> mentally disabled who do not need to be in institutions, and 3) improving conditions,
> care, and treatment for those who need institutional care. This approach is based on
> the principle that mentally disabled persons are entitled to live in the least restrictive
> environment necessary and lead their lives as normally and independently as they
> can. [GAO, 7 January 1977, p. 1]

The GAO report concludes that there are federal and state shortcomings in
providing DE leadership, and states forthrightly that the multifaceted ideal process is occurring in very few places. In effect, the authors of the GAO report
argue that DE, defined normatively, is not actually occurring. But they do not
really believe that DE as an operational phenomenon is absent. In fact, the GAO
offers evidence that DE is occurring in the fields of mental illness and retardation. The evidence is similar to other official reports; it relies on operationally
utilizing reductions in the daily census counts of publicly sponsored institutions
(see U.S. Senate Subcommittee on Long-Term Care 1974; Kramer 1977; and
Bachrach 1976).

The reduced residential population of public institutions on a census day has
become, in practice, the operational definition of DE. However, one-day or even
daily average census counts are incomplete indicators of institutional use, because this statistic does not include annual admissions and the turnover of institutional beds. As a matter of historical fact, annual admissions to state and county
mental hospitals consistently increased from 1955 to 1972; this was a period
when residential counts were going down, and DE was asserted to be occurring in the mental health field (Kramer 1977, p. 78). Whereas admissions to
state/county mental hospitals finally peaked in 1972, the number of residents on
a census day peaked seventeen years earlier in 1955. It is readily apparent that if
admissions figures rather than resident counts had been employed, 1955—the
starting date of DE most frequently cited in this problem field—could not have
been used.

In addition to the incomplete image conveyed by one-day resident counts, it can be misleading to focus entirely on public institutions. If private mental institutions, rather than state/county facilities, had been used as the sole legitimate locus for gathering DE evidence, then the global inferences about this phenomenon would have had to be modified. Private mental hospitals have not reduced their resident counts or their admissions. From 1968 to 1975, the number of private admissions increased by about 34 percent, and the one-day counts demonstrated a 10-percent increase (National Institute of Mental Health, Series A, no. 18, 1977, p. 1).

If the limits of DE's operational and normative meanings are recognized, it is possible to formulate a definition that will remain reliable and valid. Both private and public institutions for the mentally ill and retarded (as well as paupers, delinquents, and other groups) have been recognized by historians and census statisticians since the nineteenth century (Rothman 1971; Wolfensberger 1976; U.S. Bureau of the Census 1883). Analytically, a broad view of DE would refer primarily to reduced reliance on these traditional institutions, which are well known, and whose residents have been counted by the U.S. Bureau of the Census every ten years since 1850, with varying degrees of accuracy.

Distinguishing Traditional and Nontraditional Institutions

Historically, distinguishing traditional from nontraditional institutions began in the 1930s when the United States began developing a welfare state. It is my contention that the reduced utilization of these traditional institutions comes closest to the meaning implicit in the operational definition of the term. DE advocates in the fields of mental illness and retardation, child welfare, and juvenile delinquency usually refer to "community-based" alternatives to traditional institutions, even though many of these alternatives could fulfill the technical definition of an institution.

Although they are nontraditional, many of these alternatives are, in fact, types of institutional facilities. They are nontraditional not only because they emerged primarily after 1930, but also because public discussions and modern terminology often refer to a 200-bed home for the aged or a 100-bed residential treatment center for disturbed youth as a "community," not an "institutional," residential facility. At a minimum, therefore, DE refers to reduced reliance on traditional institutional facilities.

Traditional institutions include all those facilities usually set aside for the care and custody of dependent and delinquent persons. Sites for census counting include such public and private places as mental hospitals, juvenile detention homes, reformatories and training schools, local and county jails, state prisons, institutional homes for the dependent and neglected, schools for the mentally retarded, and almshouses. Aside from the almshouses (which went out of fashion after the 1930s), these types of traditional institutions are cited in the censuses of

1950, 1960, and 1970, and offer evidence regarding DE trends. The above three censuses also include some newer, nontraditional institutional types like nursing homes and residential treatment centers for children, but these post-1930 facilities can be separated from trends of traditional facilities.

This analytic, descriptive approach to DE trends is not designed to replace a normative definition. I use it to obtain an accurate depiction of traditional institutional usage. Whether or not alternatives to the traditional facilities are indeed "less restrictive" or more "normal" in practice is, of course, an empirical question. The intent is not to minimize the question, but to make certain that maintaining the distinction between the ideal and the actual can help to answer it.

Major Analytic Perspectives

Although clarifying the multiple meanings of DE is a necessary starting point for this study, other analytic perspectives were also employed. Besides pursuing comparative and general social policy purposes, this study offers a combination of analytic perspectives applied in the final stages of sifting, reading, thinking, and writing about a multitude of official documents, unpublished reports, articles, and books. While one or more of the perspectives may be found in some of the existing literature, the combination proposed appears to be unique, particularly for analysis of the comparative and social policy uses of community residential facilities. These perspectives are as follows:

1. Deinstitutionalization has multiple meanings.
2. As alternatives to traditional institutions, community residential facilities can be perceived as new types of institutions.
3. These new types of institutions, besides potentially offering medical, personal, or social care services, can also provide new sources of unofficial, publicly subsidized supervision and social control.
4. Because the majority of community residential facilities for adults are proprietary (i.e., operated for profit), these new business organizations and interests have a stake in influencing public policies regarding many aspects of DE.
5. The alternative community residential facilities have been heavily subsidized by funds associated with the welfare state, particularly those sections of the original and amended Social Security Act.
6. The reduction in daily residential populations of state institutions has often been an expedient measure—rather than a result of national or state legislation or rational planning of the allocation of resources necessary to support the deinstitutionalization effort.

The remainder of this introduction will discuss my reasons for choosing these perspectives to understand and analyze data, trends, and issues. In the process of describing these approaches to the materials, major elements of this study will also be presented.

Distinguishing Residential and Institutional Occupancies

It is generally understood that community-based placement of traditional institutional residents does not just refer to normal residential occupancies, that is, places where families and foster families reside. Rather, the new living arrangements include such nontraditional occupancies as skilled nursing homes, intermediate care facilities, domiciliary and personal care homes, group homes, shelter care homes, board-and-care homes, and residential treatment centers. How we conceptualize these post-1930 living arrangements can influence our assessment of the progress toward realizing the ideal goals of normalized living in the least restrictive environments, as set forth in the GAO definition cited earlier.

A useful point of departure is to understand the distinctions among various types of residential occupancies and to ascertain the criteria used for making these distinctions. It will then be possible to provide a definition of "institution" that will permit comparisons between the traditional and nontraditional types. Our discussion will be based on criteria employing Life Safety Code standards, minimal medical and social functions, minimum size, and nonfamilial relationships.

Life safety standards, set forth by the National Fire Protection Association (NFPA), provide a convenient starting point for a number of reasons: (1) public statutes and regulations require the use of Life Safety Code standards for some community residential facilities (see, for example, sect. 1861 [j] [13] of the Social Security Act); (2) community residential facilities must often meet state and local fire safety codes that are based on the Life Safety Code, even if federal laws and regulations do not require their level of physical safety; (3) the physical structure of a building can often influence its social uses; and (4) the standards provide a significant indicator of societal consensus regarding a "normal residential occupancy" versus all other living arrangements.

Residential occupancies are buildings where "sleeping accommodations are provided for normal residential purposes," except buildings classified as "institutional occupancies." Normal residential occupancies include: one- and two-family dwellings, lodging or rooming houses, dormitories, apartment buildings, and hotels. For our purposes, it is important to note that according to the code, one- and two-family dwellings are still considered normal, even if rooms are rented to nonfamily outsiders—but only if accommodating no more than three outside persons (NFPA 1975, pp. 101–36).

Institutional occupancies, besides providing sleeping and boarding facilities for four or more outside persons, are also "occupied by persons who are mostly incapable of self-preservation because of age, physical or mental disability, or because of security measures not under the occupant's control" (Ibid., pp. 101–11). This occupancy includes the following groups: (1) Health-care facilities—hospitals and nursing homes; (2) Residential-custodial care—nurseries, homes for the aged, and homes for the mentally retarded; and (3) Residential-restrained care—penal institutions, reformatories, and jails.

Medical and Nonmedical Community Residential Facilities

Federal statutes and regulations now specify that all health-care facilities certified by Medicare and Medicaid are required to meet the 1973 Life Safety Code
standards. In addition to using life safety standards associated with institutional
occupancies, nursing homes are also expected to provide activities beyond room
and board. Skilled nursing homes provide medical-type functions. There are
other functions that a Medicaid-certified intermediate care facility—a type of
nursing home—can provide. The definition for this type of health-care facility is
based on a broad criterion that can bridge the gap between medical and nonmedical institutional uses. Section 1905 of the Social Security Act defines this type of
facility as follows:

> For purposes of this title the term "intermediate care facility" means an institution
> which is licensed under state law to provide, on a regular basis, health-related care
> and services to individuals who do not require the degree of care and treatment
> which a hospital or skilled nursing facility is designed to provide, but who because of
> their mental or physical condition require care and services (above the level of room
> and board) which can be made available to them only through institutional facilities.
> [U.S. Senate Committee on Finance, 30 April 1978, p. 534]

The types of health-related care and services that can be provided in a state-
licensed intermediate care facility (ICF) can vary. Usually they include assistance in dressing, grooming, eating, bathing, toileting, and other personal activities. However, similar care and services can also be provided in residential
facilities not licensed as an ICF. These nonmedical residential facilities house
many persons who are aged, blind, or permanently and totally disabled, and who
are eligible for Supplementary Security Income (SSI), a type of welfare assistance. SSI regulations have recently included a definition that determines whether
SSI recipients are residing in an institution. Definitional criteria include: a minimum size that agrees with the Life Safety Code; a "beyond room and board"
level of services that agrees with the conception underlying the intermediate care
facility; an unspecified level of treatment and services not necessarily related to
health care; and a nonfamilial relationship between the proprietor and the residents that agrees with a customary Census Bureau distinction among types of
households. The complete definition is as follows: "An 'institution' is an establishment which furnishes (in single or multiple facilities) food and shelter to four
or more persons unrelated to the proprietor and, in addition, provides some treatment or services which meet some need beyond the basic provision of food and
shelter." (U.S. Office of Federal Register, April 1978, pt. 416.231 [46]).

This definition could be construed narrowly or broadly, depending on the further specification of the term "treatment or services." "Treatment" could be defined broadly to include not only guidance, counseling, and therapy, but also socialization, skills training, and general habilitation activities associated with the
field of mental retardation. "Services" could be conceived even more broadly

in that anything done for, or on behalf of, another person could be deemed a service. The breadth of potential activities "beyond the provision of food and shelter" is illustrated by a licensing code for residential and day-care facilities recently passed by the State of California. The 1973 statute defined "basic services" as including the following: "Personal care, protection, supervision, assistance, guidance or training; planned activities; food service; and incidental medical and dental care" (State of California Department of Health, 1975, Title 22, sec. 80015).

This broad approach regarding the meaning of "services" indicates that the SSI definition can include supervision and protection, as well as care, training, and guidance. What may distinguish the traditional and nontraditional conceptions of institutions may revolve primarily around the distinctions between "custody" and the "services" of protection or supervision. Traditional institutions, it will be recalled, were referred to as locations where care and custody were provided. As late as 1970 the U.S. Census Bureau referred to the institutional population as being "under care and custody." This was done even though this census included residents of nursing homes and residential treatment centers for emotionally disturbed persons—two facility types not generally categorized as "custodial." It appears reasonable to suggest that the term "care and custody" is associated with traditional institutions. Some persons would add that modernized, traditional institutions also provide treatment and habilitation/socialization training, and that care, custody, and treatment are their dominant social functions.

Care, treatment, and habilitation can be provided voluntarily or involuntarily. If they are provided involuntarily, by virtue of the civil and police powers of the state, then persons are deemed to be under custody. However, persons can be held under custody to temporarily hold, segregate, incapacitate, deter, punish, and generally control freedom of movement, as well as for the more benign purposes of care, treatment, habilitation, and diagnosis. Conceivably, persons residing in community residential facilities can also be supervised in a manner that restricts freedom of movement and involves social control. If protection or supervision of voluntary residents of a nontraditional institution involves any loss of civil rights or any restrictions on freedom of movement, then the type, degree, duration, and scheduling of these social-control practices are worth comparing to more traditional custodial activities.

Proposed Definition of "Institution"

On the basis of the varied institutional definitions and the explicit and implicit criteria associated with life safety, Medicaid, SSI, and the census, a broad definition of "institution" can be developed, which includes traditional and nontraditional institutional types, regardless of their medical or custodial classification. My definition proposes the following:

A civilian institution is a private or public establishment which furnishes (in single or multiple facilities) food and shelter to about four or more persons unrelated to the proprietor and, in addition, provides one or more of the following:

1. Medical and/or personal and/or social care.
2. Treatment and/or skills training and/or habilitation.
3. Supervision and/or custodial control.
4. Protection and/or social shelter.
5. Diagnostic assessment and/or background investigation.

Excluded from this definition are: all military establishments; educational dormitories and rooms, except for schools for the mentally and developmentally disabled; and religious training institutions.

The size requirement has been hedged to apply to possibly five or six persons, to accommodate state or local zoning definitions that include this number of unrelated individuals in a "normal residential" occupancy (Cupaiuolo 1977, p. 207). The definition is also intended to exclude foster family homes of all types, unless they exceed the minimum size of facilities for unrelated persons. The exclusions cited are in accord with focusing on residences that primarily house persons with special social problems.

In general, this definition is congruent with the new types of residential facilities that have already been included in post-1970 census activities. In 1973 the Bureau of the Census conducted a survey for the National Center for Health Statistics (NCHS) that included the following "other health facilities": all nursing homes; halfway houses for alcoholics, addicts, and mental patients; and non-hospital residences for the emotionally disturbed and mentally retarded. In 1974 the Census Bureau conducted a survey for the Law Enforcement Assistance Administration (LEAA) and included the following types of "juvenile correctional facilities": detention and shelter-care homes; halfway houses; group homes; and ranches, camps, and schools (NCHS 1973; LEAA 1977).

The only major new residential type not included in census surveys is the category known by an array of names—board and care, shelter care, domiciliary care, and personal care. Some of these facilities are licensed under state laws and are expected to provide services comparable to those provided by the California code. These clearly meet the SSI and proposed definition. Others are unlicensed, but house residents placed by public agencies that expect care and supervision services to be provided. The importance of including many of these types of residences as examples of institutional living is supported by the discussion of the next section.

Community Facilities As New Sources of Supervision and Social Control

The previous discussion about community facilities suggested that the type, degree, duration, and scheduling of supervision were of critical importance in assessing whether voluntary living arrangements excluded restrictive types of social control practices. One recent study indicates that the dichotomy of voluntary/involuntary may be a bit oversimplified. A random sample of California shelter-care facilities housing ex–mental hospital patients found that many persons were "involuntary residents" (Segal and Aviram 1978, p. 177). These involuntary placements were related to the practices of county welfare and other social agencies. Anxious to be released from the hospital, many persons accepted the proferred residential placement, but confided to interviewers that their acquiescence was involuntary. This same study found that many facilities invoked nighttime curfews and did not permit residents to control their own spending money. In addition, over 90 percent of the facilities set up a "set of rules to supervise dispersal of medication" (Ibid., p. 124).

The California code for licensing and regulating community residential facilities does not specify what types of supervisory practices are covered by the code's definition of "supervision." According to this code, supervision refers to "the assumption of varying degrees of responsibility for the safety and well-being of residents" (State of California 1975, Title 22, sec. 80053). Other state codes are more explicit and specify that supervision may include areas other than care, treatment, or habilitation. For example, a recent New Jersey investigation of board-and-care homes (similar to California shelter-care homes) recommended that the state's statutes and regulations follow the lead of New York and define supervision as follows:

> *Supervision* shall mean guidance of an individual resident as he carries out activities of daily living and social activities, including but not limited to administering or reminding a resident to maintain his medication schedule as directed by his physician, reminding him in keeping appointments and being aware of his general whereabouts even though he may travel independently about the community. [State of New Jersey, November 1978, p. 242]

Operators of residential facilities are expected to perform these checking-up activities even though the residents have not been officially designated as being "under custody." As noted earlier, many California residents can be placed in residential facilities involuntarily, but here, too, they are not deemed to be under custody. Rather, private persons are expected to perform unofficial social-control functions over other citizens, even though there have been no official commitment proceedings or orders. This peculiar social role, and its explicit or implicit legitimation in state residential licensing statutes and regulations, is a relatively recent phenomenon. California, a leading DE state, did not pass a comprehensive licensing and regulating code until 1973. By 1976, the U.S. Senate Subcommittee on Long-Term Care, in reviewing the nation's use of board-and-care homes, could cite only three states that had strict state licensing (March 1976, p. 745).

Recent federal legislation, mandating that states participating in optional supplementation of SSI shall establish and enforce standards for these types of living arrangements, will increase the likelihood of licensing laws in a majority of the states within a few years (sec. 1616 [e] 1). It is expected that these new statutes and regulations will refer to "supervision" as an integral part of the care and services provided beyond room and board. Therefore, societal legitimation for unofficial forms of potential social-control activities will probably spread rapidly to all parts of the country.

These new sources of publicly sponsored supervision of "voluntary" residents have received minimal attention in the literature. However, when examples of the use of medication as "chemical straitjackets" or "unnecessary regimentation" are cited by investigative authorities, they are usually discussed as "abuses" of the operators (Ibid., 1974, p. 7). The fact that states provide optional supplementation to SSI funds to pay for extra care and supervision, or mandate these services in statutes and/or regulations, has not been noted. The states have delegated a good deal of discretionary power to operators of nontraditional residential facilities.

Available evidence indicates that nontraditional sources of supervisory controls can provide, in practice, one or more of the following basic services in community residences:

1. Locks on exterior gates and doors and interior rooms.
2. High ratios of staff to residents to monitor and supervise activities.
3. Rules that specify that certain routines are to occur by groups only.
4. Withholding of funds, monitoring expenditures, and operator cashing of resident checks.
5. Setting up rules concerning curfews, outside visiting, and access to the community.
6. Controlling administration of the type, degree, frequency, and scheduling of medication, particularly psychotropic drugs.
7. Controlling access to, and use of, clothing.
8. Threats to have persons returned to traditional institutions.

Comparing Old and New Institutional Forms

Although the idea can be documented that operators of nontraditional settings utilize a variety of social-control practices, it can be misleading to assume automatically that former and potential residents of traditional institutions are no better off in these newer living arrangements. Many of these newer institutional forms, like nursing homes and shelter-care facilities, have been described in very negative terms by official investigators and journalists (see, for example, the thousands of pages of testimony and accounts in the hearings conducted over a ten-year period by the U.S. Senate Subcommittee on Long-Term Care). However, the overall care practices of these smaller, less traditional living arrangements have been found to be favorable in comparison to traditional facilities for mentally retarded persons in the United States, England, and Scandinavia (Balla

1976). A statewide study of former residents of state mental hospitals found that despite the "institutional overlay" of many shelter-care facilities, an overwhelming majority (84 percent) of those interviewed asserted they "would object to returning to a mental hospital" (Segal and Aviram 1978, p. 271).

The evidence indicates that although nontraditional living arrangements can be associated with custodial types of practices legitimated by state licensing laws, they may still be regarded as freer places to live than traditional institutions. Whereas the ideals of DE might suggest that complete nonrestrictive outcomes were preferable, it appears that the realization of less restrictive environments is more likely. This perspective indicates that less restrictive living conditions may have been achieved only in comparison to the custodial standards and practices associated with the traditional institutions. As the level of acceptable social-control practices is scrutinized further, many recent alternatives to traditional institutions may well be deemed new candidates for DE. This appears to have begun already in the field of aging, where many nursing homes, only a few years ago regarded as less restrictive than state hospitals, are now considered too large, lacking in privacy, and possessing "structured living environments" (GAO, 7 January 1977, p. 16). Newer standards of care, imported from Europe, now assert that "open care" in an aged resident's home is preferable to the "closed care" in nursing homes (Little 1978). Inasmuch as there are many forms of closed care environments, it will help to differentiate the new sources of social control that have been created in decentralized locations, under new sponsors, and legitimated by new statutes and regulations.

The Growth of Proprietary Institutions

Prior to the passage of the Social Security Act in 1935, there were few proprietary institutions providing care and supervision to population groups comparable to those age groups residing in state-sponsored institutions. Except in the field of child welfare and the emergent field of aging, there were few private, nonprofit facilities to rival the dominance of the public sector. Persons residing in these public and private traditional institutions were considered as "dependent" or "delinquent," receiving "care and custody" from public and/or benevolent funds.

According to the U.S. Senate Subcommittee on Long-Term Care, since 1939 the country has witnessed the birth of a nursing-home industry and a board-and-care industry, both operated primarily as profit-making enterprises. In practice, this means that out of the approximately 21,800 nursing-home facilities counted in 1973, about 77 percent were owned by proprietary operators. These facilities accounted for about 67 percent of all the resident beds existing in nursing homes during that year (NCHS, Series 14, no. 16, 1976, p. 4). Data are much more sparse for the board-and-care homes—facilities not qualifying as health-care residences. However, all of the available evidence indicates that the proportions of these facilities operated for profit would equal or surpass the figures cited for the nursing-home industry.

Nontraditional institutions housing children and youth are not nearly so likely to be dominated by proprietary operators. However, it is quite significant that there now exist proprietary facilities for children (Ibid., no. 6, p. 48). In the 1970 census of institutions, proprietary institutions for children were not even separately classified (U.S. Bureau of the Census, 1973, p. 21).

For adults, the shift toward creating nontraditional institutions has been accompanied by a shift in the proportion of aged, mentally ill, retarded, and disabled persons living under the care and supervision of proprietary operators. The move from the state-sponsored institutions is, therefore, primarily a tilting toward the profit sector of the economy. One of the most significant consequences of this shift is the creation of new interest groups with a stake in the maintenance and expansion of the new, nontraditional, institutional network of facilities. In the nursing home industry, multistate chains have already been created. It is now likely that "25 to 30 percent of the homes and 35 percent of the beds are owned or controlled by chains" (GAO, 9 January 1979, p. 2). Evidently this type of corporate concentration is likely to continue or increase.

It is important to note that this significant development does not necessarily mean that three-fourths of community-residential facilities for the aged are operated by unethical operators, motivated solely by a greed for profit, or that proprietary institutions are inferior to nonprofit or public facilities. Reality is, in fact, much more complex. For example, many proprietary nursing homes take private, as well as Medicare or Medicaid, residents and are thereby influenced by family and consumer preferences. In addition, many homeowners seek capital gains by concentrating on capital-depreciation deductions (State of New York 1976; State of New Jersey 1977).

By taking cognizance of the emergence and expansion of new profitmaking opportunities, it may be easier to understand the philosophy and politics associated with some DE issues on a local, state, and federal level. In addition, the fiscal behavior of many facilities may become more understandable if business criteria, rather than normative and professional criteria, are employed. Having legitimated—via legislation and regulations—the purchase of "services" at both federal and state levels, it should not be surprising if facility operators give high priority to the goal of maximizing capital gains and/or net income proceeds, while providing publicly subsidized "services" (Vladeck 1980).

The Role of the Welfare State in Subsidizing Nontraditional Facilities

The rapid growth of proprietary facilities in the adult, nontraditional, institutional sector was made possible to a large degree by the availability of new sources of public funding at the federal level. The nursing-home industry has been supported by welfare programs associated with old-age insurance, medical assistance to the aged, Medicare, and Medicaid, as well as small business and hospital construction funds. The board-and-care industry has received subsidization from related welfare programs: disability insurance, aid to permanently and totally disabled, old-age assistance, aid to the blind, and supplementary security income (SSI).

The availability of federal funding to subsidize alternatives to traditional institutions provided states with an opportunity to shift to the federal government a substantial part of their fiscal burden for care and custodial supervision. The shift from the public to the private sector has been accompanied by a change from the 100 percent state financing of public institutional facilities to federal financing of 50 to 100 percent for persons residing in community arrangements. This means that individual proprietors were not the sole beneficiaries of the move to new institutional arrangements; states, too, were offered fiscal advantages through involvement in the depopulation of state-sponsored facilities. This merger of private and state interests was facilitated by changes in social security legislation and regulations.

Understanding the material interests associated with DE can help us understand the timing and acceleration of depopulation trends. Although belief in an antiinstitutional ideology probably influenced the policies and activities of critical actors, the historical literature reveals that prior to the advent of the welfare state, traditional institutions had lost their attraction as a favored social policy (Rothman 1971; Scull 1977). The emergence and expansion of the federal welfare state permitted an antiinstitutional ideology to receive the material support of a funding source not committed to the traditional state-sponsored system. Welfare state funds offered public, entrepeneurial-oriented reformers a rare opportunity to capitalize on private profit motivation and state fiscal expediency. New economic incentives provided support for an ideological position that had emerged at an earlier date.

Deinstitutionalization As Emergent Policy

During the past decade public policy analysts have become increasingly concerned with the general problem of implementing desired policies (Hargrove 1975; Mead 1977; Sabatier and Mazmanian 1980). According to this analytic position, many problems associated with DE can be attributed to poor leadership, failure to plan, lax administrative and monitoring procedures, uncoordinated service-delivery operations, and other implementation deficiencies. A recent GAO report (7 January 1977) documenting these implementation problems at a federal level provides a series of recommendations based on the assumption that the administrative means for policy execution are faulty.

This mode of analysis may be appropriate for policies with clear mandates, consensual legitimation, and precise administrative and funding mechanisms. It may be useful to inquire about implementation problems with policies that possess these rationalistic, deliberative, and authoritative characteristics, in that the policies are presumed to be purposeful. However, many policies operative in a problem area (or for a problem group) have not developed in this rationalistic manner. Instead they have originated and expanded in an expedient, emergent fashion, often embedded in older policies and programs designed for other purposes and/or problems.

Various topics discussed above are examples of emergent/expedient policy formulation and execution, rather than of the ideal type often assumed in the policy analysis literature. Neither national nor state legislation set forth a policy for creating nonmedical community residential facilities according to deliberative criteria. Instead critical decision makers in state government responded to diverse opportunities to facilitate depopulating state institutions of adults. Between 1955 and 1960 many states began to use new psychotropic drugs to deal with mental patients in and out of the hospital. In 1962 changes in federal regulations permitted persons on "conditional release" from state institutions to be placed on welfare, as "permanently and totally disabled" persons. States with entrepreneurial leaders could take advantage of these opportunities and others that followed; they began to reduce daily institutional populations by a significant number without first designing and setting up alternative living arrangements, placement criteria, residential standards, or supportive services. An expedient, pragmatic approach to reducing reliance on state institutions resulted in states seeking alternative living arrangements wherever facilities could be found. In many states, released persons become concentrated in

> residential facilities previously used for other purposes but no longer competitive in these other markets. The tendency for hotels, boarding houses, and so forth to locate in a single geographic area is common. Resort areas have large numbers of beds to serve the tourist population; areas near universities have many boarding houses to serve a transient student population; and older hotels located in deteriorating urban sections now provide another source of beds for people who require community care. [Segal and Aviram 1978, p. 65]

Standards for regulating and licensing these new alternatives emerged a decade *after* their widespread usage began. Legal changes making it more difficult to involuntarily place persons in state institutions also occurred *after* many traditional facilities had reduced their daily population. The expectation that these new community residential facilities would offer care and supervision also emerged over time, as states and local communities responded to fires, bizarre behavior, and reports of abuse (U.S. Senate Subcommittee on Long-Term Care, December 1974).

DE policies cannot, therefore, be found in a single, landmark piece of legislation, or even in a designated package of laws or regulations. Instead the actual operating policies emerged over time and can be found in the laws and regulations governing Medicare, Medicaid, supplementary security income (formerly aid to the permanently and totally disabled), social-service funding, state building-construction codes, licensing laws, vocational rehabilitation, child welfare titles and regulations, and a variety of comparable sources. And since 1972, an array of court decisions at federal and state levels also provides sources of ad hoc, emergent policies.

Utilizing GAO data, it is clear that federal DE policies are embedded in the operational policies of 135 national programs operated by 11 major departments and agencies (GAO, 7 January 1977, p. 5). In addition to the 89 programs in HEW that can be used on behalf of DE purposes, there are funding opportunities from HUD, Labor, and Justice. As the GAO notes:

> Under these Federal programs almost every type of service needed by mentally disabled persons in communities can be financed wholly or partly with Federal funds. The programs generally provide income support payments directly to individuals or provide grants to states to cover part of the cost of providing services to the poor, needy or disabled. Each program generally provides for one or more services, but not for all of those needed by mentally disabled persons. Eligibility requirements, such as age, income, and degree of disability, and State limitations vary among the different programs. [Ibid., p. 65]

Given these disparate sources of operational policies and no central "lead" agency within the federal government, it is not surprising that there is a clear lack of leadership—as charged by the GAO—in any attempt at deliberate policy formulation at the national level. Since 1972, numerous court decisions have begun to compete with legislative and executive departments in setting the standards for new ideal and operational policies. The competition and search for a clear national policy is occurring between segments of Congress and the professionals within HEW (changed to Health and Human Services [HHS] in 1980), representatives of traditional and nontraditional institutions and services, and the courts and other sources of policy legitimation. This search is currently going on within each problem field, but the elements of conflict are occurring in each of the fields.

Overview of Book's Organization

The chapters that follow provide further documentation for the ideas in this introduction, and examine some areas in greater depth. To understand more fully the emergence, functions, and utilization patterns of traditional institutions—the primary targets of deinstitutionalization efforts—a historical perspective is presented in Chapter 2. Chapter 3 specifies the nontraditional alternatives that have arisen, and briefly describes their ideal and actual populations. Chapter 4 then discusses these alternatives as new sources of social control, care, and treatment.

Chapter 5 provides a summary of population trends for the total institutional system, with a special emphasis on utilization patterns in the mental health and mental retardation systems. Chapter 6 offers a provisional explanation of origins of DE, using California's depopulation of state mental health facilities as a case study.

Chapters 7 and 8 are devoted to children's institutional developments. Chapter 7 explores the birth, historical functions, and organizational auspices of the three major systems—child welfare, juvenile corrections, and mental health—and then studies the impediments to, as well as the causes of, actual population reductions of child welfare institutions. Chapter 8 analyzes trends in the other two systems, and then provides an analysis of the factors that have promoted the widespread utilization of nontraditional institutions for youth.

The final chapters transcend specific fields—or systems—by examining the search for a national policy. Three critical elements of this national policy search are discussed: (1) resolving whether to pursue a "balanced system" or a "least restrictive system" of care as a major national goal of human services; (2) resolving whether to allocate more resources to upgrade traditional institutions, or to use scarce federal and state funds primarily to expand the availability of independent living arrangements, community residential facilities, and services; and (3) resolving whether to assess, systematically, existing statutes and regulations that favor more restrictive living arrangements, in order to diminish the incentives for institutional options embedded in the welfare state's package of related policies.

None of these three policy issues is merely academic. HEW officials have responded to GAO criticisms of a lax federal effort in DE by arguing that not DE, but a "balanced system" of care, should be given the highest national priority. Many interested groups—including the GAO, a Presidential Commission on Mental Health, and federal courts—also provide support for "upgrading" state institutions for the mentally ill and retarded. However, the hundreds of millions of dollars used to upgrade traditional facilities hinders the expansion and upgrading of the new facilities and services associated with a least-restrictive policy orientation. Preferences for definitions of DE that include positive valuations of "balance" and "upgrading of care" lend support to the traditional sources of care and supervision for mentally disabled persons in the state hospital system. Besides the capital allocational decisions made in the name of "balance" and "upgrading," operational funds are expended on behalf of Medicaid, child welfare, and social services that can also support more restrictive residential placements.

It is possible, therefore, to focus on rather critical issues by assessing the recent search for a national policy—provided, of course, that there is a willingness to address directly the conflicts of ideology, values, and allocational preferences. It is hoped that a discussion of these conflicts will be informed by the perspectives and data analysis offered in the chapters that precede the analyses of issues. The discussion will also be informed by a position that favors minimal coercion of persons by direct and indirect agents of the state, even if their living arrangements are being subsidized by public funds.

PART

I

Understanding Utilization Patterns of Adult Facilities

2 Traditional Institutions: A Historical Perspective

Prior to the American Revolution, public and private expressions of mutual aid and philanthropy were distributed primarily to persons residing in "outdoor," noninstitutional homes; persons on assistance lived alone, with relatives, friends, or neighbors. Almshouses, as public modes of assistance, were found mainly in larger towns, where transients and homeless persons presented communities with special problems. By 1824, a New York survey of local practices found that only about one-third of the state's 100 largest towns provided an almshouse or a means of "indoor relief" (Rothman 1971, p. 183). This modest use of the almshouse changed dramatically by the onset of the Civil War, when the almshouse became the primary provider of relief throughout the nation. In addition, specialized institutional facilities that dealt with a variety of social problems were also developed during the antebellum era.

Funded by state and county funds or by private subscriptions, most of the new institutional facilities were founded as the critical elements of new policies for promoting social reform. These policies singled out categories of poor, unfortunate, handicapped, and nonconforming persons as objects of concern and placed them in the new institutions. Here, depending on their condition, they could receive humane care, moral treatment, reformation experiences, special education, or a disciplined, orderly life. During this period almshouses and local jails were also redesigned to become places of reformation and orderly discipline. Besides the older institutional forms of almshouses and local jails, the new system included: state and county penitentiaries to reform criminals; privately administered and publicly subsidized houses of refuge for delinquents, wayward, and "houseless" youth; privately administered orphan asylums for dependent youth; state and private schools to educate the deaf, blind, and retarded; and public and private asylums to provide care and moral treatment for the insane (Rothman 1971; Leiby 1967 and 1978; Grob 1973).

The ideals of the reformers were difficult to put into practice and were never fully realized. The end of the nineteenth century witnessed a public outcry over crowded, custodial, uncaring institutions, criticisms that continued into the progressive era. There were efforts made at reforming institutional practices, but these, too, fell short of reformer ideals (Rothman 1980). The current interest in depopulating certain types of traditional institutions expresses this generation's collective judgment that post-1900 efforts failed to realize the ideals of humane care and treatment. Before assessing recent trends and practices, it is important to understand the varied social functions performed by the traditional institutions in American society. Knowing who it was that institutions served and why persons were served in specific types of residences provides a firmer foundation for interpreting new approaches to old problems.

Multiple Uses of Institutions

Despite the enthusiasm of the nineteenth- and twentieth-century reformers, traditional institutions were not developed as part of an overall state plan, nor did these facilities house only those categories of persons for which they had been ostensibly designed. In practice, many persons were eligible for more than one institutional type; and many institutions accepted residents who, from an ideal reform point of view, did not belong in that facility. For example, the redesigned almshouse—presumably subsidized as a form of indoor relief for the local poor—continued to be used during the nineteenth and early twentieth century as: a jail for tramps and vagrants; a workhouse for the able-bodied poor; an old people's residence; a general hospital for travelers and the local poor; an orphan asylum; and a place for lunatics and idiots (Rothman 1971; Grob 1973).

These multiple uses or functions varied by community, as well as within a community, over a period of time. Depending on the time and place, a person eligible for an almshouse could have also been a candidate for residence in an orphan asylum, an insane asylum, or a school for the retarded—or, again depending on the locality and era, a recipient of outdoor relief. It could, therefore, be extremely misleading to study the utilization patterns of the almshouse without understanding its relative social functions within the *total system* of institutional types—public and private. Operationally, the almshouse performed a variety of social functions in housing a disparate assortment of persons categorically associated with diverse social problems. Ideally, the newer institutions were primarily designed to replace undifferentiated poorhouse care with specific programs for clearly defined categories of dependent persons. In practice, however, even the almshouse alternatives performed multiple functions for a mixture of social categories.

One way to gain insight into the historical uses of traditional institutions is to survey U.S. Bureau of the Census reports. By viewing the census designers and reporters as important representatives of decennial eras, it is possible to perceive both subtle and dramatic approaches to conceptualizing the boundaries of the total institutional system. The manner in which institutional types were categorized and used can also be important to an understanding of the multiple functions of these nineteenth-century social inventions. This historical overview can inform analysts about the limits of any subsequent quantitative trend analyses concerning institutional utilization. For it is apparent that the validity of any trend data is dependent on consistency in the usage of institutional boundaries, organizational types, and the mode of categorizing related types.

The Traditional Institutional System: 1850–1950

Until 1850 there was no federal census of persons residing in institutions. The decennial institutional counts of 1850, 1860, and 1870 were secured by U.S. assistant marshals as part of their duties to collect social statistics; they counted residents of almshouses, jails, prisons, and institutions for the insane, feeble-minded, and the deaf and blind (U.S. Bureau of the Census, 1910). In 1880 the first major effort to include private, as well as all public, institutions was conducted by the census. Not only was the boundary of concern broadened, but there was also a major attempt to reconceptualize the diverse array of indoor facilities associated with the emerging field of "charities and corrections." The author of the 1880 report, with the approval of census officials, titled the formal report as follows: *Report on the Defective, Dependent, and Delinquent Classes of the Population of the United States, 1880* (Ibid., 1883).

The focus was on categories of social problems per se, and not just a narrow counting of institutional residents. Persons who fit the categories of defective, dependent, or delinquent were deemed members of "special classes" of society. The *defective* classification included deaf and dumb, blind, insane, and idiots residing in institutions or in family households; the *delinquent* classification included adults in prisons and jails and juveniles in prisons, jails, reformatories, and refuges; the *dependent* class referred to paupers and "homeless children" in almshouses, in families of outdoor paupers, and in all institutions of a benevolent or beneficent character, including orphan asylums, homes for children, homes for the aged, friendless, and those "having no given habitation" (U.S. Bureau of the Census, *Benevolent Institutions*, 1910, p. 11). The inclusion of outdoor dependents and defectives indicates that the census takers were trying to define and count the problems associated with institutionalization, and not just residents per se.

"Defective" may have been a bit too strong a term; in subsequent years, it was not used in the titles of reports. Instead, the term was reserved for textual references to the "feeble-minded" and "mentally deficient" (e.g., *Insane and Feeble-Minded in Institutions*, 1910, p. 183). Because the overwhelming number of persons residing in institutions were living as dependents of counties, the state, or charity, it is possible to collapse the three-level boundary definition into a two-level conception: the dependents and delinquent classes. The 1910 *Report on Benevolent Institutions* asserted that it dealt with the "relief and care of the dependent and delinquent classes" (p. 11). A 1923 report on *Children under Institutional Care* also referred to the series of reports pertaining to the "relief and care of the dependent and delinquent classes."

In 1933, four years after the onset of the Depression, the Bureau of the Census conducted an institutional decennial census. For the first time since 1850 there was no special report on paupers in almshouses. Nor was there a reference to the "dependent and delinquent classes." With millions of Americans out of work, and hundreds of thousands of able-bodied poor moving about the country as vagrants, it may have seemed inappropriate to use nineteenth-century terms to describe problems associated with poverty. Instead, the census technicians merely produced discrete reports on the traditional institutions—without any attempt to justify the exclusion of almshouses, mission houses, municipal lodging houses, hospitals, homes for the friendless, and other adult "benevolent" institutions that had been included in 1904 and 1910 as places for dependents to receive "relief and care." One major class of institution, however, was conceptualized differently from all of the others: the "institutions and agencies caring for dependent and neglected children." This classification was the lineal descendant of the "child caring" agencies that had first been noted in 1880.

The "dependent and neglected children" category also appears in the institutional census of subsequent decades (including 1970), but the exclusions and inclusions are not similar across time. In 1933 the "dependency and neglect" category included: state, county, and municipal welfare boards; child-placing departments of juvenile courts; juvenile court detention homes providing more than sixty days care; state, county, and municipal agencies and institutions; fraternal, religious, and nonsectarian institutions; receiving homes for children awaiting placement; and maternity homes. Excluded from the definition of "dependent and neglected" were: children residing in almshouses; court-sentenced dependents residing in delinquent institutions; and children residing in detention homes from one to sixty days.

This report on children, together with the other reports, indicates that the "dependent and delinquent classes" definition had been narrowed to exclude many adults temporarily. Setting aside the omission of the almshouse and benevolent institutions for adults, the 1933 definition included the traditional (albeit renamed) categories of 1850 plus the "dependent and neglect" and "deliquent" categories (adapted from the post-1880 period). The issuance of special reports for each "special class" indicates that the census reporters believed there was still a great deal of interest in traditional population groups.

In 1940 the census definitions of the institutional population attempted to narrow the scope further, by deliberately focusing *only* on persons 14 years and older, and by utilizing an eclectic, five-part classification scheme to report all of the nation's data. The census takers deliberately focused on "certain types of institutions" that were well recognized: (1) prisons and reformatories; (2) local jails and workhouses; (3) mental institutions; (4) homes for the "aged, infirm, or needy"; and (5) "other institutions of these general classes" which could not be assigned.

The general conceptual rationale for excluding categories was not given. Patients in general hospitals with wards for mental patients and "incurables" were counted, but aged, infirm, or needy patients were excluded. Persons in monasteries, convents, and religious orders were excluded unless they "were clearly of such a nature as to place it in one of the types." Residents of tuberculosis sanitariums and lodging houses were not included. The information was offered, however, that 70,000 persons resided in sanitariums, and approximately 150,000 children lived in orphanages and in homes for dependent and neglected children.

The concerns expressed in the 1940 report indicate that "labor force," "employment," and "population" characteristics were of greater importance than conformity to traditional boundaries. However, the 1940 report is significant for signaling the emergence of another special dependent category: the "aged, infirm, and the needy." Until this year the aged had been included with other adult—or nonchild—institutions. However, this census type is not yet a clear one, since the aged grouping also includes almshouses, houses for the blind and the deaf, incurables, orphans, and disabled or aged soldiers and sailors. From a historical perspective, many members of the 1880–1923 adult "dependent" classes were in the process of being regrouped into a modern dependent category revolving around "old age."

The 1950 Census Description of the Modern Institutional System

The 1950 census provided the rationale and categories that are closest to the most recent published census—1970. Instead of merely referring to broad "classes" of "types," the 1950 census report attempted to explicate the criteria for delineating institutions from other "congregate quarters." The report also defined which categories constituted the specific and aggregate boundaries of the total system. Institutions, as a type of residence, were defined as follows:

> The places in which people live are classified in two major groups: dwelling units such as ordinary houses or apartments and congregate living quarters such as hotels, large lodging houses, residential clubs, convents, monasteries, dormitories, bunk houses, hospitals, houses for the aged, orphan asylums, prisons and jails. The persons living in a dwelling unit constitute a household and those living in congregate quarters, a quasi household. The institutional population is the population under care in certain types of quasi households.
>
> Fundamentally, *institutions are quasi households which provide care for persons with certain types of disabilities*; disabilities which, in the community at large, constitute hazards to the welfare of the person himself or to other members of the community. [U.S. Bureau of the Census, 1950, vol. 4, *Special Reports*, pt. 2, pp. 2–4; italics added]

This approach to carving out the general boundary indicated that communities provided care because of disabilities perceived as hazards, rather than because people were defective, dependent, or delinquent. Whereas the language of the nineteenth-century categories was in harmony with a charity and corrections image, the new terms appear consonant with the fields of physical and mental disability—or handicap. By dropping the phrase "relief and care," the modern definition attempts to disassociate institutions as a source of "relief from poverty." It is interesting, too, that the term "hazard" could be replaced with "dangerous" and remain similar to the civil commitment laws of virtually every state in the nation. The explicit language does not indicate that persons can be "under control" as well as "under care," but the reference to community hazards implies that this is possible.

Working within this general framework, the author of the 1950 special report discusses three other criteria that must also be present for "certain types" of quasi-households to be included:

1. USUAL RESIDENCE. The place of residence while living "under care" should be considered a "usual" residence. Therefore, "inmates are regarded as usual residents" only when the average length of stay is "great," and when a large proportion of the inmates cannot be regarded as having a usual residence elsewhere. For this reason, mental hospitals are always included, and general hospitals, with minor exceptions, always excluded (Ibid., pp. 2C–4).

2. LABOR FORCE PARTICIPATION. If the disabilities are "sufficiently serious" and the average length of stay is "sufficiently great," it can be assumed that the persons are not employable at the time of enumeration.

3. DEMAND FOR STATISTICS. Strictly speaking, residents of jails, detention centers, and child receiving homes should be excluded, in that such short-term facilities violate the criteria of "usual residence." Schools for the deaf could also be excluded because they, too, are not usual places of residence and "are similar to other residential schools" (which are excluded). The only justification for continuing to include these nonusual residents is the "demand for statistics on the prevalence of various types of disabilities"—regardless of the length of stay at their temporary residences. Therefore, this census also included tubercular and neuropsychiatric patients in general hospitals. In addition, to improve the coverage of elderly persons and chronic patients, residents of "small nursing and convalescent homes, which in some cases are not quasi households, were included in the institutional population" (Ibid.).

For all of these considerations, the census readily admits that "the definition of the institutional population is a rather specialized one." The final, specialized definition incorporates value, technical, and public demand criteria:

> In general, it constitutes the inmate population of certain places which provide care for persons suffering from various types of disabilities, in which the length of stay is relatively long; in which, by virtue of the length of stay and disability, persons under care are classified as usual residents and excluded from the labor force; and in which some general public interest attaches to the type of disability involved. [Ibid.]

From a historical perspective, 1880 census takers would have had to replace "defective" with "disability," and "dependent" with "exclusion from the labor force." As for the "delinquent" classes, they are to be counted because of their length of stay, lack of labor force participation, or "general public interest." However, in attempting to operationalize the new ideal boundary, a number of old terms reemerged. The major categories utilized in the 1950 census are defined below, with greatest attention given to "new" categories:

1. PRISONS AND REFORMATORIES. "Places in which persons convicted of relatively serious crimes serve their sentences."

2. LOCAL JAILS AND WORKHOUSES. "Places in which persons are awaiting trial or serving time on relatively short-term sentences."

3. MENTAL HOSPITALS. "Places devoted in large part to the care of psychiatric patients," but also including "psychiatric services of large general hospitals."

4. TUBERCULOSIS HOSPITALS. Besides special hospitals, this category also includes "tubercular patients in large general hospitals."

5. OTHER SPECIAL HOSPITALS. "Hospitals which could be identified as hospitals for other chronic diseases," but this category does *not* cover chronic patients in general hospitals.

6. HOMES FOR THE AGED AND DEPENDENT. "A somewhat heterogeneous group of places, which have in common only the fact that a majority of the persons under care are older persons. It is clear that, in addition to age, economic dependency and various kinds of infirmity account for the presence of many of the residents of these places." Included are "county home or poor farm" and "nonprofit houses" for the aged; "commercial boarding homes (which have increased considerably in number with the development of the old-age assistance program) and nursing, rest, and convalescent homes operating on a commercial basis."

7. HOMES AND SCHOOLS FOR THE MENTALLY HANDICAPPED. "Comprises those institutions which provide care primarily for the mentally deficient but in many instances also for epileptics."

8. HOMES AND SCHOOLS FOR THE PHYSICALLY HANDICAPPED. "Includes homes and schools for the blind and deaf, and institutions and orthopedic hospitals for crippled children and for other types of serious disability."

9. HOMES FOR NEGLECTED AND DEPENDENT CHILDREN. "Covers institutions which were known in earlier days as orphan asylums." This category presented difficulty because "there is still considerable evidence of the persistence of a pattern of care for both dependent children and older persons in the same institution"; allocations were made to homes for aged or children "wherever possible."

10. TRAINING SCHOOLS FOR JUVENILE DELINQUENTS. Public and private schools were included, although the latter contain "a somewhat more heterogeneous group ranging from institutions providing care for juvenile delinquents of essentially the same character as those who find their way into public training schools to schools providing care for problem children."

11. DETENTION HOMES. These homes provide "temporary care for juveniles who, by reason of delinquency, dissolution of the home, or other crises, present a social problem which must be dealt with immediately, before a final solution to the problem is reached."

12. HOMES FOR UNWED MOTHERS. "Ideally, this category comprises homes and hospitals providing for unmarried mothers, prenatal, obstetrical, and postnatal care." Included are those operated by "reputable social agencies with community approval and those whose status in the community is somewhat equivocal" (U.S. Bureau of the Census, *Institutional Populations*, 1950, pp. 2C5–6).

To gain an appreciation of the actual breadth of this modern conception of institutions, it is useful to compare the 1950 list of twelve major categories with that of a prior year. The 1940 census cannot be used because of its exclusion of facilities for persons under 14 years of age. The 1930 and 1923 censuses are woefully deficient in detailing the facilities for "dependent" adults. Therefore, the most recent census that provides a basis for comparing the new boundary classifications is that of 1910. This census was undoubtedly one of the most ambitious institutional surveys ever undertaken by the U.S. Census Bureau. Unlike current censuses that only conduct one-day counts of residents, the 1910 census attempted to obtain annual admission and discharge statistics. Table 2–1 lists the 1910 categories, and attempts to place the institutional populations into their 1950 counterparts. The parenthetical numbers in the 1950 categories refer to the numbered definitions noted in the paragraphs above—with the exception of (0), which refers to "quasi-households" as defined by the 1950 census reports.

A careful reading of Table 2–1 indicates that the modern conception of an institutional census is much narrower than that of its predecessors; it tends to be (in the words of the anonymous census writer) a "rather specialized one." Many temporary, or transient, residences are excluded from the 1950 institutional boundary, and are treated as examples of noninstitutional quasi-households. Lodges for newsboys, municipal shelters, Salvation Army houses, and homes for the friendless are potential examples of quasi-households. In 1910 these nonprofit institutional forms were included as the progressive period's alternatives to the traditional almshouse, workhouse, and local jail—for according to most statutes of that date transients, vagrants, prostitutes, and homeless unemployed could find official "relief and care" only if they entered the custody of one of the public, community-based facilities. Because of a diminished interest in temporary dependents, the 1950 census all but excludes the "benevolent" use of hospitals and dispensaries.

Regarding specialization, it appears that three clusters of modern differentiation have been identified. These clusters are:

1. THE AGED. This not only includes commercial boarding and nursing homes (for the first time), but also "other hospitals," to count chronic patients, many of whom are elderly.

2. CHILD-CENTERED FACILITIES. Includes not only dependent and neglected as a major category, but also detention, unwed mothers, and training schools for delinquents.

3. PHYSICAL DISABILITIES. Includes all of the physical handicaps, not just the blind and deaf and a scattering of "invalids" and "cripples."

From a historical perspective, the conceptual shift away from an institutional category of *economic* dependency is associated with a distinctive interest in *social* dependency; dependency is now associated with the social categories of the aged, children, and the disabled. The traditional categories that cover the insane, the feeble-minded, and the criminal remain, but to these must be added the "hazards" presented by the young, the elderly, and the physically handicapped. Chil-

TABLE 2–1

Comparison of 1910 and 1950 Census Categories

1910 Categories	Probable 1950 Categories
I. Paupers in Almshouse	(6) Homes for aged and dependent
II. Prisoners and Juvenile Delinquents:	
A. State prisons	(1) Prisons and reformatories
B. Reformatories for adults or juveniles	(10) Training schools for delinquents
C. County jails and workhouses	(2) Local jails and workhouses
D. Municipal jails and workhouses	(2) Local jails and workhouses
III. Insane in Hospitals, and Feeble-minded in Institutions	(3) Mental hospitals
	(7) Homes and schools for the mentally handicapped
IV. Benevolent Institutions:	
A. Children in Institutions for Care of Children	
1. Children's orphanages, homes, and asylums	(9) Dependent and neglected children
2. Lodges for newsboys	(0) Quasi-households
3. Defectives, invalids, crippled	(8) Homes and schools for physically handicapped
4. Delinquent, wayward, or truant	(11) Detention homes and (10) Training schools
5. Other homeless, neglected or indigent children	(9) Dependent and neglected children
B. Homes for Care of Adults, or Adults and Children	
1. Aged, infirm, or destitute	(6) Homes for aged and dependent
2. Soldiers' homes	(6) Homes for aged and dependent
3. Municipal shelters for homeless, wayfarers, and unemployed	(0) Noninstitutional quasi-households
4. Immigrant homes and shelters	(0) or (6) (If temporary, in quasi-households; otherwise probably homes for aged)
5. Salvation Army industrial homes	(0) Quasi-households
6. Homes for the fallen	(11) Homes for unwed mothers
7. Homes for friendless and working boys and girls	(0) (Quasi-households)
8. Convalescents and incurables	(6) Mainly homes for aged
C. Hospitals and Sanitariums	(4) Tuberculosis hospitals and (5) Other hospitals (all other general hospitals excluded)
D. Dispensaries	(0) Quasi-households
E. Institutions for Blind and Deaf	(8) Homes and schools for physically handicapped

SOURCES: The following 1910 U.S. Bureau of the Census reports: *Paupers in Almshouses; Prisoners and Juvenile Delinquents; Insane and Feeble-minded in Institutions; Benevolent Institutions;* and *Institutional Population, 1950.*

dren as a distinctive dependent category were, of course, fully recognized by 1910, but the aged and the physically handicapped were only provided peripheral attention prior to 1950.

The 1960 and 1970 census definitions continued to rely on the categorizations of 1950, despite the emergence of linguistic shifts, and additions within and among types. The 1960 definition refers to persons living in certain "group quarters" instead of quasi-households, and also refers to inmates living under "custody," as well as care. Two distinctive categories were added, "residential treatment centers" and "diagnostic and reception centers," but the latter was dropped in 1970.

The major category expansions in 1960 were "mental health" and "homes for the aged." The mental health classification was expanded to include "alcoholic treatment and drug addiction centers." The aged were provided further attention by including "chronic disease wards" as well as chronic hospitals, and the classification of "other hospitals" was changed to reflect the major focus on chronic disease. The major classification of the "aged and dependent" also attempted to specify "skilled nursing care" homes, and facilities "not known to have nursing care" (changes associated with the emergence of medical assistance to the aged).

These 1960 changes indicate that the mental health cluster gained an added emphasis: two major social problems that could have been identified independently—drugs and alcohol—were added to the general category. At the same time, residential treatment centers and diagnostic and reception centers were given the status of major categories. Both categories were defined to include potential and actual residents with emotional disturbances—a mental health concept. However, diagnostic reception centers were primarily associated with delinquent youth.

The 1960 census did not refer to "disabilities" or "hazards," but instead referred to "certain types of group quarters." The 1970 census attempted to provide a value-free definition. This census defined inmates as "persons under care or custody in institutions at the time of enumeration . . . regardless of their length of stay in that place and regardless of the number of people in that place" (p. x). The only distinguishing characteristic now is the state of being "under care or custody," inasmuch as length of stay, labor force participation, and special demand are not explicitly referred to. As a subclassification of "group quarters"—defined as a residence where "six or more unrelated persons share the unit" (p. xiii)—institutional boundaries could theoretically include all residents of general hospitals, all residents of noncommercial transient facilities, all inpatients of community mental health units, and all residents of halfway houses and group homes. However, a careful reading of the classifications indicates that the basic counting units have *not* changed from 1950 and 1960: general hospital patients are, in the main, excluded; transients in noncommercial flophouses are counted as residents of noninstitutional group quarters; and residents of community mental health facilities (inpatients), halfway houses, and group homes are evidently not yet included in the appropriate mental health, correctional, or other major categories.

Overview of the Census Description of the Total Institutional System

In 1850 the U.S. Census Bureau first took official notice that not all Americans were residing in family households, educational boarding facilities, or other socially acceptable residences; some Americans were living in institutions. The people inhabiting these special residences were soon defined by census authors as members of "special classes." By 1880 they were defined as either defective, dependent, or delinquent. The persons associated with these semiofficial labels lived in almshouses, prisons and jails, lunatic asylums, institutions for the feeble-minded, and schools for the deaf and blind. In 1880, even while stigmatic categories were being described, an array of newer alternatives was beginning to be characterized as "benevolent institutions." However, even the beneficiaries of less harsh institutional alternatives were condescendingly viewed as living in places for "the relief and care of the dependent classes."

Until 1933 children were the major beneficiaries of the alternative indoor relief and care systems. They could be conceptualized as dependent and neglected without explicitly referring to their economic status—even though the bulk of the residents of child-care institutions came from lower-income families. By 1940, several years after the first federal Social Security Act, the needy and infirm aged were added to a reconceptualized dependent category of elderly persons. The first modern attempt to delimit boundaries free from the taint of the almshouse and pauperism appeared in the introduction to a 1950 census volume. Instead of mental and physical defectives, economic dependents, and the delinquent classes, the 1950 report referred to "disabilities," "labor force participation," "a general public interest," and "usual residence."

Since 1950, along with an interest in two specific age categories (the young and the elderly), there has also emerged a specialized concern for the residence associated with the mental health and physically handicapped categories. The retention of the term "dependents" as part of the young and elderly categories is a potent reminder that the census of institutional populations has a lengthy, value laden tradition. The retention can also remind us that a significant portion of our current institutional population is perceived as receiving "relief," as well as "care and custody."

Census Examples of Multiple Functions

Reading the census reports, particularly those prior to 1933, leads one to infer that it is unlikely for any institutional type to have only one social function, regardless of its design or location. Institutions can fulfill six major functions: (1) relief/food and shelter; (2) treatment/remediation/rehabilitation/special education; (3) custody/control/incapacitation; (4) medical, personal, or social care; (5) protection/shelter/refuge/segregation; (6) receiving home/diagnosis center/holding action.

This perception of multiple functions depends on the actual practices of an institution at a given point in time, with a specific population in residence. This is a static, cross-sectional view of institutional utilization. Another approach, from a longitudinal, historical perspective, could focus on the varied uses of institutions over time. Understanding this possibility is important, because changes in institutional trends in one category can signal an actual change in the functions of institutions—not simply that there is an increase or decrease in how much these institutions are being used.

Within a total institutional system there exists an interdependence of institutions related to the mutual functions that can be performed by any institution. For example, all institutions can provide a minimum of relief and custody, regardless of their categorization. "Deinstitutionalization" *within* a category cannot be understood without an awareness of the alternative categories that could provide equivalent relief and custody for specific age/sex population groups.

In 1910 the census reporter for juveniles, R. L. Brown, noted that the Middle Atlantic and New England divisions had the highest rate of juveniles under 18 committed to all types of correctional facilities (i.e., prisons, jails, workhouses, and reformatories combined). He cautioned readers not to believe automatically that this high rate was due solely to "urban conditions." There were other policy-related reasons that should be taken into account:

> The policy of separate institutional provision for juvenile offenders has been established for a longer time in these sections of the country and has probably been developed to a greater extent than elsewhere; as previously stated, it seems very probable that there is *less reluctance* to commit juveniles to penal or reformatory institutions when there is a special institution for such offenders than where it is necessary to send them to the same institutions as adult offenders. [U.S. Bureau of the Census, *Prisoners and Juvenile Delinquents*, 1910, p. 159; italics added]

Institutions designed as prisons and jails for adults were apparently perceived as custodial, not as rehabilitative. Because special juvenile institutions could serve both functions, they were likely to be more attractive to judges in 1910. According to this line of reasoning, one could expect a rise in juvenile commitment rates when adult custodial/relief institutions were replaced by juvenile institutions that added a third function—reformation. It is important to note that this association was likely to occur when the newer, more complex institution was added to—not just substituted for—the total institutional system.

The significance of adding specialized institutions for the feeble-minded and of comparing institutional trends was also noted by J. A. Hill in 1910:

An important factor affecting comparisons of different periods is the change that has taken place in the general methods of care for the feeble-minded. Formerly, almost all of this class under institutional care were in almshouses or in asylums for the insane. As late as 1890 only 16 states had provided separate institutions . . . and the number of such institutions was only 24. In 1904 the number . . . had increased to 42. . . . In 1910 there were 63 institutions . . . ; and in an increasing number of states the statutes provide for their *transfer from almshouses* to separate institutions as rapidly as possible.

The effect of these conditions upon the statistics is apparent . . . the institutional care of the feeble-minded . . . has been almost entirely a function of the state. . . . Still another and probably the most important cause, is the increasing conviction that the *segregation* and institutional *care* of the feeble-minded is necessary, even more as a matter of *protection* to the public than of benevolence for the inmates, and that the needed care can be secured only through the *enforcement of law*, which can scarcely be intrusted to private institutions. [U.S. Bureau of the Census, *Insane and Feeble-Minded in Institutions*, 1910, pp. 183 84; italics added]

"Expert Special Agent" Hill provides testimony—backed up by other historical sources—that the special institutions for the feeble-minded had the function of "segregating" this special class, so that they would not mix with almshouse, insane, and other dependent persons. It is interesting that the segregation rather than the educational/treatment function was to be coupled with the care and custody functions in the midst of an era associated with reform—the "progressive" era.

The institution that probably attempted the most complex array of functions over time was the almshouse. The anonymous interpreter of the 1910 almshouse census commented as follows:

The relative extent of almshouse pauperism at different times or in different localities is decidedly affected by the general trend in the evolution of organized charity from a condition in which the almshouse was the *only* public agency of relief to one in which it is coming to be used only for those among the poor who do not belong to any of the *special classes*, such as the insane, the feeble-minded, and the epileptic, for whom separate institutions are provided. . . .

Furthermore, in earlier days, the almshouse was frequently used as a temporary *shelter for vagrants* and sometimes even as a place of *detention for petty criminals*, and while tramps still constitute an element in the almshouse population of most communities and petty criminals are still admitted in some sparsely settled districts these uses of the almshouses are combined with *free hospitals for the poor*, and in such localities the figures for almshouse paupers include what in other communities would have been inmates of free wards of hospitals. The statistics show a further trend in the limitation of the almshouse, namely that it is being used to a less extent than formerly for the *relief of children and women*, for whom special public and private institutions are being more commonly provided. The census statistics for benevolent institutions other than almshouses show the effect of this, since the number of women and specially of children in such institutions shows an increase between

1904 and 1910 far in excess of that for men. [U.S. Bureau of the Census, *Paupers in Almshouses*, 1910, p. 11; italics added]

In 1910 child-caring institutions were used by both private and public referral sources. One consequence of trying to care for a variety of public demands was to expand to include protective and custodial, as well as caring, social functions. The author of the *Benevolent Census Report* comments as follows:

> The children received are primarily those who are destitute and dependent upon the public for support. Of late years, however, the state has come to recognize its responsibility not only for the *material welfare* of its children, but also for their *protection from evil* influences, and in many states under the head of "dependent or neglected children" are included merely orphans and children deserted by their parents or guardians, and those without visible means of support, but also those who live in unfit or disreputable surroundings, who are growing up in the habit of begging or receiving alms, who frequent vicious places, or who in any way give indication of developing into undesirable citizens. Such children . . . may be committed to reformatories, or if the offense is slight, to some orphanage or other institutions of this class. If there is no infraction of the law, the juvenile court may still take cognizance of the case and commit the child to some benevolent institution. [U.S. Bureau of the Census, *Benevolent Institutions*, 1910, p. 26; italics added]

This class of institution might be expected to show a rise in admissions. However, at the same time that the child-caring institutions were expected to provide care, education, protection, and custody, there was also a strong movement to place children in the ideal residence—a foster family home. Many children were placed in temporary "receiving" homes, pending an agency decision. If this function were added to an institution, then the numbers institutionalized could increase, despite a commitment to "place out" in free or boarding foster homes.

Perhaps the most humorous example of the importance of understanding multiple functions is found in the interpretation of the census returns from municipal lodges (or "transient group quarters," in 1970 terminology):

> The reports for municipal shelters, immigrant homes, and private shelters for transients were not entirely satisfactory and the statistics presented probably do not represent accurately the full amount of work done by those classes of institutions. In some cases officials of municipal shelters refused information on the ground that the institutions were really a part of the *police* system rather than conducted for benevolent purposes. The information received from other institutions also proved to be somewhat vague. [Ibid., p. 44; italics added]

Aside from the issue of whether the census personnel should have classified some of the shelters as congregate "lock-up" facilities, there is the issue of how to interpret "jail and workhouse" statistics. If shelters serve multiple functions in the total institutional system available to a community, city, state, or region, then the use of shelters could be related to the trends in jail and workhouse population data.

The Multiple Uses of the Insane Asylum in California

In addition to census reporters, social historians have also discussed the varied uses of facilities originally designed for "special classes." R. W. Fox, for example, has described how the State of California used its insane asylums as a resource for detaining persons displaying "odd or peculiar or immoral" behaviors—without official records providing clear and convincing evidence that these persons were a danger to themselves or others. Using a random sample of 1906–29 legal commitments from the San Francisco courts, Fox discovered the following:

> Two thirds of all those committed were odd, peculiar, or simply immoral individuals who displayed no symptoms indicating serious disability, or violent or destructive tendencies. The reported behavior of this 66 per cent included primarily nervous and depressive symptoms and a wide variety of fears, beliefs, perceptions, and delusions. In these cases the examiners noted the behaviors which they and various witnesses deemed inappropriate, but failed to indicate any reason why the individual, for his own protection or that of the community, had to be detained. [Fox 1978, p. 148]

The primary initiators of commitment procedures against these nondangerous persons were husbands, wives, sisters, brothers, and other relatives. Not only was their behavior deemed intolerable to family members, but they had also become a social and financial burden to their families. By using the state's insane asylum, the government relieved relatives of the cost of caring for a family member deemed disturbed. As Fox notes: "Some families, no doubt, would have been willing to tolerate deviant relatives were it not for the financial burden of caring for them. But by subsidizing only institutional, and not 'outdoor,' relief for disturbed individuals, the state forced those families to turn to commitment proceedings" (Ibid., p. 97).

This use of state asylums was also beneficial to the local counties. By providing custody, relief, and care at state expense, San Francisco did not have to provide funds via outdoor relief, or via a local, institutional alternative. As the superintendent of a state hospital noted in 1886, the state "had from an early day carried along on its reports a large contingent, drawn from all quarters, of chronic incurable dements, of imbeciles, dotards, idiots, drunkards, simpletons, fools; a class, in fact, of *harmless defectives*, usually found in *poor houses* elsewhere" (Ibid., p. 42; italics added). Because the state paid for the entire cost of maintaining these kinds of persons (for an indefinite period), county officials had little incentive to provide alternative facilities. The state insane asylums could, without a formal policy, function as state almshouses, even though the state was not legally responsible for sharing with counties the costs of providing indoor relief to dependent persons.

Changing Functions of the Almshouse, 1880–1923

As noted earlier, one of the oldest institutional types—counted comprehensively by the Census Bureau for the first time in 1850—was the almshouse. The almshouse always served multiple functions, so that the residence for paupers and dependents also housed persons who by other institutional criteria could be classified as insane, feeble-minded, vagrants, orphan children, and chronically ill. Despite the buildup of institutions for various "special classes" throughout the nineteenth and early twentieth century, the almshouse did not disappear from the decennial census counts until 1933. By 1940 it had become deinstitutionalized as a "special class" institutional *category*, and was mentioned only as a *type* of "home for the aged." How the almshouse was actually used over time offers an interesting example of the dynamic character of institutional functions, as well as one example of deinstitutionalization that has apparently run its historical course.

Table 2–2 provides national trend data for 43 years of resident and admission rates (per 100,000 population). From 1880 to 1923 there was a steady downward course in both residence and admission rates. By 1923 the residence rate was almost half of the 1880 rate. At that date, the admissions rates were much lower than the residence rates, indicating that there was also less turnover in inmates in 1923 than at earlier periods.

Table 2–3 provides insights into why the turnover rate had been reduced. The almshouse had increasingly experienced a reduction in its youth and young adult population and an increase in the proportion who were elderly. In 1880 only one-third of almshouse residents were sixty years and older, but by 1923 almost two-thirds were aged.

The demographic character of this increasingly aged population is revealed in Tables 2–4 and 2–5. In 1880 there were slightly more males per 100 resident females. But by 1923 this ratio had changed dramatically—from about 116 to 223 males per 100 females. In 1923 the almshouse also had few residents classified as "able-bodied" (7 percent), although 15 percent of those admitted during the year were classified by poorhouse officials as able-bodied. The majority of residents were deemed "incapacitated" or only able to do "light work." Almost half of the residents were deemed "defective." Of those so classified, the "crip-

TABLE 2–2

Almshouse Trend Rates per 100,000 Population in Residence or Admitted during Census Year: 1880–1923

Type of Census Count	1880	1890	1904	1910	1923
Resident on census date	132.0	116.6	100.0	91.5	71.5
Admitted during year	NA	NA	99.5	96.0	58.4

SOURCE: Adapted from U.S. Bureau of the Census, *Paupers in Almshouses*, 1923, p. 5.

TABLE 2–3

Age Distribution of Persons Residing in Almshouses (in percentages)

	Census Year				
Age	1880	1890	1904	1910	1923
Under 19	16.2	9.9	4.8	3.8	3.3
20–39	24.0	20.4	13.6	11.2	7.3
40–59	26.7	27.3	28.6	29.4	22.8
60 and over	33.1	40.5	51.2	54.7	65.5
Unknown	—	1.8	1.9	0.8	1.1
N =	(66,203)	(73,044)	(81,764)	(84,198)	(78,090)

SOURCE: U.S. Bureau of the Census, *Paupers in Almshouses*, 1923, p. 10.

TABLE 2–4

Ratio of Resident Male per 100 Resident Female Almshouse Residents: 1880–1923

	Census Year				
	1880	1890	1904	1910	1923
Ratios on census dates	116.1	126.1	178.9	210.0	223.7

SOURCE: U.S. Bureau of the Census, *Paupers in Almshouses*, 1923, p. 14.

TABLE 2–5

Physical and Mental Ratings of Almshouse Residents: 1923
(Percentage Distribution)

Ability to Work	Resident on Census Date	Admissions during Year
Able-bodied	7%	15%
Can do light work	38	34
Incapacitated	55	51
N =	(75,710)	(58,807)
Classed as Defective		
Insane	6%	13%
Feeble-minded	33	29
Epileptic	3	3
Deaf-mute	1	1
Blind	8	5
Crippled	42	44
Having two or more defects	7	4
N =	(36,700)	(15,669)

SOURCE: U.S. Bureau of the Census, *Paupers in Almshouses*, 1923, pp. 32–33.

pled" comprised 42 percent, and the "feeble-minded" were the second largest group, with 33 percent. The 1923 admissions revealed that being crippled, feeble-minded, or insane were the three major "defects" for which individuals were received into the almshouse.

If we conceptualize the almshouse as an institution functionally related to the special classes of institutions for defectives, then it is plausible that the almshouse trends of deinstitutionalization are associated with a *rise* in the rates of institutionalization of the insane and feeble-minded. Data in Table 2–6 show that in 1890, insane asylums and almshouses housed virtually the same number per 100,000 population on a census date. By 1904 this parity disappeared, and by 1923 insane asylums were housing 3½ times the rate housed in the almshouse. The relative increase in the rate of feeble-minded is even more dramatic. In 1890 there were almost 14 almshouse residents for every inmate of an institution for the feeble-minded; by 1923 this disparity had been reduced to a ratio of less than 2:1.

Notice that while the almshouse was being deinstitutionalized, the general trend of the *total* system was upward—from 243 to 352 per 100,000 population. It is interesting to note that this expansion occurred at the state level. More people were now being supported by state, rather than county, funds.

Table 2–7 indicates that the decreased reliance on the county almshouse was occurring for every age-specific population category, including the aged. Although the elderly comprised a rising proportion of the almshouse residents (see table 2–3), the rates of almshouse institutionalization of those 65 years and older actually decreased between 1910 and 1923—from 910 to 851. The age-specific rates for the two "defective" institutions suggest that each age group experienced increases. The pre-1930 trends indicate that the insane asylum was beginning to compete equally with the almshouse as a residence for the aged.

Changing Functions of the Mental Health System in Caring for the Aged

Viewed historically, by 1923 the community-based almshouse had been transformed from a multifunction institution to a relatively specialized age facility. In 1940 the almshouse was recognized as a type of home for the aged. Correlatively, the trend data indicate that the expansion of admissions to the insane asylum was associated with a disproportionate use of this institutional type as a residence for the aged. However, this use of mental health institutions could shift if other types of institutions for the aged were developed and publicly subsidized. In 1950 the rate of institutionalization of the aged in state and county mental hospitals peaked at 1,150 per 100,000 population; but by 1970 the rate was comparable to the 1910 rate of 563 (see tables 2–7 and 2–8).

Table 2–8 offers a modern perspective on the institutional location of the aged. The replacement for the almshouse—that diffuse category labeled "homes

TABLE 2–6

Trends in Institutionalization of Almshouse Residents, Feeble-Minded, and Insane:
1890–1923 (per 100,000 population)

	1890	1904	1910	1923
Almshouse	116.6	100.0	91.5	71.5
Insane asylums	118.2	183.6	204.2	241.7
Feeble-minded	8.4	17.5	22.5	39.3
Total	243.2	301.1	318.2	352.5

SOURCES: Adapted from U.S. Bureau of the Census, *Insane and Feeble-Minded*, 1910, pp. 183, 187; *Feeble-Minded and Epileptics in Institutions, 1923*, pp. 12, 26; *Paupers in Almshouses*, 1923, p. 5.

TABLE 2–7

Age-Specific Rates for Three Institutional Types: 1910 and 1923
(per 100,000 population)

	1910			1923		
	under 19	20–64	65 and over	under 19	20–64	65 and over
Almshouse	8.5	89.9	910.1	6.0	56.7	851.0
Insane	6.9	324.6	554.0	9.6	387.7	700.0
Feeble-minded*	25.4	21.1	2.9	47.3	38.1	4.4
Total	40.8	435.6	1,467.0	62.9	482.5	1,555.4

*Data for feeble-minded are for under 19, 20–59, and 60 and over.
SOURCES: See Table 2–6.

TABLE 2–8

Institutional Trends for Persons 65 Years and Over: 1950, 1960, and 1970
(per 100,000 population)

	1950	1960	1970
Homes for aged/dependent	1,769	2,342	3,966
Mental health	1,150	1,074	563
Chronic hospitals	72	140	175
All others	144	118	118
Total	3,135	3,714	4,822

SOURCE: Adapted from Kramer 1977, Appendix, Table 2.

for the aged and dependent"—housed about 56 percent of all of the institutionalized aged on a census date in 1950 (1,769 out of 3,135); the mental health system housed about 37 percent (1,150 out of 3,135). By 1960 the role of the mental health system seemed unchanged, inasmuch as the rates per 100,000 aged were about the same. However, an increase in institutionalization of the aged actually occurred in the "homes for aged" category and in "chronic hospitals." In 1960 "aged/dependent" homes accounted for 63 percent of institutionalized aged; "chronic hospitals" accounted for 4 percent, still a small amount of a one-day census count.

The shift in 1970 reveals a dramatic decrease in the mental health system's role in the care and custody of the aged. Besides being only about half of the 1950 rate (563 instead of 1,150), the proportion of aged housed under mental health auspices is only 12 percent, instead of 37 percent. The societal function of the mental health system has obviously shifted; actual national rates of mental illness have not changed as dramatically, if at all.

The evidence indicates that the multifunction mental health system will continue to house fewer aged persons. By 1975 the state/county rate was at a twentieth-century low—242 per 100,000 aged persons (NIMH, 1975, *Statistical Note*, no. 146, p. 5). The transformed almshouses and special age facilities—the community-based nursing homes—are now the multifunction places of residence for those aged with mental as well as physical and social problems. In 1969 NIMH researchers estimated that more than three times as many mentally ill aged persons lived in nursing homes as in mental hospitals (Ibid., 1974, no. 107, p. 14). These trends are occurring while the *total* system for the aged has experienced a dramatic increase in total rates of institutionalization. Unlike the almshouse shift from local to state care, the current shift is from state auspices to local public and private auspices. This shift, however, is being subsidized heavily by Medicare, Medicaid, and disability funding—all federal funding sources.

Summary and Conclusions

Traditional institutions were originally designed as self-contained sites where moral treatment, reformation, and education could occur in an orderly, disciplined environment. Although they had difficulty realizing these societal expectations, they did provide a minimum level of relief, care, and custody to their residents. These primary functions of institutions could, of course, occur in any institution, for any of the "special classes." Virtually all of the institutions performed multiple functions for diverse types of persons, while attempting to fulfill their specialized mandates.

According to census writers, the following factors influenced the increase or decrease in resident counts: the proportion of state subsidies; urbanization; geographic location; availability of a complete set of institutional resources; public relief policies; modes of policing; and the activities of private charities. These factors indicate that population trends *within* an institutional category cannot be fully understood unless the *total* institutional system is taken into account. In a sense, institutions perform multiple functions for each other, as well as for the larger society. Municipal shelters could replace overnight police lockups, just as state facilities for the retarded could receive mandatory transfers from county almshouses. Recent trends indicate that homes for the aged have become the modern institutional replacements for the almshouses and the state mental hospitals.

Prior to 1930 the historical trend was toward the expansion of state-supported facilities, and the contraction of local county facilities. This trend continued until the injection of federal funds began to affect institutional utilization. Just as the county was eager to shift a part of its social problems to state support (pre-1930), so were the states eager to have external funds replace—or reduce—reliance on traditional, state-subsidized institutionalization (post-1950). It appears that the rise of a federally supported welfare state is not only associated with higher rates of outdoor relief for the aged (via the public assistance and social insurance programs), but is also associated with higher rates of indoor relief (via medical assistance programs).

3 Nontraditional Institutional Alternatives

The preceding discussion of traditional institutions relied primarily on census materials to identify changes in categories and types of facilities. Whereas several post-1930 institutional types have been included in recent census documents, knowledge about new facilities must be gleaned from other government sources. This chapter will provide information about all of the nontraditional institutions enumerated by one or more federal agencies. The discussion of these residential alternatives will provide an empirical basis for understanding the living arrangements that have been created for ex-residents of traditional institutions, or for those who might have become residents.

Nontraditional Types: An Overview

As of 1970, according to a census definition, the following types of nontraditional institutions had been identified: nursing homes; drug centers; alcohol centers; residential treatment centers. A search of the literature reveals that the following additional types have been defined and enumerated as institutional facilities by at least one federal agency: board-and-care homes; group homes; halfway houses; homes and schools for the emotionally disturbed; community mental health center inpatient units. These newer institutional types, as well as the older ones, are examples of the definition I offered in the opening chapter:

> A civilian institution is a private or public establishment which furnishes (in single or multiple facilities) food and shelter to about four or more persons unrelated to the proprietor and, in addition, provides one or more of the following:
> 1. Medical and/or personal and/or social care;
> 2. Treatment and/or skills training and/or habilitation;
> 3. Supervision and/or custodial control;
> 4. Protection and/or social shelter;
> 5. Diagnostic assessment and/or background investigation.

The following federal organizations provide information about these newer institutional types:

1. *National Institute of Mental Health* (NIMH). Residential treatment centers, halfway houses, and community mental health centers.

2. *National Center for Health Statistics* (NCHS). Nursing homes, drug centers, alcohol centers, halfway houses, and homes and schools for the emotionally disturbed.

40

3. *Social Security Administration* (SSA). Board-and-care homes.

4. *Law Enforcement Assistance Administration* (LEAA). Group homes and halfway houses.

Each of these organizations appears to be aware of the census definitions and procedures and may even contract with the Census Bureau to conduct a survey, but each has been persuaded to define the facility according to its special interest. In cases of overlapping enumerations, it is possible to infer definitional emphases.

NIMH Enumeration of New Institutional Types

The National Institute of Mental Health's enumeration of institutional populations is conducted by the Division of Biometry and Epidemiology. This division attempts to record the utilization trends of persons using specialty inpatient and outpatient facilities primarily under psychiatric auspices. General hospitals with psychiatric units are included in regular surveys and trend analyses, but hospitals without special units are normally excluded. The U.S. Bureau of the Census also adheres to this distinction. Since 1967, the NIMH has set apart inpatient data on federally funded comprehensive community mental health centers (CMHC). Also included at varying intervals are data on nonfederally assisted "multiservice mental health facilities" (not classified as hospitals or residential treatment centers).

Many inpatient CMHC facilities are not unique, nontraditional types of short-stay institutions, for only about 12 percent are "free-standing." Out of 528 CMHCs enumerated in 1976, 338 were hospital-affiliated, and 127 hospital-based (NIMH, Series B, no. 16, 1979, p. 17).

In January 1976, there were 10,193 distinguishable CMHC inpatient beds and 993 multiservice-facility beds. These facilities comprised only 4.8 and 0.5 percent, respectively, of all specialty psychiatric beds in the country. But they were capable of handling a greater proportion of persons within a year, because of the short length of stay and high turnover in bed utilization (NIMH, *Statistical Note*, no. 144, 1978, p. 15). In 1975, for example, the CMHC facilities reported about 13.8 percent of all specialty inpatient care episodes occurring in the country (President's Commission, vol. 2, 1978, p. 93). Patient-care episodes refer to "the sum of the number of patients under care of a specific type of facility as of the beginning of the year and all the admission actions to these facilities during the following 12 months" (Kramer 1977, p. 10). In 1975 two traditional institutions enumerated by the U.S. Bureau of the Census—private psychiatric hospitals and VA psychiatric inpatient service units—each had fewer patient-care episodes (President's Commission, vol. 2, 1978, p. 93).

NIMH's Division of Biometry and Epidemiology has also initiated surveys of two additional types of facilities: halfway houses and residential treatment centers for children. It is estimated that by 1969, there were a minimum of 128 psychiatric and 120 alcoholic halfway houses (NIMH, Series A, no. 16, 1975, p. 2). By 1973 NIMH identified 209 psychiatric and 597 alcoholic halfway houses, containing 7,089 and 13,296 beds, respectively. The psychiatric halfway houses had 154 admissions per 100 beds, thus serving approximately 10,917 persons in 1973 (Ibid., based on pp. 41 and 63). The alcoholic halfway houses had a much greater turnover per annum—581 admissions per 100 beds. Therefore, this new institutional type served approximately 77,250 persons in 1973.

Although at its initiation the halfway house had a distinctive meaning as a transitional facility "bridging the gap" between traditional institutions and the community, the NIMH category appears in practice to perform a wider array of functions. At a state level, psychiatric halfway houses are licensed as: rooming houses (5.6 percent), boarding houses (11.9 percent), multiple-family dwellings (1.4 percent), and residential-care facilities (13.3 percent). In addition are those with "other" functions (13.3 percent), and those facilities without license (28.7 percent). Only 25.8 percent of psychiatric houses are termed "halfway houses" by states (Ibid.). Also, not all halfway houses conform to the image of a residential-type house. Only 12 percent of the psychiatric residents and 16 percent of the alcoholic residents lived in halfway houses containing 14 beds and under. Over 48 percent of the psychiatric residents were in facilities with 100 or more beds; over 24 percent of the alcoholic house residents were in facilities with 50 or more beds (Ibid., p. 25). Evidently the term "halfway house" can have multiple meanings, despite the NIMH attempt to provide the following official survey definition:

> Residential facilities in operation seven days a week, with round-the-clock staff supervision (of a staff member living in the halfway house), and providing room and board, and assistance in the activities of daily living primarily for persons with emotional disorders or alcoholism problems. Such facilities may also be known as recovery homes, rehabilitation residences, group care homes, or foster care homes.
>
> In addition to fullfilling the above definition, to be included in the Inventory, a facility must meet these additional criteria as follows:
>
> (1) The facility must have been in operation and must have contained three or more beds as of October, 1973.
>
> (2) The facility must be "free standing," that is, it must admit residents from a variety of community sources and not restrict its intake to only residents from an affiliated health institution such as a mental hospital. [Ibid., p. 31]

The definition attempts deliberately to *exclude* the following: (1) halfway houses *not* primarily for the two disability groups, such as facilities serving primarily the mentally retarded, drug abusers, delinquents, or adult criminals; (2) facilities whose primary focus is the provision of a planned treatment program; (3) facilities that "serve all types of handicapped persons," and not primarily the mentally ill or alcoholics; (4) facilities whose primary function is to provide room and board but not a "supportive living arrangement or assistance in the activities of daily living"; and (5) "specialized" alcoholic treatment facilities.

Residential treatment centers for children were first noted in the 1960 census. This classification was intended to "include those institutions which primarily serve children who by clinical diagnosis, are moderately or seriously disturbed emotionally and which provide treatment services usually supervised or directed by a psychiatrist" (Kramer 1977, p. 54). A majority of treatment centers were originally homes for dependent and neglected children, having shifted their service focus as the demand for traditional children's institutions (i.e., dependent and neglected) continued to decline in the post-World War II years (Maluccio and Marlow 1972). By 1966, almost 300 of more than 2,500 children's institutions had redefined their function as dealing primarily with "emotionally disturbed children" (Pappenfort et al. 1970, vol. 1).

According to NIMH sources, the first reliable data about residential treatment centers (RTC) emerged in 1966. At that time these centers accounted for 8,000 "patient-care episodes" (i.e., residents on last day of year plus all additions during the following year). By 1969 this figure had grown to 21,340; and by 1971 it had risen to 28,637. The growth in both years may, in part, be due to more complete census coverage of those facilities that had redefined their functions by 1966 (Kramer 1977, p. 9; NIMH, Series A, no. 14, 1974). Since 1971 there appears to have been virtually no growth in this NIMH category of institution-alization. The figures for 1973 and 1975 were, respectively, 29,920 and 28,199 patient-care episodes (NIMH, *Statistical Note*, no. 135, July 1977).

The number of RTC facilities has fluctuated between 344 (in 1971) and 331 (in 1975). The average size of facilities was 54 and 56, but about 43 percent of the beds were in facilities with more than 75 beds (Ibid.). These facilities tended to keep youth for more than a year; in 1973 the additions per 100 beds were 64 per 100, and in 1975, 67 per 100. Although the overwhelming majority of facilities (about 85 percent) were conducted as nonprofit organizations, a number of facilities had been initiated for profit-making purposes (about 12 percent).

NCHS Enumeration of New Institutional Types

Since 1963, the National Center for Health Statistics (NCHS) has attempted to develop and maintain a "national inventory of hospitals and institutions" (NCHS, Series 1, no. 3, 1965). The surveys, conducted every two years, attempt to secure information concerning health statistics. However, surveys are also viewed as "the most efficient medium for the collection of utilization statistics for hospitals, resident institutions, and other types of health facilities" (Ibid., p. 1). The Master Facility Inventory (MFI) initially defined institutions as "establishments which are in business to provide medical, nursing, personal, or custodial care to groups of unrelated individuals who have no usual place of residence elsewhere" (Ibid., p. 2).

Besides "resident institutions," the MFI also includes *all hospitals* in the United States with six or more beds; other resident institutions can qualify if they have three or more beds. The 1963 MFI categories were similar to those used in the 1960 census, except that all mental retardation and nonhospital facilities for the mentally ill were initially excluded. In 1967 the nonmedical residences for mental disabilities were included. In the 1967 survey, it is clear that the major interest of the MFI report was nursing homes for the aged and hospitals (both general and special); all other categories were referred to as "other inpatient health facilities," and were discussed only briefly (NCHS, Series 14, no. 4, 1972).

By the time of the last available MFI survey, conducted in 1973, correctional facilities had been omitted as a "health facility," and nonhospital facilities housing drug abusers and alcoholics had been added. This survey included halfway houses for the first time. Although no definition is offered, it is likely that NCHS personnel may have initially relied on the halfway house master facility lists generated by NIMH and the National Institute of Drug Administration (NIDA). Halfway houses for the emotionally disturbed, alcoholics, and drug abusers were specifically noted, while other types were excluded. However, unlike the NIMH reports, there were no separate definitions or figures provided for halfway houses.

The NCHS operational definition of a nonhospital alcohol facility appears to be much broader than the NIMH definition of a halfway house. In 1973 the NCHS reported the following facts about alcoholic group quarters: 24,825 beds, 18,574 residents, and 106,856 admissions (NCHS, unpublished data, 1977). In contrast, the 1973 NIMH survey yielded the following approximate data: 13,296 beds, 10,295 residents, and 77,250 admissions. Insofar as the NCHS definition of a nonmedical alcohol facility yields a 28 percent disparity in admissions compared to the NIMH definition, it appears that the former's definition is operationally broader. Correlatively, it appears that a similar inference can be made concerning the definition of facilities for the nonhospitalized emotionally disturbed. In 1973, for example, NCHS data of homes and schools for the emotionally disturbed accounted for about 34,760 youth under 18; NIMH only counted 17,680 youth in RTC facilities (NIMH, Series A, no. 4, 1974; NIMH, *Statistical Note*, no. 135, July 1977; NCHS, Series 14, no. 16, 1976; NCHS unpublished data).

Whereas the NCHS operational definition of nonhospital facilities for alcoholics and the emotionally disturbed is probably broader than that used in the NIMH halfway-house survey, the definition of nursing homes appears quite similar to the category used in the 1970 census. The MFI figures reflect an adherence to a U.S. census-type definition of nursing home, first offered by NCHS in 1963:

> Establishments which provide nursing or personal care to the aged, infirm, or chronically ill. These include places referred to as nursing homes, convalescent homes, homes for the aged, rest homes, boarding homes for the aged, and homes for the needy such as almshouses, county homes, and "poor" farms. The primary factor which determines that such establishments are in the scope of the MFI is their function of providing some kind of care beside room and board. A home for the aged, for example, which *does not routinely provide nursing or personal care—that is, pro-*

*vides only room and board—is not considered an institution and is therefore not in
the scope of the inventory.* [NCHS, Series 1, no. 3, 1965, p. 3; italics added]

Nursing homes as special "care" institutions were first identified by the census
in 1950, but received no special definition at that time. The NCHS notation about
"providing some kind of care besides room and board" appears to be congruent
with the 1970 census references to homes that offer skilled nursing care or "domiciliary or personal care." The Census Bureau, besides offering the basis of the
nursing-home definition, also conducts the "other health facilities" survey for
NCHS; this assures further congruency between the two agencies' approach to
institutional counting.

In 1969 the following levels of nursing-home care were specified in the MFI
survey:

> *Nursing Care Home.* An establishment is a nursing care home if nursing care is
> the primary and predominant function of the facility. . . . One or more registered
> nurses or licensed practical nurses were employed and 50 percent or more of the
> residents received nursing care during the week prior to the survey.
> *Personal Care Home with Nursing.* An establishment is a personal care home with
> nursing if personal care is the primary and predominant function of the facility but
> some nursing care is also provided . . . [and] three or more personal services were
> routinely provided [during the week].
> *Personal Care Home.* An establishment is a personal care home if the primary and
> predominant function of the facility is personal care and no residents received nurs-
> ing care during the week prior to the survey. . . . Three or more of the criterion per-
> sonal services were routinely provided.
> *Domiciliary Care Home.* A facility is a domiciliary care home if the primary and
> predominant function of the facility is domiciliary care but the facility has the re-
> sponsibility for providing some personal care. . . . One or two of the criterion per-
> sonal services are routinely provided. [NCHS, Series 14, no. 6, p. 57]

"Criterion personal services" were defined as "rub and massage, help with
tub bath or shower, help with dressing, correspondence, shopping, walking or
getting about, and help with eating." Homes that did not routinely provide at
least one of these criterion services were defined as "not in the scope" of the
survey (Ibid., pp. 57–58). In 1973, the number of persons enumerated as residing in domiciliary-care or personal-care homes was quite small in comparison to
nursing residents, as the following figures indicate: Nursing care—824,038
(76.6 percent); Personal care with nursing—171,799 (16.0 percent); Personal
care—77,028 (7.2 percent); Domiciliary care—2,859 (0.3 percent).

Nursing homes also tend to be classified by their certification status as a skilled
or intermediate care facility, reimbursable under Medicare or Medicaid. Because
Medicare only recognizes one type of nursing facility—skilled nursing (or
SNF)—all facilites certified as meeting Medicare standards would have to be of
this type, i.e., "an institution (or a distinct part of an institution) . . . which is
primarily engaged in providing to patients (a) skilled nursing care and related
services . . . or (b) rehabilitation services under 24-hour nursing service" (So-

cial Security Act, 1978, sec. 1861 [J]). In contrast, Medicaid-certified inter-mediate care facilities (ICF) provide "care and services (above the level of room and board)," but below that of a hospital or SNF (Ibid., sec. 1905 [c]). In a 1973–74 NCHS survey, 65 percent of 1,075,800 nursing home residents lived in facilities that met SNF standards of care, 22 percent in ICFs, and 13 percent in noncertified residences (NCHS, series 13, no. 29, 1977, p. 4). About 90 percent of the residents were 65 years or older.

SSA Enumeration of Board-and-Care Homes

Other care facilities have been and are being used by disabled persons both under and over the age of 65 (see U.S. Senate Subcommittee on Long-Term Care, *Supporting Paper No. 7*, 1976). These newer types of "domiciliary-care" facilities do not provide any routine health-related nursing or personal-care services (as defined by NCHS, Medicare, or Medicaid). Instead, these board-and-care homes provide other nonmedical institutional functions: supervision and/or custody, protection and/or refuge, and personal and/or social care. Fortunately, another federal agency, the Social Security Administration (SSA), has had an interest in enumerating the nonmedical living arrangements of aged, blind, and disabled persons (physical, emotional, and mental retardation) receiving Supplementary Security Income (SSI).

Because the basic SSI grant is federally financed, and many SSI programs are also federally administered, the federal government has an interest in collecting data about recipients. However, the federal statisticians must count recipients according to their benefit and administrative status, rather than strictly by their living arrangements. Therefore, only partial data are available concerning the residential whereabouts of SSI recipients. Non-SSI recipients living in board-and-care homes are not counted by any national agency and also tend to be under-enumerated by state agencies.

Data are only available for fifteen states where the federal government actually administers state-financed, optional supplementation programs that explicitly cover extra levels of approved costs of supervised living arrangements in a non-medical care facility. Even for the fifteen states for which the SSA Office of Research and Statistics (ORS) collects data, persons in nonmedical facilities can escape enumeration if they are not subsidized by a federally administered optional state supplement.

As of 1 March 1976, nearly 107,000 SSI recipients were enumerated as resid-ing in a supervised living arrangement (funded by optional supplementation) in the fifteen federally administered states. The rates varied, however, by SSI eligi-bility. The supervised living arrangements were 5.4 percent for the aged, 4.4 percent for the blind, and 7.7 percent for the disabled (Kochhar 1977). By De-cember 1977, the total number of persons residing in a supervised living arrangement in the fifteen states had increased to about 113,000, an overall rate of approximately 6.8 percent (ORS, unpublished data, 1978).

A recent study by an ORS staff member, Satya Kochhar, provides insight into the SSA approach toward enumerating this new institutional type. Writing in the *Social Security Bulletin*, she comments as follows:

> States with optional domiciliary care provisions offer varying types of care, but one element is common among them: All provide some supervision and assistance in personal care.
>
> All facilities provide room and board, but room and board alone is not considered to be *supervised care*. A three-way classification based on the extent of care is offered under the federally administered programs.
>
> *General Supervision*. This care is for individuals who cannot function in an independent living arrangement but who do not need personal care. It may be provided in foster care homes, in family-type settings for fewer than five persons, or in a larger group or institutional setting.
>
> *Personal Care and General Supervision*. This care is for ambulatory individuals who need assistance with eating, bathing, or dressing but do not require medical or nursing care. This *level of care may be provided in domiciliary care facilities, rest homes, personal care homes, and homes for the aged*.
>
> *Custodial and Other Nonmedical Care*. This is provided in addition to personal care for those individuals who need a *more protective setting*. These persons include, for example, mentally retarded, former mental patients requiring special care, or individuals who are mentally confused because of advanced age. [Kochhar 1977; italics added]

These types of facilities, unlike the nursing homes enumerated by NCHS and the U.S. census, are ineligible to be classified as Medicare or Medicaid institutions, because there is a federal SSI grant reduction, and persons are counted as living in a medical facility. Therefore, any significant overlap with the NCHS enumeration of nursing-home residents is unlikely.

A national estimate of the number of SSI recipients living in a board-and-care home (or in a domiciliary-care facility) can be projected, using the conservative data provided for the fifteen states reporting to SSA in December 1977. At that time about 6.8 percent of SSI recipients were enumerated as residing in non-medical, supervised living arrangements. Applying this rate to the 4,230,000 national SSI recipients known to SSA in August 1977 would yield a shelter-care population of at least 288,000 persons. It is unlikely that the national figure would be below this conservative estimate, in that many SSI recipients live in states that do not have their optional supplements administered by the federal government; in addition, many persons live in board-and-care homes without any supplementation different from that received by persons living in their own homes.

This estimate also excludes board-and-care home residents not covered by SSI. In a California study of board-and-care homes serving MI residents, about

20 percent were not receiving SSI (Segal and Aviram 1978, p. 254). If this were true nationally, the conservative estimate of 288,000 would have to be increased to about 360,000 residents. Either of these low estimates would place this type as second in importance to nursing homes (as indicated by number of residents).

LEAA Enumeration of Halfway Houses and Group Homes

In the corrections field the major new types of institutional facilities—group homes and halfway houses—were not included in the 1970 U.S. Bureau of the Census counts. In 1974, the Law Enforcement Assistance Administration (LEAA) funded the Census Bureau to conduct a facility census that for the first time included group homes and halfway houses for juveniles (in both private and public facilities). At that time the category was defined as follows: "*Halfway house, group home.* A facility where juveniles are allowed extensive contact with the community, such as through jobs and schools" (Gottfredson et al. 1978, p. 754). Because NCHS no longer counts correctional facilities, there would appear to be little danger of overlap with the LEAA census. In the middle of 1974 there were 10,919 youth residing in *private*-group and halfway houses. However, of this number 2,844 youth were committed as "dependent and neglected"; 261 were classified as "emotionally disturbed or mentally retarded"; and 1,838 were "voluntary commitments" (Ibid., p. 606). It appears probable that the private sector of the correctional subsystem has a potential overlap with the child welfare subsystem (via dependent and neglected and voluntary commitments) and the mental health and mental retardation subsystems (see Chapter 8).

The public sector may also overlap with the other juvenile institutional subsystems, but the data are not provided. In 1971 there were 973 youth residing on a census date in a public group or halfway house; in 1973 there were 1,602; and in 1974 there were 1,727. The combined public and private figure, in 1974, was 12,646. Inasmuch as the traditional juvenile institutional type—the public training school—had a resident count of only 25,397 in 1974, the new institutional type—the group and halfway house—is a potentially significant omission from the usual census correctional category.

Summary and Conclusions

The definitional approach provided by the U.S. Bureau of the Census provides the initial basis for understanding the nation's total institutional system, the related categories, and the facility types. This total system was specified in Chapter 2. Since the 1950 census, the mental-health subsystem has been expanded by NIMH to include inpatient facilities in community mental health and multipurpose centers, children's residential treatment centers, and halfway houses (psychiatric and alcoholic).

NCHS efforts indicate that facilities for alcoholics, drug users, and the emotionally disturbed are not adequately enumerated by relying on the mental-health boundaries provided by the NIMH surveys or the 1970 census. The nursing-home surveys conducted by NCHS since 1970 reveal this institutional type to be of great significance for over one million residents.

The SSA highlighting of the existence of an extensive number of nonmedical, shelter-care homes, distinguished by some care and supervision characteristics, is also a significant addition to the total census boundary.

The initial LEAA foray into an enumeration of private juvenile facilities reveals the potential importance of new juvenile group quarters: the group home and halfway house. However, there may be a substantial overlap with other juvenile institutional subsystems (see Chapter 8).

It is apparent that the country has been engaging in the invention and expansion of many new institutional types since the 1930s: nursing homes (SNF and ICF); nonmedical board-and-care homes; homes and schools for the emotionally disturbed; community mental health and multipurpose inpatient facilities; group homes and halfway houses in the fields of alcohol, drugs, mental health, mental retardation, and juvenile corrections. The addition of these types testifies to an expansion of the total institutional system.

Of the new types that have emerged, the most significant ones for adults appear to be nursing and nonmedical board-and-care homes. The latter type of facility houses varied sizes of multiple-problem groups. A recent California study of persons, aged 18 to 65, with a history of a hospital stay for mental illness found that persons residing in "sheltered-care" arrangements were distributed as follows:

> Family care homes account for 26% of the facilities in California and serve 14% of residents in sheltered care. Halfway houses, which have by far received the greatest attention from mental health professionals, constitute only 2% of facilities and serve only 3% of the population in sheltered care. Board-and-care homes, which have developed in an unplanned, *ad hoc* manner, service 82% of the California sheltered care population and comprise 72 per cent of the state's facilities. The extent of service now provided by board-and-care facilities leaves little doubt that an entirely new residential care system for the mentally ill is emerging. The more familiar and well-defined facilities—halfway houses and family-care homes—have only a minor role in this new system. [Segal and Aviram 1978, p. 106]

This new type of facility varied in size from 2 persons to 280 persons and could function as an old-fashioned boarding house or be operated like a "mini-hospital" (Ibid., p. 106). The authors started with a list of 1,910 eligible facilities offering supervision and care for the mentally ill, but found that only 60 percent were actually doing so. Although the facilities studied were chosen for their likelihood of serving mentally ill persons, they were actually found to be serving multiple groups: three-fourths of the 1,155 facilities studied served more than one category of clientele—mentally retarded, drug abusers, alcoholics, physically disabled, and the aged. Segal and Aviram comment on this policy of heterogeneous grouping as follows: "This policy may indicate a step back to noncategorical care, perhaps to the old poorhouse concept where individuals are served indiscriminately. The selection criterion is simply the inability to 'make it' in society—that is, social dependency" (Ibid., p. 118).

The authors imply that the facilities not studied also had a heterogeneous population of diverse "social dependents." Although Segal and Aviram do not appear to mean that California's sheltered-care facilities are miniature "poorhouses," the reference to the almshouse is a useful reminder that the new type of group quarters houses an economically dependent stratum of society: 81 percent of the sampled residents were supported by Supplementary Security Income (SSI) payments (Ibid., p. 254). Unlike the almshouses, however, this new type of group quarters is largely managed by private operators conducting a proprietary business.

The unique social amalgam of public functions—subsidized mainly by federal and state funds, occurring in a new type of institutional residence, managed by a proprietor, and operated for profit—is, of course, a relatively recent phenomenon. The only other comparable subsystem is the nursing home "industry" (U.S. Senate Special Committee on Aging, *Supporting Paper No. 7*, 1976). At present, medically recognized nursing home residents and facility characteristics are fairly well documented by NCHS every two years. The new shelter-care industry, housing mainly a welfare population (via SSI), has not yet gained consistent statistical respectability at a federal level. If California is an example, then it is also not accurately enumerated by other states. Inasmuch as California is a recognized national leader in community-based care, this inference about the states is probably valid.

Although the data from the various federal sources are difficult to aggregate in an unduplicated fashion, the evidence cited in this section appears sufficiently persuasive to help us conclude that the actual American institutional system of 1980 is much broader and diverse than that reported in the 1970 census. It is broader, too, than that reported in the specialty areas of mental health, retardation, and juvenile correction.

4

New Sources of Social Control Practices

Historically, traditional institutions were utilized for the "relief, care and custody of defective, dependent and delinquent" persons. Many residents of these older facility types were placed there by a formal, court-approved, involuntary court commitment. In contrast, many residents of the newer, nontraditional facilities are not subject to formal court orders. Rather, they have been placed there voluntarily or by the actions of parents, spouses, relatives, guardians, and public authorities. For example, a 1976 survey of institutionalized persons determined that nursing-home residents had been admitted by the following means:

Resident	32.6%
Parent or spouse	8.2
Other relative, friends, guardian	44.5
Public authority	3.9
Court action	0.4
All other	10.3

SOURCE: U.S. Bureau of the Census, June 1978, p. 294.

Whereas the sources of admission to another nontraditional institution—facilities for emotionally disturbed—varied, only 26.4 percent of the residents were placed there by court action, and 10.4 percent by a public authority (Ibid., p. 294). This reduced reliance on involuntary commitments has changed the manner in which custodial-type supervision is administered, but it has not eliminated the use of social control functions by the newer types of institutions. Some nontraditional facilities rely upon locked rooms, wings, and buildings, as well as other forms of physical controls. But nontraditional facilities also rely on "house rules" and curfew restrictions, operator demands and/or threats, limits on use of resident spending money, and psychotropic drugs as ways to control the behavior of residents. Although the literature is sparse about these less traditional modes of control, there is persuasive evidence that the alternatives to traditional institutions are engaged in a variety of "supervisory" activities.

California's Restrictive Local Alternatives to State Mental Hospitals

California is widely recognized as a leader in the depopulation of state mental hospitals. The state system has been able to reduce its resident population from a

51

peak of 37,490 persons in 1959 to only 5,715 residents in July 1977. By 1985 California expects to reduce its state MI population even further—to 2,890 residents (State of California Department of Health, *Plan of the Community Development Task Force for Services to the Mentally Ill*, 6 April 1977). In order to implement its target, the 1978–79 county mental health plan listed the following as "priority #1": "Development of *involuntary* treatment facilities at levels and capacities adequate to handle the average demand for such service without reliance upon the state hospitals" (Ibid., p. 1; italics added).

In harmony with state mental health officials, Los Angeles county planners conceptualized their community-based local facilities into four "service types." Of the four types, only the last is deemed an unsupervised alternative to state mental hospitals. Types I and II are classified as local facilities that "would provide care to the patient population identified in the Los Angeles survey as requiring residential care in a *locked* facility and residential care with *close* supervision" (Ibid., p. 71; italics added). Type I is the 24-hour acute-care hospital; this is either a bed in a psychiatric unit in a private general hospital or a bed in an acute psychiatric hospital. Type II is a 24-hour care program in either a skilled nursing or intermediate care facility (i.e., SNF or ICF). Persons requiring "residential care with minimal supervision" would be placed in Type III, a 24-hour care program in a facility licensed by the Department of Health. Services include "personal assistance, personal hygiene, monitoring of prescribed medication, supervision and provision of social and recreational activities" (Ibid., p. 71).

On the basis of these models, the Los Angeles survey assessed October 1976 patterns of patient need for those who might have been a 72-hour admission to a *state* hospital. These need assessments included the following types of "alternative 24-hour care facilities": (1) locked facilities; (2) facilities with close supervision but not locked; (3) facilities with minimal supervision; and (4) other residential facilities. According to the survey, 433 involuntary admissions to state hospitals from Los Angeles County could be diverted by using the following "bed types":

Bed Types	Number of Beds	Percent Distribution
Locked	213	49%
Close supervision	78	18
Minimal supervision	58	13
Other residential	4	01
Independent living/own family	80	19
Total	433	100%

SOURCE: Ibid., pp. 72, 75.

The Los Angeles county planners (as well as the state planners) were quite aware that of the 433 potential diversions from the 72-hour state "holds," about 49 percent could be placed in locked county or private hospitals, and 18 percent in facilities with close supervision. Only 19 percent were deemed capable of being released directly to the community with no supervision.

Ranking Living Arrangements by Degree of Restrictiveness

A close reading of the California plans, as well as site visits to facility types, indicate that skilled and intermediate-care nursing homes, as well as psychiatric units of local hospitals, can function as locked facilities. If nontraditional alternatives are categorized according to a dichotomous medical or nonmedical classification, it is possible to compare roughly the degree of restrictiveness associated with each category:

NONMEDICAL LIVING ARRANGEMENTS
1. Own apartment; no ongoing supervision.
2. Shared apartment or living with family; minimal supervision of activities.
3. Supervised living apartment; few rules, but free to come and go under minimal supervision.
4. Family group homes (5 persons or less); resident supervision and house rules, but relatively free to come and go.
5. Board-and-care homes; resident supervision, and house rules, but free to come and go.
6. Group homes/halfway houses; moderate supervision, but some free to come and go.
7. Twenty-four hour supervision board-and-care homes and group homes.
8. Locked rooms in board-and-care homes and group homes.

MEDICAL FACILITIES
1. Psychiatric halfway houses; house rules but supervision and freedom varies, according to a treatment program.
2. Nursing homes; 24-hour supervision, little freedom to come and go.
3. Inpatient general hospitals/psychiatric units or CMHCs; 24-hour supervision, little freedom to come and go.
4. State hospitals; 24-hour supervision, little freedom to come and go.
5. Nursing homes; locked facilities, wings, or rooms, little freedom.
6. General hospitals/psychiatric units; locked units, little freedom.
7. State hospitals; locked buildings, wards, rooms, little freedom to come and go.

In general, it appears that nonmedical facilities are much less restrictive than medical institutions. Many nursing-home residents complain about a lack of freedom to come and go, even though only 14.4 percent are confined to bed (U.S. Bureau of the Census, June 1978, p. 134). Segal and Aviram's sample of ex-patients, primarily residents of California board-and-care homes, assessed their current living arrangements as follows: "Eighty-four percent of the residents said they would object to returning to a mental hospital" (Segal and Aviram 1978, p. 271). Segal and Aviram's conclusion about the shelter-care environment (see numbers 4 through 7, above), compared to hospitals, is significant, in that over 75 percent of these nonmedical facilities housed a mixture of problem groups: the mentally retarded, drug abusers, alcoholics, the physically disabled, the elderly, and the mentally ill (Ibid., p. 118). They commented as follows:

> If our study had been an evaluation, we might have painted a bleaker picture of the sheltered care environment. Instead, we looked at this environment in a way that seeks to maximize our understanding of the benefits it offers or can offer to the formerly hospitalized mental patient. It is our view, as it is the view of many of the residents we have spoken to, that *at least this environment is a place where there is more freedom* to determine one's personal life than there was in the hospital. [Ibid., p. 287; italics added]

In general, there are strong reasons for believing that medical-type facilities are associated with the greater degrees of restrictive living. Even "bleak" board-and-care homes are preferable to accredited hospital living for 84 percent of a California sample of former mental patients. The neutral language of DE tends to obscure the fact that it is the hospitals and the hospital-type imitations (e.g., nursing homes) that often constitute the most restrictive types of living arrangements.

Types of Controls in Nursing Homes

The elderly population in a nursing home might be perceived as a fairly manageable population group—in comparison to problems posed by youth in trouble, young adult MI and MR persons. However, HEW's Health Care Financing Administration issued guidelines on the mental health care to be provided in SNFs and ICFs that are "Institutions for Mental Diseases"; these included physical, chemical, and social means of controlling elderly patients (Health Care Financing Administration, 11 May 1977). Regarding physical restraints, the manual stated: "If restraints are used, the patient must be allowed to be up and about every two hours for a 15-minute period. Restraints must be closely checked to see that circulation is not impaired. Staff must sit with the patient and attempt to orient the patient" (Ibid., pt. 5, 5–81–50). No mention is made regarding the type, degree, and duration of the restraint—only the "scheduling."

Regarding chemical controls via drugs, the manual states:

> Staff must be particularly alert to giving supportive care to patients on psychotropic medications as the use of medication alone is generally not sufficient. Tranquilizers, antidepressants, vasodilators and other types of medication can be helpful, but also dangerous. . . . The staff should also be advised not to resort to punitive action against patients who are difficult to manage. . . . An acceptable principle of patient

care is that staff's establishment of trusting relationships with patients. . . . Such relationships are preferable to physical and chemical restraints. [Ibid., 5–81–40]

It should be noted that no provisions were made regarding the types, degree, duration, and scheduling of psychotropic drugs; these were left up to the staff, in accordance with plans approved by a "psychiatrist or knowledgeable physician." Relationships are "preferred" to chemical and physical restraints. Routine examinations to check up on "blood and metabolic irregularities" are to be conducted "where indicated"—rather than at specified intervals. This laxity toward regular drug checkups and testing exists even though the manual concedes that "irregularities are not uncommon when psychotropic drugs are administered for long periods of time" (Ibid., 5–81–50). Six years earlier, a study conducted under HEW auspices had found the following poor general medical practices in seventy-five nursing homes:

> Since the administration of drugs is the *primary* therapy in such homes, the study inevitably concentrated on their use.
>
> More than 30 percent of the patients had no recorded admission data, no transfer abstract, *no diagnosis nor initial treatment orders*—even though many were on digitalis and other *potentially dangerous drugs*.
>
> 73 percent had *no recorded admissions history*.
>
> 37 percent of the patients taking cardiovascular drugs (digitalis or diuretics, or both) had not had their blood pressure taken in *over a year*.
>
> 35 percent of the patients on *tranquilizers had not had their blood pressure recorded in more than a year*. Some were taking two and often three tranquilizers concurrently.
>
> Most of the patients reviewed were on one to four different drugs; and many were taking from seven to twelve drugs; some were on *both uppers and downers at the same time*.
>
> Revised treatment or medication orders had been written in the past 30 days for only 18 percent of the patients.
>
> 40 percent had not been seen by a physician for over three months.
> [U.S. Senate Subcommittee on Long-Term Care, *Supporting Paper*, no. 2, p. 253; italics added]

Besides reviewing this and other studies indicating the "misuse, high costs, and kickbacks" associated with drug use in nursing homes, the U.S. Senate Subcommittee on Long-Term Care conducted hearings in a variety of cities. In Minnesota, the subcommittee heard the testimony of witnesses, based on fifty sworn affidavits, that reported "indiscriminate tranquilization" of elderly patients to keep them quiet. Many orderlies and unlicensed aids even administered the drugs on their own initiative or increased the dosage beyond the prescription order. The executive director of the Minneapolis Age and Opportunity Center summarized the testimony as follows: "For the beleaguered nurse's aide, tranquilizers are a happy solution. If patients are sedated, they cause the staff few problems. The administrator is happy, too, because bedbound patients bring the highest rate of reimbursement" (Ibid., p. 272).

Types of Controls in Treatment Centers for Youth

If drugs are used as "chemical strait jackets" (a term coined by a pharmacologist and used by the Senate subcommittee) for the elderly, it is not surprising that they are also used on youth in trouble. A study of teen-age girls confined in the New Jersey Training School for Girls (a traditional institution) found that 76 percent were recorded as receiving sedating or tranquilizing drugs one or several times per day—even though the background information did not indicate that there was a need for this unusual proportion of psychotropic drug usage (Lerman et al. 1974, pp. 25–26). The Children's Defense Fund issued a recent report on varied institutional types, based on detailed field studies in seven states: Arizona, California, Massachusetts, New Jersey, Ohio, South Carolina, and South Dakota). It concluded:

> Children are abused in institutions *and in other group settings*. The abuse takes many forms, not only physical abuse, but the *overuse of drug therapies*, of punitive and unmonitored seclusion and of severe behavioral restrictions. Despite public concern about familial abuse, no state visited has set up specific mechanisms, nor issued specific guidelines, to monitor and eliminate the institutional abuse of children.
> [Children's Defense Fund, April 1977, p. 20; italics added]

The finding that other group settings and not only traditional institutions overuse drug therapies is not unusual. A recent class-action suit filed against the State of Louisiana charged that mentally retarded, emotionally disturbed, and other children placed in child care facilities were being mistreated and denied remediation in the least restrictive setting, even though all of the institutions were private facilities providing special treatment, located in the neighboring State of Texas (*Gary W. et al.* v. *Cherry et al.*, 26 July 1976). The suit charged that "trainable" retarded children were placed in purely custodial facilities, blind children were placed with no program for the blind, deaf-mute children were placed with no program for the deaf, and delinquent children were placed in purely custodial facilities. Many of the children were subsidized by Social Security Act funds from Title IV-A (Sec. 408) to receive a "foster care placement." According to the judicial findings, instead of receiving special treatment, they were placed in the following living arrangements:

> A. *Bagley Home for Children.* Unsafe practices are followed in storing and administering medicine. Medications are changed by the administration without medical consultation. Mentally retarded children are cared for by other mentally retarded children. There are PRN (*pro re nata*, "according to need," i.e., ward attendants are given discretion to administer changes as they deem necessary) restraint orders for most residents.
>
> B. *Balcones' Children Psychiatric Center.* Medical services are deficient. Residents have been subjected to inappropriate forms of punishment.
>
> C. *Bartley Woods House.* Patients have been tied, handcuffed or chained together to fixtures or furniture as a means of control and discipline.

D. *Beaumont Remedial Center*. Some of the witnesses criticized the medical model of the program and some of its disciplinary aspects, but on the whole, the institution appears to be an adequate one.

E. *Children's Cottage*. The administrator has abused children by hitting them with her hand or a soup ladle and by tying one child to her bed and keeping her in a high chair all day. The staff members are authorized by the administrators to strike children. Medical practices are unsafe.

F. *Dillons Home*. In general, the institution appears to meet minimal standards.

G. *Dyer Vocational Training Center*. There was excessive use of psychotropic drugs to control residents. [Ibid., pp. 395–97]

The following types of control activities can be observed in "residential treatment centers," shelters, and group homes for children and youth in other states: (1) no doors on bedrooms; (2) no access to any clothes other than those worn on that day, except by staff possessing key to locked basement wardrobe; (3) outer doors open, but inner areas locked; (4) no person moves alone without explicit permission, and all children move about as a group from activities; (5) all children assigned "buddies," who must know each other's whereabouts; (6) isolation rooms, with bars on the windows and locked doors; (7) all clothes taken away for first month, and person provided only with pajamas and slippers; (8) all activities organized and scheduled as part of "treatment plan" (personal site visits in summer 1977).

These activities are often justified on the grounds that they are part of a "therapeutic treatment environment." Even nursing homes justify similar restraints as "milieu therapy." As the SNF/ICF regulations for geriatric patients state: "Milieu therapy may also be appropriate for the aged mentally ill patient. Generally the nurse institutes milieu therapy by *regulating the patient's environment and interpersonal contacts* while at the same time stressing the importance of staff attitudes (positive) toward the patient" (Health Care Financing Administration, 1977, 5–81–501; italics added).

Types of Controls in Board-and-Care Homes

Board-and-care homes harbor no pretense about offering milieu therapy or treatment. Instead, they are expected to provide minimal supervision of multiple groups of adults. Medication is directly supervised in many facilities in California (Segal and Aviram 1978, p. 124); presumably, similar practices exist elsewhere.

The California study of shelter-care adults found that 83 percent of the operators affirmed that *they* supervised the dispensing of medications; 72 percent of the operators do not permit the patients to keep their own medication (Ibid., p. 241). In general, these patients are attended to by general practitioners, not psychiatrists. The doctors are "arranged for by the operators." The doctors, in turn, tend to maintain ex-patients on the same drugs and dosage as when they left the hospital, even though this may be extremely harmful to the MI person.

In addition to monitoring medication, board-and-care operators also rely on other forms of controlling residents' behavior. About half of the California sample set forth an evening curfew. Of those facilities exercising a curfew, many do so on an "indiscriminate basis" (Ibid., p. 124). Only about half of the ex-mental patients actually control their own spending money. Those receiving funds from the operator request varying amounts on a daily, weekly, or monthly basis; some receive no money at all. The practices of curfew rules, medication supervision, and control over spending money can create an "institutional overlay" to life in a board-and-care home.

Physiological Consequences of Chemical Controls

Virtually *all* persons taking psychotropic drugs find their effects difficult to tolerate, and report nausea, vomiting, and other unpleasant side effects. In addition, there are distinct physiological illnesses associated with antipsychotic drugs.

(1) *Akathisia* is characterized by continuous agitation or restless activities of the face and extremities or inability to sit still.

(2) *Kyskinesia* is characterized by chewing and mouthing movements, lip smacking, licking of the lips, blinking and grimacing, and continuous aimless movements.

(3) *Dystonia* is characterized by tongue-face-neck posturing, twitching of shoulder muscles, and "bizarre" muscular behaviors.

(4) *Pseudo-Parkinsonism* is characterized by rigidity, tremor, loss of associated movements, masklike faces, salivation, and an uncertain gait (Ibid., p. 235; U.S. Senate Subcommittee on Long-Term Care, pp. 273–74).

These potential side effects indicate that there is an ethical problem in administering drugs without adequate training about drug types, dosage limits, scheduling doses, individual variability, and age difference (Segal and Aviram 1978, Chapter 14). The prevalent use of drugs also raises the question of whether the benefits to "treated" persons are a sufficient trade-off for side effects and projected physiological damage to one's body. After quantifying the intake of psychotropic drugs by each member of a statewide sample of persons living in shelter homes, Segal and Aviram concluded the following about the ability of these persons to function outside the facility—on their "external integration":

> For the *severely disturbed* (16% of the study group), antipsychotic drugs exert a *positive* influence on external integration. . . . In sharp contrast to this finding is the significant *negative* association between drugs and external integration for the 29% of the population who scored in the healthiest subgroup. . . . It is clear that in the healthiest group, drugs (especially at high dosages) *hinder* external integration. [Ibid., pp. 246–47; italics added]

Similar findings occurred in relating drug usage to the ability to adapt to the internal environment of the facility. Segal and Aviram state that a "no benefit conclusion is certainly supported by our data, at least with respect to all but the most severely ill residents, if we employ internal and external integration as our outcome criteria" (p. 248). These findings indicate that medical controls, unlike other forms of social and physical controls, can often have a more powerful and long-term impact on people. Given the potency of drugs for all age groups, one can reasonably concur with this set of questions posed by the California researchers:

> If the antipsychotic drugs are effective only for a small subset of the mentally ill population, but 76% of the population are taking these powerful medications, are the drugs really therapeutic, or are they merely a mechanism of social control? If the drugs are therapeutic, why is the prescribing pattern so extensive when research has demonstrated the selective effectiveness of the antipsychotic medications? [Ibid., p. 249]

These questions take on added cogency when it is documented that in 1953, the Food and Drug Administration permitted the original psychotropic drugs to be marketed without any double-blind studies being used to establish effectiveness and safety. The first adequate double-blind studies were not performed until much later. Once studies were performed, researchers found that among persons diagnosed as "chronic schizophrenics," the results of twelve double-blind studies disclosed a mean rate of improvement that was only 17.5 percent (Scull 1977, p. 87). This documented rate of success occurred under experimental conditions. The success rate of persons receiving drugs prescribed by nonspecialists, monitored by nontrained operators, at varying dosage and schedule levels, is apparently unknown at this time—except for the Segal and Aviram data.

Summary and Conclusions

Available evidence supports the thesis that restrictive living is not only associated with traditional institutions. Newer forms of institutions, such as nursing homes, use locks, physical restraints, and seclusion. These older social-control practices tend to be associated with medical-type facilities for adults. Yet children's facilities, regardless of medical auspices, utilize physical controls in a variety of group settings.

Besides these older modes of control, the new facilities also enforce curfew rules and restricted access to the community, spending money restrictions, and psychotropic drugs. This latter mode of influencing resident behavior appears to be the most widespread control device. Psychoactive drugs have been found to be prescribed in unusual amounts and combinations in nursing homes, special children's treatment facilities, board-and-care homes, group homes, and halfway houses, as well as in special hospital units and correctional facilities.

The relative ubiquity of drugs as means of chemical control poses significant hazards for residents, in that side effects and disturbing illnesses are associated with their intake. Because the efficacy of specific drugs and drug combinations for specific problem groups and ages is not as carefully documented as might be expected, the relative benefits to residents are uncertain.

The responsibility of local and state officials—e.g., requiring supervision by operators of nontraditional facilities—is fairly clear. No states appear to have addressed the ethical issues involved in promoting medication supervision by nonspecialized doctors and untrained operators, even though the hazards of inappropriate drug dosages and combinations are now well documented.

The federal government is also involved in the range of problems associated with drugs used as "chemical strait jackets." A recent President's Commission on Mental Health estimated that about 21 percent of the nation's mental health expenditures are provided through the reimbursement mechanism of federal dollars. In 1977 the nation spent about $17 billion on "direct care for the mentally ill" (President's Commission on Mental Health 1978, vol. 2, p. 530). About 5 percent was spent for psychoactive drugs. This figure does *not* account for drug expenditures included in the expenditures for nursing homes (29 percent), state and county mental hospitals (23 percent), or general hospitals (12 percent). Using the conservative 5 percent figure, at least $850 million were expended for psychoactive drugs, of which the federal government probably paid at least $178.5 million. The share of state and local governments was somewhat larger— $263.5 million (Ibid, pp. 530–33).

Because all levels of government subsidize the multiple use of drugs, it is evident that a national approach to DE cannot avoid addressing the issues associated with the use of psychoactive drugs. The relative social costs of using drugs for control purposes include restricting personal freedom, risking unpleasant side effects, regressive emotional and behavioral activities, and potential long-term physiological harm. At present, the benefits of drugs are not at all clear on an aggregate or individual level. Nor is it clear if the decision makers at the national, state, or local level are concerned about the relative trade-offs, or even the ethics of calculating societal control benefits versus costs to the individual (see, for example, the recent GAO report, *Problems Remain in Reviews of Medicaid-Financed Drug Therapy in Nursing Homes*, 25 June 1980).

5 Assessing Recent Trends in Mental Health and Mental Retardation

A major difficulty in assessing DE trends arises because government agencies tend to present data about one category or type without providing information about related institutional types. The most systematic attempt to understand the *total* institutional system is found in the work of Morton Kramer, former chief of the Division of Biometry and Epidemiology, National Institute of Mental Health. Utilizing the decennial census and the NIMH's own data-gathering efforts, Kramer (1977) amassed and analyzed a significant array of institutional trends. This analysis provides an initial basis for understanding DE trends. However, the most recent census for which data are currently available (1970) only included information about four of the nine "nontraditional" types (see Chapter 4).

Trends of the Total System

Tables 5–1 and 5–2 illustrate the kind of data, and their potential uses, provided by an adaptation of Kramer's approach.

Viewing DE trends for all institutions from 1950 to 1970, it is apparent in Table 5–1 that there had been virtually no change in the rates of total institutionalization: from 1,035 to 1,047. However, this static image is sharply at odds with shifts occurring within specific categories or subsystems. The prime site of 1950 institutionalization—mental hospitals—has reduced its resident rate by 47 percent and has been surpassed by homes for the aged as the major facility for institutional residence. This latter category, it will be recalled, first emerged in the 1950 census, and consists primarily of the types of nursing homes described in Chapter 3. The other major institutional gainer is another category that houses a preponderance of elderly patients: chronic disease hospitals. This category experienced the largest growth of any category.

Aside from mental hospitals, the two other significant losers of resident population are TB sanitariums and homes for dependent children. From earlier census data, we are aware that the decline of TB sanitariums and juvenile orphan asylums is a long-term trend, whereas the reduction in the mental health category began in the late 1950s and early 1960s (U.S. Bureau of the Census, 1950; Kramer 1977, p. 75; and see Chapter 7, below).

Aside from the difference in trends for specific categories, there are also sharp differences according to demographic characteristics. Table 5–2 reveals that DE is age-, sex-, and race-specific. For persons under 20, only white males (545 to

TABLE 5–1

Resident Institutional Trend Rates, by Census Categories: 1950, 1960, and 1970
(per 100,000 population)

Categories included in Census Counts	1950	1960	1970	Percent Change
Mental hospitals/residential treatment centers	406	351	214	− 47%
Homes for aged and dependent	196	262	456	+133
Adult correctional institutions	175	193	161	− 08
Homes and schools for mentally handicapped	89	97	99	+ 11
Homes for dependent and neglected children	64	41	23	− 64
Tuberculosis hospitals	50	36	08	− 84
Training schools for juvenile delinquents	24	26	33	+ 38
Homes and schools for physically handicapped	14	14	11	− 21
Chronic disease hospitals (excluding TB and mental)	13	24	33	+154
Detention homes	03	06	05	+ 67
Homes for unwed mothers	02	02	02	0
Diagnostic and reception centers	NA	01	NA	NA
Total (all institutions)	1,035	1,052	1,047	+ 01%

SOURCE: Adapted from Kramer 1977, Table 3, p. 21.

432) and females (390 to 239) have experienced a reduction in resident rates. The rates for young black males are up sharply (641 to 1,003), while black females are up about 10 percent (301 to 342).

If we set aside the trends for those who are 65 and over, then white male and female rates are either down, or are stable for age categories between 20 and 64 years. Black male rates behave in an opposite direction for ages 20 to 64: they are all up. Rates for black females are similar to those for white females, ages 20 to 64. Finally, the rates for both black and white males and females are up for senior citizens, with the sharpest rise occurring among females.

Mental Illness (MI) System

As noted earlier, Kramer's total institutional trends rely on census data. A major drawback of this data base (aside from the newer types omitted) is the omission of admission and/or discharge data. In the mental illness (MI) subsystem, this omission can be quite important, in that admissions have risen dramatically since

TABLE 5–2

Rates of Persons in U.S. Institutions by Sex, Color, and Age: 1950 and 1970
(per 100,000 age-specific population)

	Whites		Blacks	
Males	*1950*	*1970*	*1950*	*1970*
Under 20	545	432	641	1,003
20–24	1,111	1,117	3,750	4,749
25–44	1,102	868	3,217	3,287
45–64	1,599	995	2,355	1,964
65 and over	3,097	3,798	2,031	3,039
All ages	1,176	1,005	1,998	2,090

	Whites		Blacks	
Females	*1950*	*1970*	*1950*	*1970*
Under 20	390	239	301	342
20–24	395	274	640	458
25–44	545	306	807	466
45–64	988	649	1,148	798
65 and over	3,366	5,843	1,644	3,054
All ages	825	1,004	694	655

SOURCE: Adapted from Kramer 1977, Table 4, pp. 24–25.

1950: in 1950 there were 152,286 admissions to state and county mental hospitals, while 512,501 were resident—or a ratio of .297 admissions for every resident. In 1970, by contrast, there were 384,511 admissions and 337,619 residents, or a ratio of 1.14 admissions for every resident. By 1974 this ratio had increased to 1.74 (Kramer 1977, p. 78).

Another indicator of usage—utilized by the NIMH Division of Biometry—counts all inpatients cared for in a facility for one year, thereby including not only all persons resident at the beginning of the year, but also all admissions for the year. This indicator is referred to as "inpatient-care episodes." According to NIMH data, the 1971 inpatient-care episode rate in specialized facilities was nearly *four times* the resident census rate of 1970: 839 to 214 (Kramer 1977, p. 77; and table 6–1). Since 1955 the inpatient-care episodes from all specialized psychiatric facilities surveyed by NIMH have increased about 6.5 percent—based on rates per 100,000 population. In 1955 the rate was 795; in 1965 the rate was 817; and in 1975, it was 847 (President's Commission, vol. 2, 1978, p. 93).

The trends in the specialized mental health sector reveal fewer people in institutional residence on a specific day, probably staying for shorter periods of time, while admissions have increased to a point where the number of admissions exceeds the number of residents. Therefore, the total number of persons actually experiencing an MI institutional stay in a given year has probably *not* gone down (even controlling for population increase). This conclusion is reached without counting inpatient- or resident-care episodes of potential mental patients residing in homes for the emotionally disturbed, halfway houses, or group homes, for inpatient care in these facilities was not included in the census or in NIMH trend analyses.

The NIMH report series emphasizes specialized mental health sites, and omits short-term general hospital usage occurring in nonpsychiatric units. In 1977 general hospitals, with and without psychiatric units, reported discharging about 1,625,000 patients with a *primary* diagnosis of "mental disorder." They stayed an average of 10.8 days and yielded a rate of about 766 per 100,000 (NCHS, Series 13, no. 41, 1979, pp. 38–39). Using general hospital psychiatric units and inpatient community mental-health center units, NIMH data for 1975 revealed about 813,000 inpatient-care episodes, or about one-half of the total general hospital discharges (see President's Commission 1978, and NIMH, *Statistical Note*, no. 133, 1977). For short-length stays, inpatient-care episodes would be comparable to annual admissions discharge data; therefore, the NIMH reliance on specialized short-term facilities underestimates the annual use of local general hospitals by about 50 percent.

The omission of about half the psychiatric patients of general hospitals mars the current statistical image of institutional usage; it also hinders an interpretation of trends. From 1946 to 1975 the inpatient-care episodes of general hospitals *with* psychiatric units increased from 78 to 268 per 100,000 population. Not only has this nontraditional site of institutional care been growing at a faster rate than the entire MI system (see earlier discussion of inpatient-care episodes), but it has also become a significant form of inpatient care. In 1975, a total of about 1,791,000 inpatient-care episodes occurred in all specialty MI facilities, according to NIMH statistics. However, as noted earlier, about 813,000 episodes occurred in psychiatric units of general hospitals and inpatient community health centers (primarily located in general hospitals). Therefore, after subtracting this contribution from specialty facilities, it seems that only about 978,000 inpatient-care episodes occurred in the other specialized MI sites. Using the 1977 data for general hospitals, it appears that almost a comparable number were being handled in hospitals without psychiatric units—about 812,000 discharges. The fact that approximately 1,625,000 episodes occurred in a short-term general hospital—with and without specialized psychiatric units—is enormously important, in that far fewer were served in a longer-term specialty facility. The major locus of care and length of stay has shifted, but neither the Bureau of the Census nor the NIMH specialty series sufficiently captures this facet of deinstitutionalization. There has been a movement from traditional specialty sites to less specialized facilities, and from long-term institutions to short-term types.

Table 5–3 examines the significance of the shift in the locus of inpatient care and custody, by providing data for all available inpatient facilities, traditional and less traditional. Traditional MI sites include state/county hospitals, VA psychiatric units, and private/nonprofit hospitals. This classification accounted for 274,206 *specialized* beds in January 1976. A total of 941,000 inpatient-care episodes occurred in 1975 in these facilities. The inpatient-care episodes varied from 2.66 to 8.52 per bed.

The less traditional inpatient sector tends to consist of facilities not fully counted until the 1960s (CMHCs, residential-treatment centers, and other multiservice facilities); that had experienced rapid growth since the end of World War II (general hospitals/psychiatric beds); or those facilities usually omitted from NIMH statistics (general hospitals/nonpsychiatric beds). These less traditional facilities probably handled about 730,000 more inpatient-care episodes than the usual MI types.

Except for the residential treatment center (primarily for youth) and general hospital/nonpsychiatric, the less traditional inpatient-care episodes per bed tend to be much higher, indicating a far shorter length of stay. The general hospital/nonpsychiatric stay is actually shorter than general hospital/psychiatric, but the ratio method fails to capture this fact because the million beds are used by *all* types of disorders, not just a specialized type. Except for the residential treat-

TABLE 5–3

Distribution of Inpatient Beds and Patient-Care Episodes by Facility Type: 1975–1976

Traditional MI	Beds in 1976[a]	Episodes in 1975[b]	Episodes/Bed
State/county	222,202	590,000	2.66
VA-psychiatric units	35,913	214,300	5.97
Private/nonprofit	16,091	137,100[c]	8.52
Nontraditional MI			
Gen. hosp.-psych. units only	28,076[d]	566,000	20.16
Gen. hosp.-nonpsych. beds	1,002,356[d]	812,000[e]	0.81
Comm. mental health centers	10,193	246,900	24.22
Residential treatment centers	18,029	28,200[e]	1.56
Other multiservice facilities	993	24,100[f]	24.22

SOURCES: [a]Number of beds for types, except general hospital/nonpsychiatric. NIMH, *Statistical Note*, no. 144, February 1978, p. 13.

[b]Patient-care episodes. From President's Commission on Mental Health, vol. 2, 1978, p. 93, except where noted.

[c]Patient-care episodes for residential treatment centers. NIMH, *Statistical Note*, no. 135, July 1977, p. 15. This figure was deducted from private hospital episodes (in source [b]) to obtain inpatient-care episodes from private hospitals.

[d]General hospital psychiatric beds (from source [a]) were deducted from total general hospital beds. NCHS, Series 14, no. 16, May 1977, p. 30.

[e]See NCHS, Series 13, no. 41, March 1979, for 1977 total "mental disorders" as "first-listed diagnosis." The *estimate* of 812,000 was obtained by subtracting the episodes for hospitals with psychiatric units and community mental health centers.

[f]Because these facilities are equivalent to CMHCs in function, an episodes/bed ratio of 24.22 was multiplied by the number of beds (from source [a]).

ment center, all of the less traditional MI facilities tend to keep their patients for relatively short periods of time, and process many more patients per bed. The residential treatment center is closer to the state/county hospital in bed utilization than any other MI type.

Although complete trend data are difficult to obtain, it is evident that the shift from traditional utilization patterns is a phenomenon that has occurred within the past twenty years. Using a descriptive meaning of DE, more people are under care and custody in a year in less traditional facilities, even without including board-and-care homes, group homes, homes for the emotionally disturbed, and halfway houses. If all types could be enumerated in an unduplicated fashion for an entire year, it would appear that more persons are experiencing institutional living today than in 1950.

The Mental Retardation (MR) Subsystem: Trends in the Public Sector

According to the U.S. Bureau of the Census, the traditional MR subsystem has included all public and private residential facilities that provide care and custody for the retarded. However, this orthodox view underestimated the traditional institutional population, in that MR residents have been noted in mental-illness facilities since the census of 1923. Table 5–4 displays the trends in the *public* sector of the traditional MR subsystem. (Private facilities data are much less complete.)

In 1950 the traditional state/county MI hospitals housed 48,000 MR residents, or about 27 percent of all public MR residents. In 1970 MI facilities housed only 32,000, or only about 15 percent of all public MR residents. By 1974, the last year for which data are available, the number had decreased to 20,000, or only 10 percent of all public MR residents. In addition to showing a decreasing reliance on MI facilities, Table 5–4 also reveals that DE was not occurring uniformly for both parts of the public MR subsystem. From 1950 to 1974, MI facilities have decreased their resident MR population by 58 percent. This rate of decrease is comparable to that obtained for *all* MI residents (see table 5–1). Since 1950 public MR facilities actually increased their resident population by 38 percent. However, the population peaked in 1967 and has since been on the decline—from 193,000 to 176,000. Recent data from a University of Minnesota survey indicate that as of 1977, public MR use has continued the decline—to 152,000 (University of Minnesota, Brief no. 3, March 1979).

In a four-year period, 1970–74, public MR facilities were only decreased by 5,000 residents. In contrast, MI facilities decreased their MR residents by 10,000 (or over 33 percent) in one year, 1973–74.

Table 5–4 also presents limited admissions data. It is apparent that the MI sector has increased the number of admissions since 1946, although a peak may have been reached in 1971. However, in that year about 40 percent of all MR admissions occurred in MI facilities. The high point of public MR admissions

TABLE 5–4

Population Trends of Public MR Facilities: 1950–1974

Resident population	1950[a]	1967[a]	1970[a,b]	1973[b]	1974[b,c]	Per-centage Change 1950–74
MI facilities	48,000	NA	32,000	30,000	20,000	−58%
MR facilities	128,000	193,000	181,000	NA	176,000	+38
Total	176,000	193,000+	213,000	NA	196,000	+11%

All Admissions during Year	1946[a]	1955[b]	1965[b]	1971[b,c]	1975[d]	
MI facilities	1,764	NA	NA	10,000	7,000	
MR facilities	NA	13,000	18,000	15,000	NA	
Total	NA	13,000+	18,000+	25,000	NA	

SOURCES: (1) Resident Population
[a]President's Committee on Mental Retardation (PCMR), 1976, pp. 15–35.
[b]NIMH, *Statistical Note*, no. 146, March 1978, p. 12.
[c]Scheerenberger, February 1976, p. 32.
(2) Admissions Data
[a]Kramer 1977, p. 121 (first admissions *only*).
[b]PCMR 1976, p. 16.
[c]NIMH, Series B, no. 5, 1975, p. 33.
[d]NIMH, *Statistical Note*, no. 146, March 1978, p. 9.

TABLE 5–5

Trends of Residents of Public MR Institutions in Five States: 1963–1974[a]

	1963	1971	1974	Percentage Change 1963–74
Maryland	2,690	3,260	2,800	+ 4%
Massachusetts	7,100	7,200	5,790	−18
Michigan	12,740	10,970	7,340	−42
Nebraska	2,220	1,480	1,070[b]	−52
Oregon	2,870	2,845	2,220	−23
U.S. total[c]	175,000	181,000	176,000	+ 1%

SOURCES: [a]GAO, January 1977, p. 10.
[b]Ibid., 1975 data.
[c]President's Committee on Mental Retardation, 1976, p. 15.

y have occurred in 1965. (Recent data from a University of Minnesota survey indicate that this admissions trend has continued in public MR facilities; there were about 10,000 in 1977 [Ibid.].) These national trends are, of course, gleaned from available state data. Table 5–5 compares data for five states studied by the GAO, and compares state trends with national trends.

As Table 5–5 discloses, there is a great deal of variability between the five states chosen by the GAO. For this period the national trend reflects virtually no change. Maryland increased by 4 percent, although there is a downward trend between 1971 and 1974. The Massachusetts decrease occurred only in the past three years, although the overall rate is −18 percent. Michigan, however, has displayed a steady decrease since 1963, for an overall resident reduction of 42 percent. Nebraska displays a similar pattern, and at the time of the GAO survey was considered one of the nation's leading DE states in the MR field. Oregon's pattern is similar to that of Massachusetts—steady from 1963 to 1971, and downwards from 1971 to 1974.

In addition to variability between states, the public MR subsystem also discloses an intrastate variability. For example, data are available for a single state hospital in Minnesota—Cambridge State Hospital. The trends for Cambridge and the rest of the state are outlined in Table 5–6.

From 1962, DE in Minnesota has occurred as in Michigan and Nebraska—and at about the same statewide rate. However, within the state, Cambridge State Hospital reduced its population by over one-half—by 67 percent from a peak population of 2,008. The rest of the state also experienced a decrease, but not to the same extent.

The MR Subsystem: Assessing the Private, Less Traditional Sector

Because the MR field has lacked a national data-gathering capability comparable to the NIMH Division of Biometry and Epidemiology, it has been difficult to ob-

TABLE 5–6

MR Resident Population Trends of Cambridge State Hospital Compared to Public MR Institutions in Minnesota[a]

Public institutions	1962–63	1972	1975	Percentage Change 1962–75
Cambridge State Hospital[b]	2,008	935	658	−67%
Rest of Minnesota	4,517	3,062	2,751	−39
Total	6,525	3,997	3,409	−48%

SOURCES: [a] State of Minnesota Department of Public Welfare, Mental Retardation Program Division, February 1977, p. 1.
[b] State of Minnesota, Cambridge State Hospital, 29 May 1975.

tain information about the private sector and less traditional types. Fortunately, the University of Minnesota has completed a 1977 survey of community, as well as public, residential facilities. If these data are analyzed along with additional information gathered from two leading DE states (Minnesota and Pennsylvania), it is possible to gain an understanding of recent trends in the MR subsystem.

According to the University of Minnesota survey, a "public residential facility" (PRF) was defined as "a state-sponsored and administered facility which offered comprehensive programming on a 24-hour, 7-days-a-week basis as of June 30, 1977" (Ibid., p. 1).

The definition of a "community residential facility" (CRF) obviously excludes all state-sponsored facilities, regardless of location, and is, therefore, primarily a definition of private facilities. CRF is defined as "any community-based living quarter(s) which provide 24-hour, 7-days-a-week responsibility for room, board, and supervision of mentally retarded persons as of June 30, 1977" (Ibid., p. 1).

This definition deliberately excluded: single family homes; nursing, boarding, and foster homes not formally licensed or contracted by the state as mental retardation service providers; and independent living (apartment) programs without resident staff. The Minnesota survey noted that the resultant CRF definition included a variety of residential types: group homes, halfway houses, residential schools, and sheltered care homes. Although the CRF definition was quite broad, fewer than half of the facilities initially enumerated—5,038 out of 11,351—were able to meet the criteria set forth.

If we use the CRF definition as a recent indicator of private MR facilities, it is possible to understand the trend since the 1970 census. Table 5–7 provides the relevant data for the private/CRF and public-residential facility (PRF) sectors.

Data in Table 5–7 disclose that there has been a sizable increase in the number of MR residents living in a private/CRF, and a moderate decrease in the number residing in public/PRF. However, the total resident number in any institutional type appears about the same—slightly above 200,000. The table also indicates that controlling for population, the total rate is still about 99/100,000 population. However, about 29 percent of MR persons lived in a private/CRF in 1977, as compared to 12.8 percent in 1970. It appears that the increased reliance on the private/CRF sector has offset the decreased use of the public sector.

Using the criterion of size, it is possible to compare the two types according to the proportion of MR persons living in residences with: fewer than 20 persons; from 21 to 50; from 51 to 100; and over 100 persons.

The data in Table 5–8 provide potent evidence that the public sector remains far from the normative ideal of a small facility. Over 98 percent of public/PRF residents live in a facility with over 100 residents. As a matter of fact, 46 percent live in a PRF with 1,000 or more residents, and 35 percent in facilities with between 501 and 1,000 beds. Although in the private/CRF sector 43.8 percent of MR residents live in facilities close to a numerical ideal (see O'Connor 1976), almost one-fourth live in facilities housing more than 100 persons. If the total institutional MR population is assessed, regardless of facility auspice or type,

TABLE 5–7

Comparison of Resident Data for Private/Community Residential Facility and Public
Residential Facility: 1970[a,b] and 1977[c]

Numbers Resident on Census Day[a]	1970	1977
Private/CRF	25,900	62,400
PRF	176,100	152,000
Total	202,000	214,400

Percent Distribution of Residents, by Facility Type		
Private/CRF	12.8%	29.1%
PRF	87.2	70.9
N =	(202,000)	(214,400)

Rates/100,000 Population, by Facility Type		
Private/CRF	12.7	28.8
PRF	86.7	70.3
Total	99.4	99.1

[a] All figures are rounded to the nearest 100.
SOURCES: [a] U.S. Bureau of the Census, *Persons in Institutions and Other Group Quarters, 1970,* July
1973, p. 21.
[b] NIMH, Series B, no. 12, 1977, p. 61, for 1970 total rate/100,000 population.
[c] University of Minnesota, Brief no. 3, March 1978, pp. 2 and 8.

then only 16.4 percent resided in a facility with fewer than 50 residents in 1977.
Whereas this represents progress since 1970—when only 4.9 percent of all institutional MR residents lived in comparable facilities—it is evident that over 80
percent of the total still reside in large institutional types.

The MR Subsystem: Assessing Ideal CRF-Types in the States

In the MI field, the halfway house is usually described as one of the ideal community residential facilities for adults (see NIMH, Series A, no. 16); for children, residential treatment centers have been singled out for attention (see
Chapter 7). In contrast, leaders in the MR field have attempted to identify residential types that would be useful to persons along an age and disability continuum. Information obtained from Minnesota and Pennsylvania—two states
that have achieved CRF resident rates above the national rate of 28.8/100,000
population—offers further insights into the implementation of normalization
ideals.

In 1971 the Pennsylvania Office of Mental Retardation in the Department

TABLE 5-8

Distribution of MR Residents by Facility Type and Size: 1977

	Facility Type		
Size of Facility	Private/CRF	Public/PRF	Total
Under 20	43.8%	0.5% (under 50)	16.4%
21–50	16.6		
51–100	15.0	0.9	5.0
Over 100	24.6	98.6	78.6
Total	(62,397)	(151,972)	(214,369)

SOURCE: Adapted from University of Minnesota, Brief no. 3, March 1978, p. 3.

of Public Welfare established a "Community Living Arrangements Program" (CLA). This program was designed to provide a "progressive continuum" of residential programs, so that MR persons of "all ages and all levels of handicap" could live in "culturally normative and typical residential settings within the community" (State of Pennsylvania Department of Public Welfare, *Community Living Arrangement Plan*, 1976, p. 1). By 1977 the state had achieved a CRF rate of 51.8 and a PRF rate of 80.4, for a combined rate of 132.2. Although the combined rate is above the national rate of 99.1 per 100,000 population, it is quite likely that the CLA plan contributed to the relatively high distribution of MR persons living outside of the state institutions (39 percent compared to a national norm of 29 percent).

According to the CLA plan, there were to be nine different types of community living arrangement programs within the continuum:

1. *Developmental Maximization Unit.* An educational and developmental residential program for the medically complex, multihandicapped, profoundly retarded individual. Each person has developmental growth potential and can learn self-help skills. The primary objective is to move each individual into a more normative residential and educational setting as quickly as possible. Maximum size is 20.

2. *Infant Nursery.* For children up to the age of 4, who do not need maximization service, but do need nurturant help to learn such basic self-help functions as walking, eating, some communication, and some toilet training. Maximum size is 6.

3. *Intensive Behavior Shaping.* For persons age 4 and over who do not fit into higher functioning programs. A short-term service, with an emphasis on shaping and maintaining basic habits. Maximum size is 6 persons per home, or 2 individuals per apartment.

4. *Structured Correctional.* For youths who are MR and delinquent, displaying serious behavior problems. This program will use a "highly structured approach and intensive supervision." Maximum size is 6, grouped by ages 8–13 and 14–18.

5. *Child Development.* A program for children from birth to age 18; it should have a broad range of ages. This program can occur in foster homes, apartments for 2 children, or homes with a maximum size of 6.

6. *Adult Long-Term Sheltered.* For persons not capable of finding or holding employment in a competitive industry. Residents will participate in vocational services or day activity centers. Maximum size is 8 individuals, or apartments with 2 to 3 individuals per apartment.

7. *Adult Short-Term.* A one-year program to help persons learn vocational skills, obtain employment, and learn self-sufficiency skills. Maximum size is 8, or apartment units of 2 to 3 persons.

8. *Adult Minimal Supervision.* This program could be operated by a "program-oriented landlord in a rooming or boarding house," or by less direct supervision. Persons residing here are capable of holding jobs in competitive or sheltered employment, but may have difficulty holding a job, working out problems of daily living, or using leisure time. This program can occur in a rooming and boarding house, an apartment cluster, a co-residence apartment, or maximum independence apartment.

9. *Family Relief.* A residential or nonresidential service to provide short-term care and supervision for persons residing with their families. The service is designed to deal with crises or relieve family stress. Maximum stay should be for one month at a time and no more than three months during a year. Homes as well as apartments can be utilized, with a maximum size of 12.

As of 31 March 1976, the plan had been operationalized as reported in Table 5–9.

Table 5–9 illustrates that, in practice, the continuum was reduced to seven basic types, because the infant nursery program (no. 2) was transferred to the child development category (no. 5), and two adult programs (nos. 6 and 7) were combined into an "adult training" classification. It is important to note, too, that the 220 CLA units may be group homes, apartments, or family foster homes. The table provides evidence that the CLA program is skewed toward a heavy concentration of adults (nos. 6, 7, and 8): 1,593 out of 2,048 residents were adults (78 percent). Because these adult programs can take place in board-and-care homes, it is apparent that this is a significant offering in the Pennsylvania continuum of services. In conforming with the aim of having small facilities, the average size is only 9 persons.

The Pennsylvania typology also makes reference to length of stay in various programs. Although data are lacking by program type, there is evidence that a total of 1,220 persons have been "dispersed" from CLAs. This means that a minimum of 3,268 persons have been served. Inasmuch as the admissions-to-resident ratio is about 0.6:1, it appears that length of stay is longer than one year per facility. Out of the 1,220 dispersals, about 48 percent were classified as residing in "independent living," and 27 percent were residing with their maternal parents—a total of 75 percent in normalized living arrangements. The remainder were dispersed to state MR institutions (12 percent), foster homes (5 percent), nursing homes (2 percent), and all other (6 percent) (State of Pennsylvania, Joint Legislative Budget and Finance Committee, August 1976, p. 7).

The Minnesota typology was developed by the Minnesota State Planning Agency as a 1975 report, "Community Alternatives and Institutional Reform

TABLE 5-9

Pennsylvania CLA Typology

CLA Type	Number of CLA Units	Number of Persons	Average Size
Developmental maximization unit (no. 1)	2	32	16
Habit shaping (no. 3)	5	62	12
Structured correctional (no. 4)	0	0	0
Child development (nos. 2 and 5)	49	351	7
Adult training (nos. 6 and 7)	137	1,278	9
Minimal supervision (no. 8)	25	315	13
Family relief (no. 9)	2	10	5
Total	220	2,048	9

SOURCE: State of Pennsylvania, Joint Legislative Budget and Finance Committee, August 1976, p. 6.

(CAIR): Planning Alternatives for the Developmentally Disabled Individual." However, serious efforts to set up specially designed CRF facilities began in May 1971, with the passage of a combined licensing law for community and institutional facilities and programs (Minnesota Statutes 1969, Chapter 252, Amendment 252.28, 1971). The legal power to regulate all types of programs also empowered the commissioner of Public Welfare to "establish uniform rules, regulations, and program standards for each type of residential and day facility or service for more than four retarded persons, including state institutions under control of the commissioner and serving mentally retarded persons" (Ibid.).

The critical departmental regulations implementing this enhanced power to license, review, and supervise agencies—Rule 34—state the following:

> The purpose of the licensing law and these regulations is to establish and protect the human right of mentally retarded persons to a normal living situation, through the development and enforcement of minimum requirements for the operation of residential facilities and services. Moreover, these regulations serve an educational purpose in providing guidelines for quality service. [State of Minnesota, Department of Public Welfare, *DP Rule 34*, 17 November 1972, p. 1]

By 1977 Minnesota had the highest CRF rate in the nation (79/100,000 population). Its PRF rate was 75.9 (slightly above the national figure of 70.3). The total rate was the highest in the nation (154.9), but the distribution was 51 percent residing in nonstate institutions.

The Minnesota "Community Alternatives and Institutional Reform" (CAIR) typology was also designed to offer a "continuum of residential programs." The program descriptions included: a definition, a location, population and program characteristics, size, duration, staff, licensing standards, educational support services, and community support services. Brief descriptions of the eight types are as follows:

1. *Developmental/Medical Program.* For individuals having severe, chronic health problems requiring a life-support program in conjunction with training in adaptive behaviors. This program will be located in large communities having comprehensive hospitals and medical personnel. Maximum size is 25, and duration of stay may be intermediate to long term.

2. *Family-Living Developmental Program.* Serves individuals with severe developmental handicaps, but who do not have severe, chronic medical problems. It is expected that primary education and training would occur outside the residence; however, a formal training program to accelerate the development of adaptive behavior would be provided within the CRF. Location would be near schools in communities of varying sizes having the requisite support services. These support services include infant-stimulation programs, pre-school programs, special-school programs, and special-class programs for persons 0–21 years. For persons 16 years or over the support services would include adult day-activity centers, work-activity centers, sheltered workshops, comprehensive rehabilitation facilities, and competitive work-training programs. Maximum size is 6–8 individuals, and duration is short term to long term.

3. *Five-Day Board and Lodging Program.* Serves individuals (3 years of age and over) from sparsely populated areas attending community training programs and electing to return to a home base on weekends. Location would be in communities having the required education/training support services. Maximum size is 6–15 individuals, and duration is short term to intermediate.

4. *Developmental Foster Program.* Serves individuals having a wide range of developmental handicaps. Location can be in communities of varying sizes. Maximum size is 1–3, depending on the number of natural children in the family; duration is short term to long term.

5. *Social-Vocational Training Program.* Serves individuals (14 years and over) who have acquired the basic self-care skills but require basic training in independent-living skills and vocational skills in a group environment. Location should be in community settings close to schools, shopping, transportation, and vocational opportunities. Maximum size is 10, and duration is short term to intermediate.

6. *Supervised Apartment Training Program.* Serves adults (18 years and over) attending community vocational-training programs, sheltered employment, supervised, or independent employment. Location should be in existing apartment complexes close to shopping, transportation, and vocational opportunities. Maximum size is less than 10 units with a maximum of 2 persons per unit. Duration can be short term to long term.

7. *Minimally Supervised Apartment Program.* Serves persons who need little outside support to assume independent roles in community settings, but are able to use occasional visits by a counselor. Location is the same as the other apartment programs. Maximum size is for units of 1 to 4 persons, and duration is intermediate to long term.

8. *Behavior Training Developmental Program.* Serves persons on a short-term basis to eliminate serious maladaptive behaviors and to improve behaviors to a level appropriate for placements in developmental foster homes, family living developmental residence, or five-day boarding homes. Location is in small or large community centers on a regional basis. Maximum size is 10, and duration is short term.

It is evident that this typology is quite similar to the Pennsylvania CLA continuum, focusing on developmental tasks, chronological age, and medical/multiple handicap complications. However, the Minnesota CAIR descriptions are much more detailed regarding location and requisite educational and community support services. A study of 121 CRFs open as of 1 May 1976 provides some insight into the ability of the state to implement the proposed typology.

TABLE 5–10

Minnesota CAIR Typology

CAIR Type	Number of Units	Percentage
Developmental/medical	5	4.1
Family living/developmental	73	60.4
Five-day boarding	0	0.0
Developmental/foster	0	0.0
Social vocational trng.	34	28.1
Supervised apartment trng.	6	5.0
Minimum supervised apt. trng.	3	2.5
Behavior trng.	0	0.0
Total	121	100.0

SOURCE: W. Bock, February 1977, p. 45.

In Minnesota, as in Pennsylvania, the typology was reduced in practice. In Pennsylvania the continuum was reduced from nine to seven types, but only six were actually in use (Developmental Maximization, Habit Shaping, Child Development, Adult Training, Minimal Apartment Supervision, and Family Relief). In Minnesota the eight CAIR types were reduced, in practice, to only five types. The two typologies can be further reduced and compared as follows (with the number of units in brackets):

Distribution of 220 Pennsylvania CLA Types

1. Developmental Maximization and Habit Shaping (7)
2. Child Development (49)
3. Adult Training (137)
4. Minimal Supervision (25)

5. Family Relief (2)

Distribution of 121 Minnesota CAIR Types

1. Developmental/Medical (5)
2. Family Living/Developmental (73)
3. Social Vocational Training (34)
4. Supervised Apt. Training, Minimally Supervised Apt. Training (9)

Except for the family relief type, the typologies are similar regarding the four major types of CRFs. (However, the fourth type may not fit an institutional definition of four or more unrelated individuals.) About 65 percent of the Minnesota effort is the CRFs for the youngest age groups (Developmental/Medical and Family Living/Developmental)—78 or 121 CRFs. In Pennsylvania 58 out of 220 CRFs appear to be children (Developmental Maximization Unit, Habit Shaping, and Family Relief)—or about 27 percent. This difference, however, may be deceptive, in that Pennsylvania has been able to keep the size of the units within its ideal goals (see table 5–11), whereas Minnesota has not been able to reach the ideal CAIR goals.

Though about two-thirds of the facilities offer fewer than 15 beds, only about 29 percent of the state's CRF beds were located within this size of facility. Instead, over half (57 percent) were located in facilities with 33 or more beds. These are mainly adult board-and-care facilities that the state inherited from the period of 1962–72, prior to the enactment of Rule 34. Minnesota included these older board-and-care facilities within the CRF programs and then attempted to upgrade them to meet the special Intermediate Care Facility/MR standards (ICF/MR) promulgated by Medicaid. Between 1972 and 1974, sixteen of these older CRFs were closed for various reasons, reducing the CRF capacity by 160 beds (Bock, 1977, p. 51). Pennsylvania, on the other hand, did not include existing board-and-care facilities as legitimate CRFs. Therefore, the Pennsylvania data do not refer to the non-CLA adult facilities where MR persons reside in nonspecialized CRF facilities.

Adults comprise about 69 percent of all CRF residents (Minnesota Department of Public Welfare, Report to the Minnesota Legislature, 28 February 1977). This distribution of *persons* (not CRF units) served by special MR programs is much closer to the Pennsylvania figure of 78 percent. However, the average size of these inherited adult CRFs (which are probably of the board-and-care type) is about 46 beds per unit, instead of the 9–13 beds noted in the Pennsylvania data. The size per facility for children appears to be almost exact—about 12 per unit both in Minnesota and in Pennsylvania (tables 5–9 and 5–10).

Another way a state like Minnesota can adhere to the goal of smaller living units is to mandate that the larger facilities be broken down into primary living units of 15 or fewer beds. This requirement is set forth in Rule 34 and is in harmony with national ICF/MR standards (which Minnesota personnel helped write, before drafting the 1971 licensing amendments and Rule 34). In February 1977 it was estimated that 117 of the 121 Minnesota CRFs would be able to meet a deadline of 1 March 1977 for state compliance with federal ICF/MR standards (even though this deadline has since been repeatedly postponed). It appears reasonable, therefore, to assess Minnesota's compliance with its own (and federal) standards according to the primary living-unit size, rather than the facility's total number of beds. However, ideal normalization implies that the unit size will coincide with facility size.

TABLE 5–11

Minnesota Licensed Capacity by Size of CRF

Number of beds	Number of Facilities	Percentage	License Capacity No.	Percentage
0–15 beds	80	66	818	29
16–32	17	14	416	15
33 +	24	20	1,639	57
Total	121	100	2,873	100

SOURCE: W. Bock, February 1977, p. 44.

Summary and Conclusions

Assessment of the best available evidence indicates that there have been reductions in the use of traditional institutional facilities. However, the total rates of institutionalization also support the inference that as many Americans resided in an institution in 1970 as did in 1950. The total institutional rates display relative stability in this period, even though there are marked shifts for certain categories, as well as for sex, age, and racial differences. This assessment did not include admissions or resident rates for some of the new institutional types not counted by the census.

In the MI field, reduced reliance on the traditional types has occurred since about 1955. It has been accompanied by rising rates of admission, shorter lengths of stay, and heavy reliance on general hospitals or community centers associated with local hospitals. These trends, based on NIMH or NCHS data, do not include the use of group homes, alcohol and drug centers, halfway houses, homes for the emotionally disturbed, and board-and-care homes. If these newer types had been susceptible to unduplicated counting, they would have added a significant number of inpatient-care episodes to the total figure cited in Table 5–3.

The MR subsystem began to rely less on the traditional, public sector about 12 to 15 years later than did the MI field. Since that time there has been increased utilization of private, community-based residential facilities (CRF). Whereas CRF rates are up—controlling for population—and the percent of MR persons living in such facilities has also increased, the total national MR rate displays a marked stability from 1970 to 1977.

Data in Chapter 4 disclosed that over 48 percent of the residents of psychiatric halfway houses lived in facilities with 100 or more beds. In contrast, MR private/CRF facilities only had 25 percent living in such large facilities. This attempt to realize the ideal of smaller living units has been operationalized in the field of alcohol abuse (see Chapter 4), as well as in the private/CRF sector of the MR field. However, the great majority of MR persons still reside in large state institutions.

Examining data from two states with above-average CRF rates indicates that the MR field has been successful in developing at least three distinct types of nontraditional, smaller institutional facilities: developmental/medical, child development, and adult training. Supervised apartment living has also been used in Pennsylvania and Minnesota, but this type of residence does not fit an institutional definition. To the extent that MR planners can realize normative ideals, there appears to be an emphasis on specialized care and educational functions within a facility. The MI field seems to emphasize facilities with specialized care and treatment functions.

6 Explaining Deinstitutionalization: California As a Case Study

Many studies of policy changes begin with the assumption that new directions are guided by purposeful legislation or executive decisions on behalf of a set of target-specific, ideal outcomes. This ideal conception of policy development sharply contrasts with the reality of recent patterns of national deinstitutionalization (DE)—particularly in the field of mental health. Instead of following a model of national development, DE appears to have occurred with a great deal of interstate variability. Reform-minded states differed in their ability and willingness to take advantage of the opportunities created by expansion of the welfare state.

Beginning in 1935 with the passage of the Social Security Act, and with subsequent amendments, the federal government began to share the costs of subsidizing Old Age Assistance, Aid to Permanently and Totally Disabled, Medicaid, Supplementary Security Income, and Aid to Dependent Children. Although the expansion of these grant in aid programs was a major cause of the rapid decrease in the resident counts of traditional institutions—particularly the state and county mental hospitals—other factors were also operative. It is important to emphasize that the federal government could not—and did not—mandate that categorical grant-in-aid programs be used to depopulate state institutions. States had to discover and choose this discretionary option. Factors that could have influenced state use of federal programs to reduce populations of traditional institutions could include the following: the growth of humanitarian, antiinstitutional values; cost savings; overcrowding pressures; new treatment drugs; federal and state court decisions concerning patient rights; state fiscal crises; and special mental disability legislation funding noninstitutional programs (U.S. Senate Special Committee on Aging, 1976, pp. 720–23; Kramer 1977, pp. 34–36; Scull 1977, p. 135; Witkin 1976, p. 4).

To assess the relative importance of these and other factors in explaining DE, we will examine the timing, population targets, and acceleration trends in California, a leader in the MI field. Understanding the factors that contributed to California's performance can help elucidate the types of significant causes associated with DE in other states. Before examining the California experience, it is important to specify the basic facts pertaining to reductions in the population of traditional institutions—state mental hospitals. The analysis will not deal with how and why the admissions and turn-over patterns to state hospitals also changed during the same time period.

Four Factors in the Depopulation of Mental Institutions

According to the official reports of the National Institute of Mental Health, deinstitutionalization of the mentally ill began nationally in 1956 (Kramer 1977; Pol-
lack and Taube 1975; Witkin 1976). A review of U.S. census data confirms that
one-day resident counts of state and county mental hospitals peaked in 1955 (at
about 559,000), after having risen steadily from earlier census dates: 248,000 in
1923; 354,000 in 1934; and 463,000 in 1946 (U.S. Bureau of the Census, *Patients in Mental Institutions, 1939 and 1946*).

An important fact about DE, and a helpful starting point for understanding it is
timing, using national data. (Inasmuch as England's mental hospital population
also peaked about the same time, 1954, it appears that the mid-1950s is significant to an inquiry into the origins of DE [Wing 1979; Bennett 1979]. Although
this analysis will not examine English trends, the simultaneity of occurrence is a
rather striking fact.)

As noted earlier, the timing of DE refers only to resident counts, not admissions data. As a matter of historical fact, admissions to state and county mental
facilities continued to increase past 1955. The peak year for admissions appears
to be 1971 (Kramer 1977; Milazzo-Sayre 1978). If we control for population,
then the rate per 100,000 for first admissions was about the same in 1972 as it
was in 1946—68.2 versus 69.4 (Kramer 1977). In contrast, resident rates per
100,000 decreased from 344.4 in 1955 to 133.1 in 1972—and down to 90.6 in
1975 (Kramer 1977; Milazzo-Sayre 1978).

A second major fact about DE refers to the annual *rate variability* of the decline since 1955. Between 1955 and 1960, the number decreased by an average
of 0.8 percent per year; from 1960 to 1964, it decreased by 2.1 percent per year;
and from 1964 to 1972, it decreased by 5.5 percent per year. From 1972 to 1974,
the decrease was a relatively high 10.8 percent per year (Witkin 1976); in 1975
the annual decline reached 11.2 percent (Milazzo-Sayre 1978).

In addition to timing and rate variability, explanations must also account for
marked *interstate* differences and the relative *concentration on the aged* by high
DE states. Between 1955 and 1969, for example, California's mental hospital
population decreased by 56.4 percent. Virginia did not decrease its institutional
population during this period, but Texas decreased by 19.7 percent, New York
by 25.8 percent, and Illinois by 47 percent (Aviram et al. 1976). The national
decline was 33.8 percent (Kramer 1977).

Leading DE states like California and Illinois also decreased their aged population by a much larger proportion than other states and the national average.
Table 6–1 compares two time periods: 1955–69 and 1955–75. It is clear that
California had a strikingly different DE pattern from New York between 1955
and 1969. New York did not decrease its aged MI resident population, but it did
manage to reduce its under-65 population in mental hospitals by more than one-
third (36.9 percent). In contrast, California reduced its aged institutional population by a greater margin than its under-65 group (73.5 percent vs. 49.4 percent).

TABLE 6-1

Resident Population Changes in State and County Mental
Hospitals of Persons over and under 65 Years: 1955–69
and 1955–77 (in percentages)

	65 Years and Over	
State	1955–69	1955–75
California	−73.5%	−94.6%
Illinois	−41.7	−89.9
New York	+ 1.2	−43.9
Texas	−24.8	−69.4
Total U.S.	−29.6%	−65.8%

	Under 65 Years	
State	1955–69	1955–75
California	−49.4%	−66.8%
Illinois	−49.5	−77.4
New York	−36.9	−70.4
Texas	−18.0	−49.5
Total U.S.	−35.5%	−65.8%

SOURCES: Aviram et al. 1976; Milazzo-Sayre 1978; Kramer 1977.

These critical facts provide a starting point for determining how and why California became such an early leader in depopulating its state mental institutions. The following analysis will utilize a case study approach in order to assess the relative potency of explanatory variables that exist in the literature on DE. Among the variables that will be assessed are: the invention and utilization of psychotropic drugs; changes in treatment ideals and modalities; growth in humanitarianism and antiinstitutional values; the emergence of innovative federal-state court decisions concerning patient rights; changes in welfare regulations and legislation; and state fiscal readiness to shift expenditures from state to federal budgets (Aviram et al. 1976; Bachrach 1976; Enki 1972; Kramer 1977; Leiby 1978; Mechanic 1980; Scull 1977; Stanford Research Institute 1974; U.S. Senate Subcommittee on Long Term Care, 1974; U.S. General Accounting Office, 1979; Witkin 1976).

Early Efforts to Control California's Institutional Population

California built its first institution for the "insane" in 1853. Throughout the nineteenth century, the state added additional institutions as each became overcrowded. Beginning in 1910 the State Board of Charities and Corrections recommended a series of programs to alleviate the constant population pressures. These included: using "parole" as a means of testing an inmate's potential for discharge from the institution's "books"; supporting local hygiene clinics as a means of fostering preventive work; and handling persons not "dangerously insane" under the provision of a permissive psychopathic parole act, in conjunction with the establishment of "psychopathic wards" in two county hospitals. In setting up these progressive measures California was emulating the innovations that had emerged in Massachusetts and other leading states (Cahn and Bary 1936; Grob 1973). In addition, sterilization of parolees was actively promoted and implemented in California (Fox 1978).

Parole work was supervised by untrained workers directly responsible to each institutional superintendent. In the 1930s regulations required that committed patients could be paroled only if someone in the community signed an agreement accepting responsibility for the parolee. In addition each responsible person had to "give such security as may be necessary, to cover the cost of returning the patient to the institution if it should become necessary to return the patient from his parole" (Department of Institutions, Rule no. 17, 1937, cited in Aviram 1972, p. 3).

In January 1939, Dr. Aaron J. Rosanoff was appointed director of the Department of Institutions. The author of a *Manual of Psychiatry and Mental Hygiene* (1938), and of numerous journal articles, Rosanoff had also accumulated administrative experience in New York public hospitals. Within a few days of assuming the post, he set forth a "plan of attack on the problem of overcrowding in state hospitals" (Rosanoff 1939). He analyzed the problems in an unusually dramatic and forthright fashion:

> The great fact is that our overcrowding is so great as to be physically and mentally unhygienic, esthetically revolting, and altogether intolerable. This problem is neither new nor peculiar to the State of California. On the contrary, it has existed now for fully a century, in more or less marked degree, in practically every state in the Union. The obvious lesson to be learned, not only from our own experience, but also, and even more impressively, from that of older and more populous states, is that the building of new hospitals, or the enlargement of existing ones, or both, no matter on how large a scale, seems to afford but partial and temporary relief at best. Every state in the Union has had under way for many years an almost continuous program of hospital construction; and none have as yet gotten caught up with its over crowding. [Ibid.]

He proposed a plan whose features had been "thoroughly tried out in various places in this country and throughout the world over periods of years or even decades." What was new was his proposal to organize the features in a "fully comprehensive manner." He called for:

1. Using available and new funds to increase bed capacity by 4,000 beds and thereby relieve the "intolerable" living conditions.

2. Establishing a 200-bed acute neuropsychiatric unit in the University of California Medical School and Hospital in San Francisco, and later, in Los Angeles. With the aid of an outpatient unit, mental diseases would be recognized in their

"incipiency," and appropriate treatment offered at a time when it would be most effective. These units would use the most recent medical innovations, like insulin shock therapy. If carried out on an adequate scale, state admission rates of the most important psychiatric groups would be reduced, and the state would "no longer maintain its institutions as mere passive receptacles for end products of psychotic disease committed to them for custodial care as a desperate measure of last resort."

3. Increasing the number of patients on parole from about 2,800 to about 5,000. This large-scale extension of "extramural care" is justified because even in "many chronic cases" where "recovery could be quite out of the question," patients can be helped. Further, "it may be *estimated conservatively* that in this way the percentage of cases on parole can be raised from 11 percent to 20 [italics added]." A similar proposal can be applied to the institutions for the "feeble-minded."

4. Developing and using "family care homes" housing from 1 to 5 patients who are "too disabled physically, mentally or both to earn their board and room." The state would pay a rate that corresponded to the per capita cost of maintenance in the institutions.

5. Arranging the parole of some reimbursing patients, in order to transfer them from state hospitals to "licensed private institutions."

To generate support for his expanded parole plan (soon to be called "convalescent leave"), Rosanoff addressed an "open letter" to "all patients in state hospitals, their relatives and friends, state hospital employees and officers, judges of the superior courts of the various counties and others whom it may concern" (Aviram 1972). In the letter he asserted that patients having recovered from "distressing situations" often remained institutionalized because "no one initiated proper release procedures."

To further his plan Rosanoff obtained the agreement of the governor, leaders of the legislature, and the Department of Finance, that if he could recruit a sufficient number of trained social workers, the goal of 5,000 parolees would be attained by 30 June 1941. The social workers and their supervisor, Nathan Sloate, were to be directly responsible to the central administration, rather than to the individual institutions. By the target date the new social workers reported that Rosanoff's goal had been surpassed. Writing to the NIMH staff in 1949 about the significance of this purposeful control of institutional population movement, Rosanoff's deputy director commented as follows:

> The significance of these figures was great. They established that there were many patients ready for extramural care. They proved that a social service program with institutional cooperation could expedite and sustain their leaves. They showed a method whereby for the first time in the department's history the annual rate had been checked. [Aviram 1972, p. 40]

In retrospect, the impact of Rosanoff's plan went beyond the reduction of annual population growth. The ideas implicit in the plan involved a strategic approach to mental health policy development, the communication of these ideas to future leaders of the Department of Mental Hygiene, and the creation of an organized mechanism, centrally administered and controlled, to facilitate the release of patients. Strategically, Rosanoff appeared to view the problem as one that involved the state and other units of government, as well as the private sector. In today's parlance this would be viewed as "involving the community." It was necessary to involve the community for two major reasons: it was here that the flow of admissions to the place of "last resort" could be reduced, and it was here that persons released from the institution would have to reside and adjust— even if not "cured." Attaining this cooperative could help control popular movement into and out of the institution.

Whereas political support, goodwill, and the sharing of humanitarian objectives could be useful in procuring cooperation, it was also necessary for the State of California to budget mental health funds to promote, develop, and maintain "new" community resources. These new funds could be used to build acute, short-term, psychiatric units in metropolitan areas (at a cost of $2,500 per bed, instead of the $1,500 per bed allocated for state institutions); or the new funds could be used to finance "supervision of extramural care," social workers, outpatient units, and even board-and-room grants to families who would care for disabled persons (Rosanoff 1939).

This approach to mental health policy implied that proposed building construction of state units was only permissible on humanitarian grounds, to deal with the "altogether intolerable" living conditions of overcrowding. The 4,000 beds symbolized a holding action; they allowed the innovative treatment methods associated with acute, intensive hospitals (at a local level), with the new methods of psychiatric social work, and with subsidized welfare (i.e., family care payments) to begin to deal with the underlying causes of the overcrowding problem. According to Lawrence Kolb—Rosanoff's deputy director, and later acting director—Rosanoff believed that ultimately as many as 65 percent of the patients living in a state hospital could live elsewhere (Aviram 1972, p. 34).

The Ideological Assumption of Early DE Proposals

Some of the ideas that formed the basis of Rosanoff's "plan of attack" can be found in the 1927 and 1938 editions of his *Manual of Psychiatry*. However, the Rosanoff writing in 1927 would never have contemplated proposals for a 65 percent goal. In 1927 Rosanoff had written that most mentally ill aged persons were "best cared for in homes for the aged"; that "many patients who have chronic psychosis" could be released because they "can get along safely on parole"; and that "*up to*" 20 percent of an institution's population could be paroled under adequate supervision (Rosanoff 1927, pp. 332, 396; italics added).

Although a pragmatic and humanitarian approach is apparent in Rosanoff's views on the aged and safe "chronic" patients, he also believed that "bad heredity" was the "cause of causes of mental disorders" and that a *"movement for the prevention of mental disorders will lead the race in no mistaken path if it concentrates the bulk of its energies on the problem of bad heredity"* (Ibid., p. 437). To further this aim he actually proposed that California increase its total institutional population from 12,000 to 40,000, inasmuch as community surveys had revealed that one person in a hundred required "segregation" (p. 471).

However, the 1938 edition of his *Manual of Psychiatry* revealed that Rosanoff had undergone a marked change in his views about hereditary causes and a eugenics policy. He now argued in favor "of the all-pervading influences of social and economic factors in the etiology of mental disorders and human maladjustments" (p. viii). This edition also noted that a eugenics policy was "more complicated" than realized, inasmuch as the balance between heredity and environment had to be assured in every case. In "many cases" heredity factors were "of minor importance," and, therefore, "the issue of eugenics does not exist" (p. 750). Thus, there was no longer any need to expand institutional capacity, and this proposal was deleted.

Rosanoff's successive writings symbolize the progression of influential psychiatric thought in the United States concerning the role of heredity and environment (Hofstadter 1955; Grob 1966). Persons believing that "bad heredity" was the "cause of causes" were unlikely to be policy proponents of a 65 percent population reduction. An environmental emphasis appeared to presage receptivity to a reduction in the custodial, social-control function of mental institutions. Given this change in intellectual orientation, parole, too, could change its social functions. In 1927 Rosanoff had supported it as a mechanism for relieving overcrowding and for "testing" eugenic capability for social adjustment. In 1939 he proposed using parole as a means to minimize custodial care and supervise a "convalescent leave." Instead of serving as an extension of specific institutions, parole work could be used as a centrally guided organizational mechanism for achieving broad reform goals in the "community."

Because Rosanoff left his position in 1942 due to illness (and died shortly thereafter), his radical idea about releasing patients beyond a 20 percent reduction rate was not able to be fully tested in the immediate postwar period. Between 1942 and the appointment of Dr. Daniel Blain in 1959, no other leader of the state's institutional system advocated a drastic reduction in daily population. In retrospect, Rosanoff's views could be viewed as a premature "environmental" aberration of the Great Depression, in that DE did not occur in California until the end of the 1950s. Such a view might be shortsighted, however, for it underestimates the organizational mechanism and leadership that survived Rosanoff's brief tenure. When Blain arrived in 1959 he found an experienced, politically astute Bureau of Social Work (BSW) still led by Nathan Sloate, the personal choice of Rosanoff. Sloate and the BSW regional leadership were quite ready to operationalize a radical DE goal of a 65 percent reduction. In addition, Rosanoff's ideas strongly influenced other postwar leaders of California's community mental health movement (Segal and Aviram 1978, p. 35).

Proinstitutional Policies of the 1940s and Early 1950s

By the end of the war, California's rate of institutional growth had been slowed, but the total population had not been reduced. Instead of continuing a DE policy to accommodate postwar population pressures, California's new mental health leadership helped launch a $90 million building program, including a maximum security unit of 1,000–1,100 beds (American Psychiatric Association, *Mental Hospital Institute Proceedings*, 1950, p. 15). In embarking on this policy they, as well as leaders of other states and of the American Psychiatric Association (APA), were emulating the policies of the Veterans Administration (VA). The acknowledged leader of institutional psychiatry in the postwar decade, the VA had also embarked on a building program using U.S. Public Health Service (USPHS) architects and standards.

Architectural standards set by USPHS were presented to APA state hospital administrators as the best guides for expanding and upgrading state facilities (Ibid., pp. 5–11). The California Deputy Director of Mental Health, Carl E. Applegate, reported to the APA's 1950 Mental Hospital Institute that USPHS standards were used as a "guide" in planning the state's large building program (Ibid., p. 15). USPHS standards could be utilized by states in two primary ways: to project statewide bed capacity requirements, and to determine the physical characteristics and layout of mental hospitals.

According to the USPHS, a modern state system required five mental hospital beds per 1,000 population (Council of State Governments, 1950, p. 58). This standard was half of the 1927 institutional goal proposed by Rosanoff: segregating 1 person per 100 population (or 10 per 1,000). Even at this lower standard the country, in 1950, was projected to "need" an increase in mental hospital bed capacity of over 70 percent (Ibid.). Projections were made by USPHS on a state-by-state basis, and could be utilized to evaluate state applications for federal subsidies under the 1946 Hospital Survey and Construction Act—usually referred to as Hill-Burton funds. Although federal regulations favored the construction of these mental-hospital beds near centers of population and in proximity to (or inside) general hospitals, traditional state facilities were not excluded from procuring federal subsidies. By mid-1965, Hill-Burton funds had been used to add 19,300 state mental hospital beds and 10,000 general psychiatric beds (Connery 1968, pp. 26–27). Unlike other states, however, California chose to use these funds for the construction of psychiatric units in general hospitals (Enki 1972). Whether this deliberate choice was influenced by Rosanoff's 1939 ideas about the role of local psychiatric facilities is unknown, but the inference seems plausible.

In 1950, state hospital administrations were advised by USPHS architects to allocate new bed capacity in a building program according to the following standards: an entering and receiving service for intensive observation and treatment—10 percent of the beds (based on an average stay of six months); a medical-surgical service for regular operations and psychosurgery—4 percent;

continuing treatment services—55 percent; and a geriatric service—30 percent (APA, 1950, pp. 5–11).

Federal building standards were, therefore, used to promote (even without subsidies) the retention of aged persons within state hospitals. Because fewer persons died in hospitals, there were, in fact, more aged persons in state hospitals after 1945 than in prior years (Kramer, in APA, *Mental Hospital Institute Proceedings*, 1953, pp. 106–9). The USPHS standards appeared to treat this demographic occurrence as an ideal goal, even though this position had been questioned in the 1920s by some leaders (e.g., Rosanoff). In contrast to USPHS, the 1948 *Report to the Governor's Conference* recommended that the aged might be better served in "community facilities," with the aid of old age insurance and public assistance programs (Council of State Government, 1950, p. 4). California chose to follow the USPHS position; by 1955 aged persons constituted 29 percent of the MI resident population (Aviram et al. 1976). The national average was 28 percent (Kramer 1977).

Although treatment modalities were not specified by USPHS standards, building space had to be provided for the most widely practiced "modern" procedures. A special 1948 survey, conducted for the Council of State Governments, revealed the following major treatments offered by a 187-hospital sample: electric shock—177 hospitals; hydrotherapy—144; insulin shock—103; psychosurgery—102; group psychotherapy—97 (Ibid., pp. 182–86). The 1956 edition of APA *Standards for Hospitals and Clinics* referred only to hydrotherapy and electric shock treatment. The standards noted that in place of hydrotherapy, "some hospitals prefer to use electric shock treatment for the *management* of agitated and excited patients" (APA, 1964 ed., p. 19; italics added).

California's Early Stages of Deinstitutionalization: 1955–1965

By keeping up with the perceived demand for institutional facilities, it is not surprising that California's "total admissions" continued to outpace "net releases." Population counts continued to expand yearly until 1956. There were slight drops in population in 1956 and 1957, but fiscal 1958–59 witnessed an increase. For California this was the zenith year: 37,489 residents. From 1959 on, there were annual reductions. DE of California state institutions had begun.

By 1962 there was a 6.8 percent reduction for a four-year period. Beginning in fiscal 1963, the *annual* reduction matched or surpassed this four-year reduction. Annually, the reductions were as follows from 1963 to 1969: 6.7, 7.4, 12.2, 17.3, 14.1, and 14.4 percent each year. (Aviram 1972, pp. 224–25).

A major event occurred in 1955, when the California state legislature explicitly "appropriated funds to purchase the new wonder drugs for use in state hospitals" (Enki 1972, p. 3). On a national level, Witkin reports that 1956 "coincided with the large-scale introduction of psychotropic drugs" (Witkin 1976, p. 1). National dissemination of information about these new drugs was spurred by two

American Psychiatric Association publications reporting recent research at two regional conferences held in 1955. Both reports were prepared with the financial assistance of a pharmaceutical company, and published within six months of the conferences (APA, July 1955, and April 1956). In addition, the Association for Research in Nervous and Mental Disease published the proceedings of a 1957 meeting of the association on *The Effect of Pharmacologic Agents on the Nervous System* (1959).

The speedy diffusion of the new drugs, between 1955 and 1957, occurred despite the fact that "double-blind control studies" constituted only "a small scattering in the enormous literature devoted to new drugs in psychiatry" (Ibid., p. 3). By 1962 only twelve double-blind studies could be located in a review of this literature (Scull 1977, p. 87). A 1969 review found few studies that had even controlled for dose levels of drugs (Segal and Aviram 1978, p. 237).

Despite the fact that California institutions began widespread drug use by 1956, the impact on resident counts appeared negligible. Between 1955 and 1958 the population figures stabilized around 37,000. In 1958, however, the resident count increased to the highest number in California's history. The decrease slowly began in 1959, and then accelerated from 1963 onward.

Whereas greater sophistication in drug use may have been achieved from fiscal 1959 through 1962, two significant social developments also occurred: in 1959 Dr. Daniel Blain was appointed director of the state's Division of Mental Health; in 1960 the U.S. Congress passed the first major medical assistance program for the aged (MAA).

Blain had served as medical director of the APA from 1948 to 1958. As such, he had been the prime organizer of the APA-sponsored annual Mental Hospital Institute. He was also the editor of the APA's journal, *Mental Hospital*. In 1956 he availed himself of the opportunity to publish in this journal an article summarizing his views on the "Changing Patterns of Mental Hospital Patients." Drugs were barely mentioned; instead he discussed alternatives to state mental hospitals: day hospitals, night hospitals, general hospital psychiatric inpatient units, halfway houses, residential diagnostic and screening centers, and sheltered workshops. He ended his review by advocating that professionals "find an alternative to hospitalization," shorten the "duration of stay" when hospitalization occurs, and "facilitate discharges." These views fit quite well with the views of Sloate, the BSW, and other California mental health leaders interested in "breaking down the walls between the hospital and the community" (Bardach 1972, p. 93). They also agreed with the paradigm about hospitalization that had first been introduced to a nationwide audience at the 1950 Mental Hospital Institute. This paradigm stated that people do not go to hospitals to get well, but to get "well enough to go home where treatment continues" (APA, *Mental Hospital Institute Proceedings*, 1950, p. 64).

With Blain's arrival, the BSW's hospital release efforts received renewed support. Besides supporting legislative requests for new social work positions, Blain also included BSW personnel as part of the central administration's critical leadership group (Bardach 1972). Sloate became the first nonmedical assistant to become a division head, assuming the leadership of Community Services (Aviram 1972, p. 221). With others, he participated in the creation of a "long-range plan," which recommended that the BSW program be intensified in order to move patients back to the community. The plan explicitly favored private care and local government administration in the provision of mental health service (Ibid.). The California Medical Association applauded this effort in an editorial, thereby assuring state leaders of support from the private medical sector (*California Medicine*, 1963).

Support for intensifying convalescent-leave programs was also forthcoming directly from the legislature. In 1963 some legislators wanted to offer the BSW about 100 more social workers than even the pro-leave leadership had requested. Sloate had to persuade these supporters to proceed more cautiously (Aviram 1972).

Besides the critical change of internal leadership, new federal legislation in 1960 also offered the states an opportunity to provide Medical Assistance to the Aged. This program, aside from subsidizing general hospital care and chronic hospitals, also provided nursing-home services and home health-care services. It provided these services not only for elderly welfare recipients, but also for *income eligible elderly citizens* who qualified according to any "reasonable standards" of income proposed by a state plan (*U.S. Senate, Compilation of Social Security Laws*, 1962, Title 1, secs. 2 and 6). For the first time, elderly citizens could receive medical assistance without being labeled a "welfare case." Continuing the original 1935 Social Security policy, state institutions or mental hospitals were deliberately prohibited as service sites. However, public general medical facilities were included, along with their psychiatric units. Proprietary nursing homes and nonprofit medical and health-related services were also eligible for governmental reimbursements (Vladeck 1980). These fiscal conditions were well suited to a plan that favored private care and local administration of mental health services.

In 1962 the activist leadership in control of DMH policy and central headquarters were given two new major sources of federal funds. As a result, beginning in 1963 the rate of resident reduction so accelerated that there was as much depopulation in one year (6.7 percent in 1963–64) as had occurred during the previous four years (1958–62).

On 15 June 1962, HEW issued new regulations that permitted patients other than elderly recipients to claim Aid to Permanently and Totally Disabled (APTD) while on convalescent leave from the hospital. Regulations were drafted that permitted payments to APTD recipients while living at home, in a family care home, or in larger nursing and board-and-care homes (Aviram et al. 1976). Besides regulatory changes, 1962 Social Security amendments expanded the medical assistance program to APTD recipients and provided social services at a matching rate of 75 percent federal and 25 percent state. Social services could be provided to former or potential, as well as actual recipients (*U.S. Senate, Compilation of Social Security Laws*, 1962, Title 14). The definition of social services included placement and after-care activities. The service eligibility requirements were so open-ended that federal dollars could be received on the basis of unverified state agency reports (Derthick 1975).

California took full advantage of these open-ended, discretionary, grant-in-aid programs. In 1962 California had 6 percent of the nation's APTD recipients; by 1970 the state had 20.1 percent (U.S. Department of HEW, 1964, table 10; and Ibid., 1972, table 14). In addition, in 1970 California had 22.6 percent of the nation's APTD persons classified as disabled due to mental illness, as compared to only 3 percent of the mentally ill APTD recipients in 1962 (Ibid.).

The year 1963 also witnessed federal passage of the Community Mental Retardation and Community Mental Health Centers Construction Act. Staffing grants were not added until 1965. Although these acts could have helped California add to its developing community mental health program, the evidence is clear that the depopulation of state institutions was more closely linked to federal welfare—rather than mental health—programs. Of greater symbolic importance, in 1963, might have been the public assertion by a president of the United States that institutionalization could be reduced by 50 percent in a "decade or two" (Mechanic 1969; Connery 1968; U.S. GAO 1977).

Besides these developments, California legislation of 1963 initiated a program to reduce geriatric *admissions* to the mental hospital system (U.S. Senate, Special Committee on Aging, November 1971, pp. 62–75). Instead of just relying on the terminal end of the institutional process, the DMH leadership persuaded the legislature to authorize special funds for a "geriatric screening project." For the first time, California was deliberately attempting to influence entry into the state system.

The project was carried on outside of the traditional state intake mechanisms; screening personnel were based in the prestigious Langley Porter Institute in San Francisco (built as a result of Rosanoff's 1939 initiatives). The project team was composed of an internist, a psychiatrist, and two psychiatric social workers. The unit's task was to screen older persons facing a legal petition for commitment to a mental hospital, in order to avoid state institutionalization. Diagnostic assessments took place preferably in patients' homes. During four years of operation the project was successful beyond expectation. The number of admissions to local general hospitals for psychiatric evaluations was reduced by 65 percent. Only 4 percent of the persons evaluated by the geriatric screening unit were committed to state hospitals over a three-year period. Prior to the project, from 1961 to 1964, the county had averaged 486 commitments per year; but from 1965 to 1967 the county committed only 18 geriatric patients per year (U.S. Senate, Special Committee on Aging, November 1971).

By 1965 the DMH presented the geriatric screening program as a proposed standard for all counties in the state. DMH also applied the standard internally. Federal resources, unavailable for elderly persons institutionalized in the traditional state mental hospitals, could be used to prevent or reduce this type of hospitalization.

Increased Acceleration of DE: 1965–1969

In 1965 DE proponents in DMH and the legislature were provided with an additional federal resource that could be used to subsidize medical and health-related services outside the state hospital system. Medicare for the elderly and Medicaid for all age groups permitted an expansion of federal resources available to potential, former, and actual state hospital patients. The 1965 legislation, patterned after MAA, made Medicaid available to those persons defined by each *state* (and not by the federal government) as qualifying for medical services without having to be on the welfare rolls. Medi-Cal was California's program that qualified for Medicaid reimbursement. As in the MAA program, these Medi-Cal services could include general hospitals' inpatient and outpatient psychiatric services and skilled nursing facilities (SNFs); the choice was up to each state. In 1967 federal legislation was amended to further facilitate social service programs and to subsidize a form of nursing care below the level of SNF-intermediate care facilities (ICFs). The California leadership responded to each new opportunity with accelerated vigor.

Given these expanded definitions of eligibility, types of social and medical services, and service sites, as well as an organization experienced in depopulation techniques and skills, the DMH—with legislative support—set out to close two hospitals deemed obsolete. They proposed to accomplish this goal not by adding new wards to other hospitals, but by means of a drastic patient reduction program. Three California researchers described the projects as follows:

> The depopulation projects are an excellent example of how California used the new opportunities in order to reduce the population of its state mental institutions. In 5 years the resident population of the two state hospitals mentioned above was reduced by 3,500, and in 1969 the state closed one of the hospitals. Many of those chosen for discharge were either *senile aged* or *chronic schizophrenics*. It seemed unlikely that continued hospitalization would improve their mental condition. It appeared they could be maintained, *some on chemical control*, in the community without danger to themselves or others. [Aviram, Syme, and Cohen 1976, p. 575; italics added]

By 1966 any state, if it were organized and aware of opportunities, could use Old Age Assistance (OAA), Aid to Permanently and Totally Disabled (APTD), Old Age and Survivor Insurance (OASI), Medicare, and Medicaid to subsidize alternative care/custody arrangements. Any state could also use drugs as an outpatient management device, to replace inpatient shock treatments. In addition, states might receive federal reimbursement for placement, after-care, and other social services to former, potential, and actual welfare recipients. A DMH planning group proposed that many BSW activities might be reimbursed by the federal government at a 75–25 percent matching level, if the placement and supervision services (defined as casework services) were transferred out of DMH and provided under the auspices of the State Department of Welfare (Aviram 1972, pp. 267–78; Bardach 1972, pp. 120–82). The reorganization was accepted by the state legislature and Washington and quickly executed in 1967. By 1969 California paid 61 percent of the total BSW budget—instead of 100 percent, as occurred prior to fiscal 1967. This was direct and actual "cost savings," in comparison to the paper savings associated with half-empty, but fully staffed, state hospitals.

As Derthick points out, in order to take advantage of such fiscal opportunities, state governments have to make claims and have them approved by federal administrators. According to Derthick, as regards the use of the open-ended social service amendments of 1962 (and slightly modified in 1967), "*the first and for several years the only state to do this in a big way was California*" (Derthick 1975, p. 29; italics added). From 1967 through 1971 California received from 25 to 36 percent of the nation's total federal expenditures for social services and training grants. The BSW fiscal gains were only one example of the state's "skill factor" in promoting and subsidizing state objectives with federal funds; other programs, like vocational rehabilitation, also profited by creatively interpreting regulations (Ibid.).

The California Plan for Future Use of State Hospitals

Data on interstate variability indicate that California was a leading DE state between 1955 and 1970. By 1975 the rest of the country had achieved a similar population reduction rate for persons under 65; however, the reduction of California's aged MI population from state institutions had still not been surpassed by 1975 (see table 7–1). With California's plan for 1985, it is likely that the state will again assume a leadership role in reducing the under-65 state institutional population and probably become the first large state to eliminate senior citizens totally from state mental hospitals (State of California, April 1977).

By 1985 California plans to reduce its state MI population to 2,890 residents. How state planners propose to accomplish this goal reveals a great deal about the projected future functions of the traditional hospital within the state's total mental health system. On the basis of numbers alone, it is likely that the social functions for 2,890 residents will differ from those performed for 37,489 residents (in fiscal 1958). The future manifest purposes of the state hospitals are revealed by the following target projections (Ibid.):

1. Phasing out all programs geared to the following diagnostic groups: alcoholics, drug abusers, autistic children, and geropsychiatrics.

2. Eliminating all surgical services at state hospitals and reliance on local general hospitals.

3. Utilizing local facilities for observation and evaluation of all 72-hour involuntary detention cases.

4. Admitting involuntary persons from local facilities, after a 72-hour period, only if they: (a) exhibit "acute" psychotic symptoms; (b) require continuous treatment beyond a "14-day certification" period; and (c) represent "so substantial a danger to others that they require a degree of security that cannot be provided by community inpatient settings" (Ibid., p. 13).

5. Accepting as "voluntary" patients only children and adolescents.

6. Retaining involuntary adults only if they display chronic psychoses requiring care and treatment in a "highly structured setting" *and* are: (a) physically aggressive, assaultive, destructive, and severe escape risks; or (b) multihandicapped in problems of daily living (i.e., exhibit problems in taking medication regularly, maintaining a proper diet or other life-sustaining regimen, or training to maintain personal hygiene, or wandering and getting lost easily); or (c) unable to be provided with sufficient appropriate community resources.

7. Complying with a new law, whereby judicially committed sex offenders can be treated on a local level if they do not require "substantial security" (Ibid., p. 17).

The plan expects that more state prisoners will be transferred to state hospitals. Aside from this category the only other group for which gains are projected or designed are children (ages 6–12) and adolescents (ages 13–18). Regarding children and adolescents, hospitals are to be used for the "acutely longer-term psychotic child" and "the severe acting-out behavioral disturbance." Criteria for admission would include, besides diagnosis, a need for "continuous close observation" or "treatment in a secure 24-hour setting" (Ibid., p. 7).

It is evident from this description of the 1985 plan that state hospitals are considered to be the most secure mental health facilities in the state. It is apparent that the planners are relying on less secure MI facilities at the local level (see Chapter 5). State hospitals are also defined as places of last resort for the most difficult psychiatric cases, exhibiting multiple handicaps or life-functioning problems. Given these limited functions, for well-defined groups, state hospitals are to give up their traditional roles in dealing with cases of senility, alcoholism, drug abuse, and autism. In addition to eliminating any bed needs for these nonpsychotic groups, state hospitals are also expected to cease all surgical procedures.

These "delimited" state hospital functions are sharply at variance with the functions included in the USPHS architectural "standards" of 1950. Recall that on the basis of these standards, beds were to be set aside as follows: observation and intensive treatment (10 percent); medical-surgical (4 percent); and geriatric service (30 percent). Besides totally eliminating 44 percent of the "standard" beds, the 1985 plan reduces the categories of persons who can use the remaining "continuing treatment" beds. In the future, more attention will have to be paid to "greater security" for adults and "treatment in a secure 24-hour setting for children." Both of these emphases indicate that custodial, social-control functions are likely to receive renewed prominence in the California state hospital of 1985.

Explaining the National Acceleration of 1972–1974

As noted earlier, national data disclosed a low rate of population reduction during the 1960s. Not until 1972–74 did the national rate of resident reduction reach a level achieved earlier by California: 10.8 percent (Witkin 1976, p. 4). The most likely cause for this belated acceleration was the passage in 1972 of a new welfare program, Supplementary Security Income (SSI), whereby an older categorical program for the permanently and totally disabled (APTD) was phased out in favor of a minimum, 100 percent federally funded assistance level. With state fiscal sharing totally eliminated for the basic grant (except for optional state supplementation), "late blooming" states could engage in accelerated DE without increasing their own welfare assistance rolls (after the federal assumption of fiscal responsibility).

In anticipation of the January 1974 starting date of SSI, many states hurried to "blanket in" eligible categorical recipients to qualify for 100 percent federal funding of aged, blind, and disabled persons (physically and mentally). Prior to SSI, from 1962 to 1970, the number of adult APTD recipients grew from about 421,000 to 866,000—a gain of 106 percent in eight years. In only four years, from 1970 to the eve of SSI on December 31, 1973, the number of adult APTD recipients soared to about 3 million persons—a gain of 247 percent (U.S. Department of Health, Education, and Welfare, June 1964, table 10; HEW, September 1972, table 14; and Callison, June 1974, table 1). Not surprisingly, the national DE rate of state mental hospitals also became "relatively high" (Witkin 1976, p. 4). States could place ex-patients on APTD, knowing full well that SSI legislation required that the federal government automatically include any pre-1974 disabled welfare recipients.

Assessing DE Factors, 1939–1969

FISCAL FACTORS. As noted at the outset, DE continued in California subsequent to 1969. There are plans to decrease the state population even further by 1985, to 2,890—or a 92.2 percent reduction since 1955 (State of California Department of Health, April 1977). The post-1969 DE efforts—both realized and planned—represent substantial reductions in population. However, it is important to emphasize that by 1970 California had already reduced its 65-and-over population by 73.5 percent and its under-65 population by 49.4 percent (Table 6–1).

It is clear, therefore, that events following these large-scale reductions cannot account for the origins of DE. This means that the rather significant changes in California's commitment laws, state and county planning and monitoring mechanisms, new state funding allocations, and procedures for local and state services cannot account for pre-1970 events (Bardach 1972; Enki 1972). Since 1970 these changes had, and will continue to have, a major impact on the delivery of mental health services in California. However, they are not relevant to an inquiry into the pre-1970 period. In similar fashion, significant federal legal decisions that have a bearing on DE (e.g., *Wyatt* v. *Stickney*) cannot account for pre-1970 events, in that these decisions began in 1972 (President's Commission on Mental Health, 1978, vol. 4, pp. 1359–1516).

The assessment of fiscal factors is more complex, in that costs for institutional care and attempts to determine how much of these costs should be borne by states, localities, and the family have been perpetual issues in mental health policy (Grob 1973; Cohn and Bary 1938). A. T. Scull, in his provocative book *Decarceration* (1977), has argued that "the drive for control of soaring costs is seen as the primary factor underlying the move towards decarceration" (p. 140). A year earlier, the Senate Subcommittee on Long-Term Care had reached a similar conclusion about DE of the aged. Commenting on cost savings, the subcommittee asserted that "this is undoubtedly the primary reason for removal of thousands from state hospitals into nursing homes and other facilities" (U.S. Senate Subcommittee on Long-Term Care, March 1976, p. 723). The subcommittee referred to the big differential in annual costs between a state hospital and a nursing home. It also referred to the fact that states assumed 100 percent of the cost for state hospital beds and only 50 percent for Medicaid beds (Ibid., p. 724). Scull claimed, in addition, that the proportion of total state expenditures devoted to state mental hospitals decreased steadily for all states, but particularly for California.

Although some legislators may have believed that actual state costs were being reduced, the fact is that state costs for the *total* mental health budget were increasing. In California, $68.5 million was budgeted for state hospitals in fiscal 1957, and that amount increased steadily until it peaked in 1966 at $116.7 million; in 1969 the hospital budget had receded to $112.8 million (Enki 1972, p. 6). After a decade of sharp population reductions, *actual* cost savings had not yet materialized. In addition, the state's budget for local programs—termed Short-Doyle—was increasing from less than $1 million in fiscal 1957 to $53.4 million in 1969. If this cost is included in state expenditures for mental health, then actual total mental health costs increased from $69.3 million in fiscal 1957 to $166.1 million in fiscal 1969—a gain of about 140 percent.

Neither Scull nor the Senate subcommittee provided data on *actual* state budgets, nor did they refer to nonhospital costs. The funds allocated for Short-Doyle programs were not the only increased costs incurred by the State of California. Although precise data are not available, it is clear that the State of California also sustained increases in expenditures from general revenue funds for the state's share of welfare costs related to the care of released persons residing in family care homes, board-and-care homes, nursing homes, and their own homes. Adding up these diverse costs, and others, is a complex task. The General Accounting

Office noted, in 1977, that on the basis of a variety of studies, "HEW believes that the state of the art of determining the costs in alternative long-term care settings is still in the early states of development" (GAO, 7 Januay 1977, p. 6).

This line of analysis does not mean that fiscal considerations had no role in the efforts of DE activists. It is not necessary to equate a desire for fiscal sharing—or transfer—of costs with actual cost savings. It appears almost axiomatic that one unit of government is usually attracted to the idea that other units pay for traditional expenditures—providing, of course, that actual costs do not increase. Before the advent of SSI, federal funds were not often used to replace "old" money—funds allocated by states to pay for traditional expenditures. The only major program in which it probably did occur, in many states, was in pre-1972 social services (Derthick 1975). Instead, federal funds were used as "new" money to subsidize increased release efforts, diverse living arrangements, and support services. In the process, old state hospital money continued to support the traditional institutional system.

The new federal money usually involved a match of new state funds. When California increased the number of mentally ill persons eligible for the APTD public welfare program, it was required to pay a state share for about 37,400 persons in 1970—instead of only 1,300 in 1962 (U.S. Department of Health, Education, and Welfare, 1962 and 1970). New money also had to be found for increased Old Age Assistance, Medical Assistance to the Aged, Medicaid, and for the social workers required to administer the transfer of payments. There is little doubt, therefore, that in California (and probably in other states as well) DE for the first fifteen years involved the financing of two systems of care: the emerging community-based system, and the old state hospital system.

Thus, in the short run, there were no actual savings, but rather added costs. Of course in the long run, phasing out many units (and buildings) within the traditional institutional system might save the state annual maintenance costs. Of greater importance were the deferred capital construction costs. Given the assumptions associated with the postwar Public Health Service "Standards," continued construction of new beds would have been required merely to keep pace with California's increasing general population and the utilization of state hospitals to care for an increasing aged population. Although California did not achieve rates per 100,000 population as high as New York's (291 vs 608 in 1955), it is quite probable that periodic construction of more units would have occurred—at state expense (Robertson 1974, p. 63).

It appears, therefore, that it is *future* savings that may attract astute legislators, executives, and administrators. But these potential savings involve taking fiscal risks in current budget years, thereby adding to the short-run costs. Because of political, social, and fiscal costs, states differ in their willingness to engage in this type of public entrepreneurial behavior. For many years California has been an entrepreneurial state in capturing federal dollars for new programs and sharing costs (Derthick 1975). Viewed from this perspective, fiscal factors played a critical role in accelerating DE. However, it is unlikely that California sought federal funds for released mental patients just to capture new grant-in-aid dollars. Federal funds provided valuable new money to *accelerate* the creation and maintenance of nontraditional resources for providing the supervision, care, and treatment of former and potential state patients. From this perspective, the precipitating factors associated with the onset of DE must be sought elsewhere.

HUMANITARIAN VALUES AND CHANGING CONCEPTIONS. The growth in humanitarian values and the dissemination of psychoactive drugs are two other reasons often cited to explain the occurrence of DE. Antiinstitutional criticisms about state hospitals have been voiced since the middle of the nineteenth century (Scull 1977, pp. 108–14). Grob has documented that since the late nineteenth century, criticisms of state mental hospitals had "steadily mounted" (Grob 1973, p 347). This growth in humanitarian sentiment helped to diminish "restraint and seclusion," promote a more "liberal leave policy," support a limited "family care" program, and provide limited support for clinics and "mental hygiene" educational efforts (Ibid., p. 350–52). Despite these efforts, from about 1912 to the eve of World War II, the numbers residing in state hospitals continued to increase, often under conditions that were "altogether intolerable" (to use Rosanoff's pungent wording).

Humanitarian sentiment was not sufficient to induce substantive change. Evidently just being against *specific* institutional abuses and in favor of specific reforms was not enough to generate a general mental health policy shift. Other ideas, related to conceptions of the mentally ill, the social functions of institutions, and the aims of treatment also had to change before alternative approaches to custody and care could be actively pursued. The discounting of bad heredity as the "cause of causes" and the corollary emphasis on "social and economic factors" helped change the image of persons who were objects of humanitarian concern. Changing terminology—"parole" became a "convalescent leave" and a form of "extramural" or "after" care—symbolized the shift in the conception of the mentally ill that began to emerge on the eve of World War II. Instead of "inmates on parole," the mentally ill were now perceived as "patients on leave." Ideally, up to 65 percent of a resident population could be released.

One difficulty with this new conception of the patient was that "mentally unhygienic" places were unsatisfactory sites for providing active treatment. Alternative places of treatment and care had to be created and subsidized with public funds. Instead of being places of first choice, state institutions were to become places of last resort—when all else had failed. In addition, they were no longer to be used as places of eugenic "segregation," in that the ideological rationale for this societal function had been undermined by the changing conceptions of mental illness.

Hospitals for the insane also underwent a change. The local "psychopathic hospital" had existed since 1912, but its primary functions were to serve as an "observation hospital for acute cases" and to screen those cases that required long-term care in a state hospital (Grob 1973). By 1940, they were expected to function as places of active "neuropsychiatric" treatment. By 1950, a Canadian psychiatrist reported to a meeting of the American Psychiatric Association that during the war, because of a shortage of personnel, "day hospital" treatment had been introduced. Accompanying this local development was a conscious reformulation of the aims of hospitalization and psychiatric treatment: patients did not go to hospitals to get cured, but rather to "get well enough to go home where treatment continues" (Cameron 1950, p. 64).

PSYCHOACTIVE DRUGS. Changing conceptions about mental illness, the social functions of state and local hospitals, and the aims of hospitalization were encompassed by advanced psychiatric thinking *before* the advent of psychoactive drugs. It appears reasonable to infer that given the resources, DE could have started immediately after World War II. Instead, a significant amount of state resources was devoted to expanding and upgrading traditional state hospital systems. Now they, too, could become places of active treatment. Proinstitutional policies were guided by standards that legitimated a massive building program. There was a division of opinion over whether state hospitals should be the sites of long-term care for the elderly, but this did not prevent allocating 30 percent of the new beds for persons 65 years and over.

State hospitals eagerly made plans for the postwar forms of treatment: insulin and electric shock, as well as psychosurgery. As perceived by Rosanoff (1939), this vast building program, "no matter on how large a scale [afforded] but partial and temporary relief at best." In order to handle increased numbers more efficiently, electric shock was administered in maintenance treatment doses, especially on "chronic wards" (Noyes 1953, p. 559). This use indicates that state hospital leadership had not yet accepted the notion of noncustodial functions and aims. By 1955, therefore, there still existed conflicting ideas about the social functions and aims of state hospitals. In the context of a conflict over public policy, the invention and dissemination of psychoactive drugs could be used for diverse purposes. For proponents of an active role for state institutions, the new "wonder" drugs could take the place of electric shock therapy. Noyes and Kolb's authoritative *Modern Clinical Psychiatry* (1958) summarized the social-control use of drugs in the mid-1950s as follows: "Formerly electroconvulsive therapy was extensively used as a maintenance treatment of chronically disturbed patients, especially those suffering from schizophrenia. While such treatment given once every week or ten days facilitated the care of these patients it has been largely replaced by the use of tranquilizer drugs" (p. 613).

Drugs could also be used to increase release rates and thereby bolster the claim of institutional effectiveness. But unlike electroconvulsive therapy, the new medical technology could also be used on an outpatient basis. Although the cultural "fit" between the values of the state hospital and drugs was also compatible, it had a unique "fit" for "community based treatment." Drugs could be given anywhere: in nursing homes (U.S. Senate Subcommittee on Long-Term Care, January 1975); in board-and-care homes (Segal and Aviram 1978); in residential treatment centers (NIMH, Series A, no. 15); or in general hospital psychiatric inpatient units (NIMH, *Statistical Note*, no. 141). In addition, drugs were much cheaper to administer than electroconvulsive therapy.

Deciding how drugs were to be used—on behalf of institutional treatment goals or DE objectives—was a matter of ideology and judgment by critical decision makers. Until 1959, the State of California had not yet made a clear choice, as indicated by resident population figures. With the selection of a new director who supported the policy of community alternatives, the political balance was tipped in favor of the use of drugs for a DE policy. Professional leadership and the availability of an existing organizational mechanism (Nathan Sloate, head of BSW, for example) facilitated the development of a long-range plan. They were able to utilize the new technology on behalf of DE objectives. As a California administrator told a national audience, drugs were used as "a significant bridge from control of the mentally disordered person to his socialization. For a few cents a day in medication, many persons who previously could look forward to little more than residence in controlled settings in our large institutions became able to return to life in the community" (Robertson 1974, p. 65).

From 1959 on, a number of factors supported a clear DE policy in California: leaders in critical positions, at central administrative levels, committed to the nontraditional conceptions of mental illness, new state hospital functions, and a modern treatment paradigm; a patient-release organization legitimated by law, experienced in placement development and supervision skills, politically protected at a central level, and led by a person with extensive contacts in the legislature, the judiciary, and in local communities; a new medical technology that was relatively inexpensive and easily adaptable to any type of placement decision; and a state executive leadership and legislature sympathetic to, and supportive of, entrepreneurial approaches to public policy development. When the new federal funds were made available, the state could take advantage of the opportunities with alacrity and enthusiasm. Reformers could refer to "breaking down the walls," and conservatives could appreciate projections of deferred capital construction costs.

This view of the impact of drugs appears to be congruent with the known facts. However, others might be more attracted to D. Mechanic's formulation about the role of drugs: "The use of drugs gave the staff greater confidence in its own efficacy and helped dispel the feeling of hopelessness and apathy that had captured the mental hospital. All these conditions gave impetus to administrative changes such as eliminating restraints, minimizing security arrangements, and encouraging early releases" (1969, pp. 61–62; 1980, p. 87).

In contrast to the view that drugs may have given "impetus to administrative changes" that promoted DE policies, this analysis has thus far emphasized that prior to the introduction of psychoactive drugs, there existed a viable subgroup of mental health leaders favoring alternative approaches in state mental health organizations. In addition to California, there is evidence that Massachusetts also had leaders committed to DE (Cole et al. 1978). States that lacked this antiinstitutional leadership were probably not as ready or willing to take full advantage of the drugs and opportunities offered by the expanding welfare state of the 1960s.

SOURCES OF AGE SELECTIVITY. Although the use of psychoactive drugs is probably critical to an understanding of the national timing of DE, interstate variability is best accounted for by leadership, organizational, and philosophical differences. Acceleration, as suggested earlier, is related to the entrepreneurial use of social welfare regulations and legislation. This leaves the last fact to be explained: the selectivity of choosing aged persons among leading DE states. As the least dangerous group, whether from a community or eugenic perspective, Rosanoff proposed their removal from state hospitals as early as 1927. The Council of State Governments' *Report on Mental Health* made a similar proposal in 1949. In addition, California had a history of giving special attention to the aged, a concern that expressed itself in the 1930 creation of a Division of Old Age Security to provide state welfare payments—one of nineteen states to pass a pre-1935 old-age pension law (Cahn and Bary 1938, p. 180; Leiby 1978, p. 215). Sentiment in California on behalf of the elderly was also expressed in the 1930s by the home-grown Townsend clubs, which expanded into a national movement on behalf of a federally funded old-age pension law (Piven and Cloward 1971).

This ideological sympathy for the problems of the aged was later realized on a national level by higher welfare benefits and by the first medical assistance program based not on a narrow welfare definition, but on a state definition of economic need for persons 65 and over (1960). This medical assistance for the aged was followed by the nation's first entry into national health insurance coverage— for the aged only (in 1965). Fifteen years later the nation is still without a universal health insurance program for all ages. There has been age selectivity in the operation of the welfare state since its inception in 1935.

For persons interested in an accelerated DE policy, the aged offered a good strategic target. The target group was a large one (about 30 percent of the resident population), with easier eligibility requirements for procuring a wide variety of federally funded benefits, and the age group with the lowest rates of crime and dangerous behavior. The risks associated with controlling admissions and accelerating the release of this age group were much less than in any other category associated with the state's hospitals.

CONTRIBUTION OF COMMUNITY ALTERNATIVES. This assessment has given little weight to the development of local mental health treatment resources as a major contribution to DE. Although California was one of the first states to fund local programs, these efforts were devoted to *voluntary* patients until legislative changes in 1963 (Bardach 1972; Enki 1972). Even after 1963 and 1969 legislative changes in state funding ratios (from 50:50 to 75:25, and then to 90:10), local programs were not greatly involved in the after-care of released patients

(Ibid.). A research team sympathetic to local programming concluded in 1972 that "a shift in funding to counties did not appear to have significantly increased after-care services" (Enki 1972, p. 177). Prior to the 1969 shift in greater funding to counties, BSW staff (renamed Community Service Division) "had responsibility for after-care of most patients released from state hospitals" (Ibid., p. 171).

If, prior to 1970, state-funded local programs had little to do with DE patients, then California community mental health centers—federally funded under the Community Mental Retardation and Community Mental Health Centers Construction Act of 1963–also "had little or no official role in providing after-care" (Ibid.). A General Accounting Office report in 1977 found that the national result was similar, even as late as 1974: "Public mental hospitals accounted for fewer referrals for CMHCs than any other referral source reported, except for the clergy" (GAO, 7 January 1977, p. 68). The report also stated that the resident population of state mental hospitals "had been substantially reduced before many CMHCs became operational." Despite this knowledge, the GAO opened its lengthy report on DE with the assertion that by passing the 1963 CMHC Act, the government embarked on a "bold new approach" to provide "alternatives to institutional care" (Ibid.).

Rhetorically, federal officials and sympathetic legislators and staff may have believed that the 1963 CMHC act symbolized a "bold new approach." But analysis of fiscal data provides evidence that, aside from implementation deficiencies, mental health program funding by the federal government did not even match the efforts of one state—California. In 1971 the National Institute of Mental Health (NIMH) spent about $110.2 million for CMHC and freestanding outpatient clinics for direct care and facilities development (Levine and Levine 1975, table 1). In fiscal 1971 California budgeted $115.7 million for state and county expenditures to local programs (Enki 1972, p. 7).

Actually, the bold new approach on behalf of mental health did not come from NIMH expenditures, but rather from other parts of the welfare state. In 1971, the federal government directly expended a total of $2,338,600,000 for mental illness, to be used for civilian and nonpenal purposes (Levine and Levine 1975, table 1). The expenditures were as follows: NIMH and other Public Health Service—$432.7 million (18.5 percent); Medicaid—$816.6 million (34.8 percent); welfare and social rehabilitation services—$622.0 million (26.6 percent); other welfare transfer payments—$201.0 million (8.6 percent); all other—$266.3 million (11.4 percent). The distribution revealed that the Social Security Act (as amended over the years) constituted the bold new program, in that Medicaid, welfare and social rehabilitative services and other welfare transfer payments were funded by authority of this legislation—for a total of about 70 percent of all federal MI costs in 1971. The federal government has funded varied DE efforts primarily with welfare dollars—not mental health budgets.

Summary and Conclusions

Mental health policies in the United States have always been influenced by national and state factors as well as ideological, organizational, and technological practices peculiar to the state hospital system (Grob 1973). It should not be too surprising, therefore, that external as well as internal factors shaped the timing and development of DE trends and policies. Careful attention to historical factors and sequence of shifts, as well as empirical changes and trends, is necessary in order to discern the relative influence of external and internal variables.

From a historical perspective, state mental hospitals have always delivered a variety of social functions to diverse population categories. By providing relief, care, custody, and protection inside segregated institutions, state mental health policies have been intimately related to existing policies toward the "dependent and defective classes"—or, in today's terminology, toward welfare and deviant groups. A review of Chapter 2 supports the view that state hospitals have traditionally housed persons who were former candidates for local almshouses and jails. Although moving welfare and deviant persons away from these local facilities represented a distinct departure in American social policy, the shift into more specialized institutions was circumscribed by a distinct preference for helping diverse poor and troubled persons primarily inside asylums (Rothman 1971; Grob 1973).

The American predilection for institutional handling of the mentally ill was buttressed by an economic relief policy openly hostile to helping individuals and families "outdoors" in their own homes. This anti-outdoor relief policy began to change in the early part of the twentieth century, but not without a great deal of hostility from the leaders of private philanthropy (Lubove 1968). Even when outdoor relief was provided through meager "pensions" to widows and the aged (in some states), it was done without federal assistance until the middle of the Great Depression. Although a few states offered subsidized "family care" for paroled mental patients, the funds came out of institutional budgets (Grob 1973). Until the 1930s, even when noninstitutional relief was given to ex-mental patients, it was provided under institutional auspices. This was congruent with funding parole staff out of institutional budgets.

An institutional approach to social problems was also supported by the widespread ideological acceptance that "socially maladjusted" and mentally ill persons were carriers of "bad heredity" (Hofstadter 1955). In 1927, Rosanoff's text on psychiatry and mental hygiene promoted eugenic policies that envisioned an expansion—not reduction—of segregated institutions for "defective" persons. As an advocate of paroling "up to 20 percent" of an institution, and thereby "testing" the ability of inmates to conform and not be considered "defective," Rosanoff's views were considered progressive for the period (Rothman 1980, p. 365).

The ideological shifts in Rosanoff's thinking paralleled an emerging "modern" conception of the importance of: social and environmental factors on mental health "adjustment"; the state hospital as a place of last resort; and the aim of relieving "distressing symptoms," rather than seeking a "cure" for illness. These changing views occurred at a time when Americans belatedly accepted public responsibility for the welfare of citizens in their own homes—including the initiation of a federal welfare state. Although DE did not occur in the 1930s, it is now clear that a new federal responsibility for economic misfortune, childhood dependency, and assistance to the elderly was coupled—in the initial Social Security Act of 1935—with a public antagonism toward traditional forms of indoor relief. Old-age assistance could not use federal funds "on behalf of any individual who is an inmate of a public institution (except as a patient in a medical institution) or any individual who is a patient in an institution for tuberculosis or mental disease" (Title 1, sec. 6). Aid to families with dependent children could only use federal funds to support children living "in a place of residence maintained by one or more of such relatives as his or their own home" (Title 4, sec. 406).

These federal-welfare prohibitions against "public institutions" and institutions for "mental disease" were upheld in the 1950 addition of a new beneficiary category: Aid to Permanently and Totally Disabled (APTD) (Title 14, sec. 1405). When Medical Assistance to the Aged (MAA) was passed in 1960, the definition of MAA again excluded payments for inmates of public institutions and facilities for mental disease (Title 1, sec. 6). When APTD recipients became eligible for medical assistance in 1962, prohibitions against traditional institutions were again included (Title 16, sec. 1605). Federal public policy clearly favored assisting persons living in their own homes, with relatives, in medical hospitals, or in other nonmental-disease facilities. Although these ideological changes and the emergence of new welfare policies supported noninstitutional strategies, the historical record reveals that depopulation of the mental hospitals began after 1955—not 1945. Other variables had to exist to trigger population reductions in state institutions.

The national onset of DE is clearly associated with the widespread introduction and utilization of psychoactive drugs. However, the California data disclose that the appearance of a new treatment technology did not automatically lead to stable population reductions. A different type of leadership—favorable to DE ideas, and strategically located at a centralized level of state organization—had to possess the power to use a pharmacological innovation on behalf of an explicit population-reduction policy. Changes in state mental health ideology, goals, and leadership, as well as drug technology, facilitated the initial stage of the reduction in state hospital populations in California (1959–62).

Accelerated reductions in the 1960s were associated with the availability of significant new fiscal resources from an expanding welfare state. Taking advantage of these new federal funds required that a state also provide new matching funds for the specific grant-in-aid programs. The willingness to fund new welfare programs relied on public entrepreneurship capability and skills, as well as philosophical agreement with the objectives of a long-range plan. California risked providing new grant-in-aid funds in order to capture anticipated benefits in the future—the closing of hospital units and buildings, and deferring new construction costs. This type of public entrepreneurship can come into maximal play in a federal, pluralistic, political system when federal programs provide incentives, have diffuse eligibility boundaries, vague definitions of services, and are openended in funding (Derthick 1975).

Besides using new federal funding opportunities to reduce daily population counts, California also used new welfare legislation to reduce admissions of aged persons into state hospitals. Utilizing the country's first geriatric screening project, California demonstrated that admissions, as well as discharge, could be brought under strict organizational control. The new DE goal could be accomplished successfully if interested staff maximally utilized the great variety of welfare programs available to the aged prior to an involuntary commitment to a state facility—because persons became ineligible for federal subsidization if residing in a public institution.

The analysis in this chapter is based on a single case study. Analyses of other states might yield new explanatory factors, or perhaps stimulate a reassessment of variables associated with DE trends. However, the examination of national institutional trends following the passage of new federal legislation in 1972, the Supplementary Security Income (SSI), provides fuller support for the idea that acceleration of DE is associated with the availability of new welfare resources. The availability of 100 percent federal funding to subsidize former or potential mentally disabled persons (i.e., APTD eligibles) reduced the state problem of finding new money on a long-term basis—in that after 1 January 1974, no state funds would be necessary to pay for the basic SSI grant. States could wait until the 100 percent funding date, but they risked having ex-patients declared ineligible by *federal* standards. By placing persons on convalescent leave, or directly discharging them—using state eligibility standards—states were assured that these persons would be subsidized by the federal government for an indefinite period. All state-eligible persons had to be carried over on SSI rolls after assumption of 100 percent federal funding. Of course, even the more cautious states could wait until 1 January 1974, to accelerate DE.

It is reasonable to infer that since 1972 many states have been attracted to the unprecedented opportunity to transfer traditional state costs on to a 100 percent, permanent federal funding source. None of the earlier federal programs had offered this type of long-term incentive. It also appears reasonable to infer that the national jump of DE in state mental hospitals (and in institutions for the retarded) was influenced by public entrepreneurial calculations. The expansion of the welfare state and the existence of public entrepreneurship appear to be intimately associated with the acceleration of DE at a national level, as well as at a state level. Not surprisingly, the varied opportunities for public entrepreneurial behavior also stimulated conditions for the expression of profit making behaviors in the private sector—via the growth of the nursing home and boarding home industries (see Chapter 10).

PART II

Understanding Utilization Patterns of Youth Facilities

Dependent and Neglected Youth: Institutional Care versus Home and Foster Care

Removing youth from older institutional types has long been a matter of concern to reformers. Long before there was a strong repudiation of forcing impoverished adults to live in almshouses in order to receive public relief, there was a growing consensus to stop housing dependent youth in the local poorhouse. There was also a movement to empty jails and prisons of "wayward" and delinquent children. As alternatives, special child-oriented institutions were created during the nineteenth century: juvenile and orphan asylums for poor, houseless, and neglected youth, and houses of refuge and juvenile reformatories for delinquent and wayward youth (Lciby 1978; Rothman 1971). Detention facilities were created after 1900 to house dependent/neglected, status offenders, and delinquents awaiting court action (Schlossman 1977).

The late nineteenth century witnessed increasing disillusionment with the special institutions for children and youth, particularly in the field of dependency and neglect. DE of dependency/neglect institutions did not, however, occur nationally on a large scale until after the passage of Title 4 of the Social Security Act of 1935—Aid to Families with Dependent Children (AFDC). Disillusionment with the traditional, long-term, juvenile correctional facilities occurred later and did not yield substantive results until the late 1960s and early 1970s.

As DE of traditional child welfare and long-term, public, juvenile correctional facilities progressed, new institutional alternatives were again created, as they had been in the previous century. In the process of developing new residential treatment centers (a post-1950 social invention) and other community-based forms of group care and supervision (a post-1960 invention), a new set of relationships developed between the fields of child welfare and juvenile corrections. The public child-welfare system promoted and subsidized private residential alternatives for the "voluntary" placement of youth 12 years and older, often described as "acting out" and "needing structure" and "treatment." Many of the youth were actually or potentially in trouble with police and court officials, inasmuch as their behaviors were often classifiable as offenses under the juvenile code statutes of the fifty states. Juvenile courts also began to use these correctional alternatives for youth; the courts processed youth who were "acting out" and in need of "structure." These systemic changes were facilitated by amendments to federal welfare legislation, permitting the subsidization of foster care maintenance and social services related to residential placement.

Because of the growing predilection to refer to youth in trouble as exhibiting "acting out" symptoms indicative of an underlying "emotional disturbance," the mental health system also became involved in providing treatment and "structure." Beginning in the 1960s, an increasing number of youth were admitted to inpatient psychiatric units in general hospitals and community mental health centers (usually associated with a general hospital), private mental hospitals, and state/county mental hospitals. New federally assisted medical welfare programs (Medicaid), as well as third-party insurance payments, helped promote this new system's coverage of youth in trouble.

These developments indicate that to understand DE trends and issues pertinent to youth, it is necessary to understand changes within and among the three major youth-serving systems from a historical perspective. This and the following chapter will depict and analyze developments and trends on two levels: intrasystem and intersystem. In addition, they will offer an assessment of the social factors that inhibited, as well as promoted, changes in youth custody, care, and treatment. The summary and conclusions for this chapter are incorporated at the end of Chapter 8 in order to facilitate a holistic discussion of the three systems.

The First DE of Children: Separation from Adults and the Emergence of Separate Systems

As noted earlier, the separation of youth from adults living in local almshouses and jails began in the first half of the nineteenth century. This separation, however, was not completed within a short time period. Many communities did not totally remove youth from almshouses until the latter part of the nineteenth century. A few, primarily in rural areas, continued to mix adults and children in almshouses until 1923. According to census figures, 16.2 percent of the nation's almshouse resident population were persons under 19 in 1880, and 9.9 percent in 1890; by 1923 this age category dropped to 3.3 percent of the total population, as the almshouses had become transformed into places primarily for aged and near-aged persons (see table 2–3).

The difficulty in eliminating children from public almshouses was mirrored in the utilization patterns of private adult institutions. In 1923 about 140,300 children were residents of institutions "primarily for the care of dependents." Of this number, about 10,000—or 7 percent—were still residents of institutions for adults: homes for the aged, infirm, or destitute; or temporary shelters for the homeless or unemployed (U.S. Bureau of the Census, 1923, table 1).

Moving children out of local jails and adult correctional facilities appears to have been even more difficult to accomplish on a national basis. By the time the juvenile court was invented, at the beginning of the twentieth century, a variety of public training schools and reformatories had already been created for violators of criminal statutes, truancy laws, and status offender statutes. However, in the 1904 census, about 33 percent of the juveniles formally committed by a court (excluding detentions) were sent to adult penal institutions: jails, workhouses, state prisons, and young-adult reformatories. In 1923, the census estimated that this figure had been reduced to about 20 percent—12 percent in local jails and workhouses, and 8 percent in prisons and young-adult reformatories (Ibid., p. 295). Census data for 1933 revealed that progress had been temporarily reversed, in that about 27 percent of youth committed during that year were sent to an adult-type correctional facility (U.S. Bureau of the Census, *Prisoners, 1933*, pp. 1, 30; Ibid., *County and City Jails*, 1933, p. 40).

Separating youth from adults—particularly from almshouses and jails—constituted America's first effort at deinstitutionalization. It appears that faster progress was made in moving dependent youth into alternative care facilities, than in moving delinquent and wayward youth into alternative correctional facilities. This difference in policy implementation was reflected in the distinctive organizations and practices associated with the two classifications of youth: "dependents" and "delinquents." The former category, together with physically handicapped and socially neglected youth, became the primary responsibility of private organizations, which were often subsidized by state and/or county public welfare authorities, or the child welfare system. The delinquent category, with its criminal and status offenders, usually came directly under the aegis of the state and/or county juvenile courts, and state and/or county detention and training school organizations—or the juvenile correctional system.

The Three Youth-in-Trouble Systems: A Pre-1933 Assessment

Although both systems of juvenile care and control tended to handle youth according to a specialized delinquent or dependent categorization, some overlap continued into the first part of the twentieth century. The juvenile correctional system had a more diverse mixture of youth in trouble than did the child welfare system. According to the 1923 census, out of the 140,300 youth enumerated as residing in a dependent/neglected institution, only 1,670 were formally classified as "delinquents separately reported"—less than 2 percent (U.S. Bureau of the Census, *Children under Institutional Care*, 1925, p. 14). By contrast, in the same year about 7 percent of the youth classified as residents of "special institutions for delinquents" were also categorized as "dependents separately reported" (Ibid., p. 14).

But the largest amount of diverse mixing occurred in local, publicly operated "detention homes." In the 1923 census the proportion of youth classified as dependent residents in ninety "homes" reached about 55 percent. About 30 percent of all admissions during three months of 1923 were categorized as dependent youth (Ibid., p. 345).

By the time the first national welfare programs were initiated during the Great Depression, the child-welfare and juvenile-correctional systems were well established at local and state levels—albeit with multiple uses by the juvenile correctional system, particularly in local detention facilities. Mental health—the third modern system for handling youth in trouble—was only beginning to develop as a new resource in the 1920s, primarily as court-attached or free-standing "child guidance clinics." Between 1921 and 1927 these clinics multiplied from only 7 to 102, primarily because of funding by the Commonwealth Fund (Leiby 1978, p. 184; Bremner et al. 1971, vol. 2, pp. 570–74). Many of the clinics furnished diagnostic work-ups and made recommendations for "habit" training, but offered little treatment (Ibid.; Robins 1966). Institutionalization of youth for psychiatric reasons was a rare event. Part of the reason so few residents of hospitals for "mental disease" were youth was due to an ideological belief about the age of insanity. As reported in the 1923 census of mental hospitals:

> Mental disease occurs principally in adult life. Psychopathic disorders appear in children, but as a rule these are not serious enough to require commitment to a hospital for mental disease. . . . It will be noted that only 0.2 per cent of the total patients were under 15 years of age and only 1.5 per cent were under 20 years. [U.S. Bureau of the Census, *Patients in Hospitals for Mental Disease, 1923*, p. 26]

By the 1960s this view of the mental health system changed dramatically. But until recently, those problems of youth deemed serious enough to warrant removal from the home were allocated to the two older systems.

DE of the Dependency/Neglect Institutions: The Emergence of Alternatives

In 1899, almost seventy-five years after the first youth institution was founded in New York City, the leading private social welfare organization of the era—the National Conference of Charities and Corrections—officially endorsed, for the first time, the following policy: when a dependent child requires substitute care, consideration should first be given to a foster family arrangement (Kadushin 1974, p. 401). A decade later, participants in the first White House Conference on Dependent Children reiterated this position by stating that "the carefully selected foster home is for the normal child the best substitute for the natural home" (Bremner et al. 1971, vol. 2, p. 365). Actually, both of these statements were a belated recognition of activities that had occurred since 1854, when without charge, Charles Loring Brace "placed out" New York City children in Middle West farm communities (Ibid., p. 291; Brace 1972; Warner 1908, pp. 263–96).

The "free foster home" activities begun by Brace were picked up by other children's aid organizations; the idea was extended to using homes near cities, as well as placing out in the West. By 1868, the Massachusetts Board of State Charities began experimenting with "boarding out" payments to foster families to pay for substitute care and supervision of "state pauper children" in lieu of institutional residence (Bremner et al. 1971, vol. 2, pp. 322, 330). By 1882, Massachusetts legislation provided that "indigent and neglected" children could be directly boarded out with a "suitable person," without passing through a state-operated "primary school" (for dependent children). By the time of the 1909

White House conference, boarding out children in foster homes as an alternative to institutionalization was widely used in Massachusetts, Pennsylvania, the District of Columbia, New Jersey, and California, and to "a lesser degree in the other states of the union" (Ibid., p. 329).

The other alternative to institutional care that received broad support from the first White House conference on children was direct assistance to families so children could be kept at home. Because of a concern that support would be provided only to "persons of worthy character," the conference leaders were careful to couch their recommendations in conditional and restrictive language. Sponsored by the esteemed leaders of private charities organizations, the "home care" resolution also included a distinct preference for providing economic assistance "in the form of private charity rather than of public relief." Because the recommendation became the accepted policy of the private welfare sector for at least a quarter of a century, and influenced subsequent public welfare policies and procedures, it is worth quoting in full:

> Home life is the highest product of civilization. It is the great molding force of mind and character. Children should not be deprived of it except for urgent and compelling reasons. Children of parents of worthy character, suffering from temporary misfortune, and children of reasonably efficient and deserving mothers who are without the support of the normal breadwinner, should as a rule be kept with their parents, such aid being given as may be necessary to maintain suitable homes for the rearing of the children. This aid should be given by such methods and from such sources as may be determined by the general relief policy of each community, preferably in the form of private charity rather than of public relief. Except in unusual circumstances, the home should not be broken up for reasons of poverty, but only for considerations of inefficiency or immorality." [Bremner et al. 1971, vol. 2, p. 365]

Despite the widespread acceptance of home care and foster care as ideal alternatives, there does not appear to have been a reduction in the actual number of youth residing in institutions designated for the care, education, and supervision of dependent and neglected children. Although census categories were not always comparable in 1910, 1923, and 1933, the following figures appear to provide the best approximate indicators of one-day census counts of children residing in all institutions for "dependents" (for children only and children with adults, excluding almshouses): 1910—136,500; 1923—140,300; 1933—140,350 (see table 7–1 for sources).

Whereas the actual number of youthful residents appears to rise slightly between 1910 and 1923, and then stabilize, a slightly different image is conveyed if rates per 100,000 youth are used (instead of raw numbers). Table 7–1 provides information on the utilization of institutional and foster home residences, controlling for the number of youth under 14 years of age (the accepted census age of "adulthood" until the post-World War II censuses).

The information in Table 7–1 suggests that, controlling for the youth population, the institutional rate of 1923 probably dropped from that of 1910. The slight increase in actual numbers institutionalized did not keep pace with the sharp in-

TABLE 7–1

Youth under 14 Residing in Institutions for Dependent/Neglected and in Foster Homes:
1910, 1923, and 1933 (per 100,000 youth population)

Year	Under-14 Child Population	Resident Institutional Rate	Foster Home Rate	Total Out-of-Home Rate
1910	27,806,000	491	NA	NA
1923	33,032,000	425	222	647
1933	32,742,000	429	313	742

SOURCES: Institutional and foster home figures are from U.S. Bureau of the Census, *Benevolent Institutions*, *1910*, and *Children under Institutional Care*, 1923 and 1933. Population figures are from U.S. Bureau of the Census, *Historical Statistics of the U.S.*, *Colonial Times to 1957*, 1960.

crease in the under-14 population. The 1933 rate per 100,000 youth, however, is slightly above the 1923 figure—primarily because of a decrease in youth population.

Foster homes were not counted separately in 1910; therefore, data are available only for the prewar years of 1923 and 1933. The number of youth residing in foster homes (whether free or subsidized) increased from 73,300 in 1923, to about 102,600 in 1933. Because this large increase occurred despite the drop in the youth population, the foster home rate rise was disproportionately higher than indicated by just using the raw numbers.

This analysis indicates that the modest amount of DE that occurred between 1910 and 1933 (about 13 percent) was primarily due to an increase in the population at risk. No actual depopulation of dependent institutions appears to have occurred at a national level, despite public declarations and rhetoric in favor of home care or foster care. Instead, there appears to have been an increase in the total number of youth under the direct supervision of social welfare agencies. This inference is supported by the increase in the total number of out-of-home youth, as well as the total out-of-home rate per 100,000 youth (see table 7–1). At a national level, it appears that the greater use of foster homes was independent of the use of institutions, inasmuch as the foster home rate increased (from 222 to 313), while the institutional rate stabilized (from 425 to 429). This curious phenomenon warrants a more complete examination.

Pre-1933 Increase in Number of Youth under Supervision and Care: The Critical Role of the Juvenile Court

The increased use of foster homes (independently of any diminution of institutional use) occurred for those receiving "boarding home" payments. "Free" foster home use actually declined between 1923 and 1933 (see table 7–1 for sources). This heightened concern for dependents was paid for primarily with public funds. In 1933 about 84 percent of boarding home children were supported by public funds, in contrast to only 46 percent of the institutional residents. This disparity in support is also revealed by the 1933 administrative auspices of care: 84 percent of institutionalized children were under private agency care and supervision, whereas voluntary agencies supervised about 53 percent of those in foster care (free and boarding homes combined) (U.S. Department of Health, Education, and Welfare, 1966, p. 9).

The reasons for this greater public concern are quite diverse. Mothers' pension laws, as a means of helping poor families, received wide political support, and were entered into the statute books of forty states by 1921 (Bremner et al. 1971, vol. 2, p. 385). In addition to the growing concern about the impact of poverty on family life and children, particularly for blameless widows, the Progressive era was also a time for child labor reform, and renewed interest in children's health, education, nutrition, recreation, and character building organizations (Ibid.; Leiby 1978). In addition, between 1899 and 1923, virtually every state enacted juvenile court legislation to separate adults and children in local jails and courtrooms; many states also built new detention homes (particularly in large urban areas).

The juvenile courts in many urban areas served as the critical authoritative source for dealing with child welfare protective cases involving dependency or neglect. As the 1909 White House resolution stated, homes could be justifiably "broken up [for] consideration of inefficiency or immorality." Courts granted private and public agencies the leverage to do so, as well as to oversee the handling of other problems of youth in trouble.

Juvenile courts, until they were "domesticated" by due process in the 1960s, exercised an enormous amount of discretion in the implementation of broad jurisdictional boundaries. Early statutes referred to general conceptions of "delinquency," "neglect," and "dependency." Often similar dispositions were permissible, regardless of the jurisdictional basis for the court petition. Perhaps the most significant indicator of the breadth of judicial interest, jurisdiction, and power was the use of local detention facilities. In 1923, as noted earlier, more than half of the daily residents of secure detention homes were youth categorized as "dependents." The court, according to the census reporter of this statistic, should be considered a primary child welfare agency. The census author believed that "the agency that has come most distinctly to the front in assuming children's protective functions is the juvenile court" (U.S. Bureau of the Census, 1923, p. 26).

Juvenile courts were perceived to have "performed a protective and educative rather than a penal function" (Ibid., p. 261). In addition to these protective and educational judicial roles, judges were often chosen to administer the new laws providing mothers' pensions (Lubove 1968; Bremner et al. 1971, vol. 2, p. 320). Using his diverse powers, a judge could authorize payment of public assistance, placement in a foster home, probation, detention, residence in an institution for the dependent/neglected, or commitment to an institution for juvenile delinquents. As for jurisdictional clarity in the use of these discretionary powers, many judges behaved as if they shared the views of the 1923 census author: "The dividing line between dependency and delinquency is often so vague that in practice both types of children may be found in the care of organizations intended primarily for the care of a single class, and there is a growing tendency for organizations for dependents to accept predelinquents and the milder delinquents" (Ibid., p. 11).

DE of Dependent/Neglected, and the Fight for Home Care

If juvenile court judges were helping to populate detention homes and dependent and neglected institutions for a variety of social purposes, why didn't other leaders of the child welfare system attempt to reduce institutional use for the clearly dependent child, so that "the home should not be broken up for reasons of poverty"? The likely candidates were those leaders chosen to participate in drafting public policy at the 1909 White House conference. Yet, they were unable to perform this function because the overwhelming majority of charity and child-care organizations were unalterably opposed to a home-care policy where public funds replaced private charity. They were opposed to any form of public outdoor relief—whether it was termed mothers' or widows' pension, mothers' aid, poor relief, or public assistance. They were uncompromising in their opposition to mothers' pension legislation in virtually every state, even though home care could have promoted DE. In addition, they believed that private charity could meet the task of helping poor families. Therefore, they did not propose any new stable, voluntary, funding sources to prevent institutionalizing poor children (Lubove 1968).

The activities of one of the leading private social welfare organizations in the nation—the Charity Organization Society (COS) of New York City—provides an example of their policies about "home care." Beginning in 1898, COS, together with other societies, opposed a state legislative proposal that the City of New York, "instead of supporting children in private institutions should pay parents the cost of their support and thus prevent the evils of the separation of families and of institution life for children" (Bremner et al. 1971, vol. 2, p. 353). COS leaders argued that "owing to the certainty that great moral injury would be sure to result to the character of the people by this return to public outdoor relief," they were "obliged to oppose" the legislation. In an effort to stave off mounting public support for mothers' aid, they launched an experiment to demonstrate how to provide private assistance to poor families as a means to avoid the commitment of children to a "benevolent institution."

For emergency economic aid COS relied on the existing "Provident Relief Fund or some other cooperating relief agency." If there was a need for a regular monthly allowance, COS issued an individual "newspaper appeal" or solicited the existing "various sources of relief when such are available." (Ibid.). The

COS "friendly visitors" who administered this uncertain private relief program found that the "poor worthy parents" chosen were also the persons who most often applied for commitment of their children to an institution. In many cases, according to COS, "parents usually apply for the commitment of only part of their children, expecting to be able to support the remainder." Three "typical" cases were cited by COS in *Charities*, a leading philanthropic journal:

> "(1) A widow with 6 children, two of whom were able to work, applied for the commitment of the three younger children. . . .
> (2) A mother with five children was living with her brother who could not continue to keep them. She applied for the commitment of four children. . . .
> (3) A deserted woman with three children asked for the commitment of two in May 1901, though she was very anxious to keep her children with her." [Ibid., pp. 354–55]

The private welfare leaders of New York City were not content merely to demonstrate the moral superiority of private charity—as opposed to public assistance—to impoverished families. Rather, they campaigned actively against public assistance, until its passage in 1915. They were not novices in politics; their organizations had succeeded in outlawing public outdoor relief of any kind in Brooklyn in 1879 (Warner 1908, p. 230; Lubov 1968, p. 224). Later this prohibition was extended to other boroughs in New York. But political activism against any form of public outdoor relief was not confined to New York: "By 1900 more than half the cities in the country with populations over 200,000, where the need was greatest, gave up public outdoor relief. These included New York, Philadelphia, St. Louis, Baltimore, San Francisco, New Orleans, Washington, Kansas City, and Louisville" (Leiby 1978, pp. 86, 519; Warner 1908, p. 236).

Homer Folks—President Theodore Roosevelt's choice for chairman of the 1909 White House Conference on Youth—viewed a mothers' pension as a type of "outdoor relief to families at their homes" and, therefore, "harmful to the poor" (Lubove 1968, p. 101). As head of the New York State Charities Aid Association, Folks joined with other leaders to oppose the pro-pension efforts of the 1914 New York Commission on Relief for Widowed Mothers. Among those supporting Folks were Mary Richmond (director of the Charity Organization Department of the prestigious Russell Sage Foundation and the leading casework theorist of the era) and Edward T. Devine (head of the New York School of Philanthropy, which became the Columbia University School of Social Work) (Ibid.).

Although private welfare leaders in New York and elsewhere lost the battle against mothers' pensions at the legislative level, their views were highly influential in the implementation phase of this new form of public assistance. Very few states actually voted appropriations out of state general revenues. By 1921, only 12 of the 40 states actually authorized any funds to share with the counties the cost of administration or of financial aid (Bremner et al. 1971, vol. 2, p. 392). Even though most states did not actually participate in funding the pensions, virtually all set payment standards for the first and subsequent children. A national survey by Lundberg of the Children's Bureau found that the legislative standard was far below the average amount paid by private agencies for foster boarding homes—a minimum of one-third to two-thirds below the boarding home average payment (Ibid., p. 389). But even the statutory maximum was rarely granted, in that "local economy and inadequate appropriations set a minimum entirely insufficient for the proper maintenance and safeguarding of the children" (Ibid., pp. 391–92).

The inadequate legislative standards, skimpy appropriations, and meager assistance allowances were congruent with COS values. Taken together they increased the certainty that poor families would not suffer "moral injury" by relying on funds below a substandard level of living. Moral injury was also prevented by the manner in which eligibility was established and assistance offered. According to the new public officials, mothers' pensions were to be considered part of a social treatment plan. Public officials believed that they were to administer relief as "laid down by the charity organization society for the work of private charities." As a type of "sympathetic casework," the public child worker "studies each individual's need and tries to lift him out of it by personal services" (Lubove 1968, p. 233). This, too, was congruent with the COS view that the poor needed "personal service" rather than money to "lift" them out of a need for charity (Ibid., p. 107).

The Public Sector's Responsibility for Initiating DE of Dependent/Neglected Youth

The record indicates that DE of dependent/neglected institutions could have progressed much faster than actually occurred prior to 1933. The 1909 White House conference preference for "home life" merely expressed a consensus that had begun to develop in the last quarter of the nineteenth century—when "free" and "boarding out" placement of children gained wide acceptance as an alternative to institutionalization. Public assistance to widowed and deserted mothers, and caring for children in their own homes, was also widely accepted as an institution alternative. But ideology alone could not promote DE. As the battle over mothers' aid revealed, other values and interests were also at stake. Private welfare leaders firmly asserted that traditional principles about outdoor relief and private charity would be accorded priority when confronted by newer value preferences for "home life" and public in-home support for "parents of worthy character." Preventing unnecessary commitments, and maintaining family cohesion could only be justified if they occurred under private auspices, with charitable funds and services. If this outcome was not politically acceptable (and it was not), then public funds should be spent as if they were being dispersed by a private charity organization society.

While the private welfare sector's opposition to mothers' aid directly inhibited the use of this alternative to an institutional commitment, the other alternative—

boarding out—could have been employed to accomplish DE objectives. The State of Massachusetts used boarding out between 1880 and 1910, to reduce institutional use. Comparing Massachusetts with New York offers insights into why subsidized foster care, by itself, did not automatically result in DE.

As noted earlier, Massachusetts began experimenting with boarding out in 1868. By 1882 legislation was passed to use this method to reduce both commitments and the length of stay of those placed in the State Primary School. To prevent any abuses of this use of public funds, the work "proceeded slowly and cautiously" (Bremner et al. 1971, vol. 2, p. 322). Boarding out costs were designed to be no higher than two dollars per week—the approximate cost of a week of institutional living. However, when the cost of an initial "outfit of clothing" was added to maintenance and quarterly allowances for new clothing, "the cost to the state for the first year is *slightly above*, but for two or more years it is somewhat below, the $2 per week presented by statute" (Ibid., p. 323; italics added). A boarding home policy required investing state funds in order to realize later benefits. By 1908, a contemporary review of the Massachusetts approach to the problem of dependency and neglect disclosed the following:

> In Massachusetts, the tendency has been to substitute the placing out method for the care of children in institutions. The building of new orphan asylums has practically ceased, and no less than 13 orphan asylums and children's homes have been closed within the last few years, family care being substituted. Among the institutions closed were: the Massachusetts State School at Monson; the two homes of the Boston Children's Aid Society; the home of the Boston Children's Friend Society; the home of the Boston Children's Mission; the Boston Female Asylum.
>
> The Boston child-helping societies have substituted home care for institutional care, even in cases where the child is only to be under care for a day or two. [Ibid., p. 329]

The unique achievement of Massachusetts is also supported by 1923 census data. At a time when the nation reported that about 64 percent of all children under dependent care were in institutions, Massachusetts had only 28 percent. With less than 4 percent of the nation's population, Massachusetts paid for over 24 percent of the nation's total number of children classified as "boarding family homes" (U.S. Bureau of the Census, 1923, pp. 18, 20). In 1908, this alternative to institutionalization was primarily funded as follows: state treasury—$346,000; City of Boston—$75,000; private organizations—$50,000 (Bremner et al. 1971, vol. 2, p. 329).

This estimated allocation of funding for the state's new policy toward dependent children reveals that the public sector played the leading role in policy implementation. The policy was also formulated by state leaders. Formal state leadership began in 1863, when the state set up the first State Board of Charities to supervise the "general and systematic improvements in our methods of public charities" (Abbot 1937, p. 104). Dr. Samuel Gridley Howe, the board's first chairman, enunciated the "general principles of public charity" in the Second Annual Report of the Massachusetts State Board of Charities. According to

Howe, the first principle to "bear in mind" was that if, by investing one dollar, we prevent an evil the correction of which would cost ten cents a year, we save four percent" (Ibid., p. 104). This investment should be based on separating and diffusing the dependent classes, and enlisting "the greatest number of individuals and of families, in the care and treatment of the dependent." Institutions were to be used as a "last resort," and, if used, "we should not retain the inmates any longer than is manifestly for their good, irrespective of their usefulness in the institution" (Ibid.).

By backing up these principles with significant funds, Massachusetts investments yielded an institutional rate of less than half the national rate in 1933: 206 per 100,000 youth under 14, compared to 429 (based on sources in table 7–1). The achievements of Massachusetts indicate that clear public goals, consistent public leadership, and an entrepreneurial willingness to invest state funds for the future could yield a much lower institutional rate. Although other states belatedly began to fund more foster home placements, this evidently took place without leadership committed to making certain that a "last resort" policy was being followed. New York, for example, had virtually the same number of youth in dependent institutions in 1923 as in 1933, despite the fact that the number of youth boarded out increased from 3,905 to 19,026—a gain of almost 400 percent (U.S. Bureau of the Census, 1923). In contrast to Massachusetts, the new method of boarding out was grafted onto a stable institutional system that although nominally private and sectarian was actually heavily subsidized by public funds (Warner 1908, pp. 404–13). Although the public paid more than half of the institutional bills, the sectarian private agencies controlled admission and discharge policies. In effect, the private sectarian institutions dominated public policies concerning rates of institutionalization.

Federal Outdoor Relief and the Acceleration of DE

The accelerated removal of children from dependent/neglected institutions finally occurred in 1935, after the nation accepted and funded a federal share in the provision of outdoor relief to needy children and their families. Aid to Families with Dependent Children (AFDC) legislation did not define economic need, nor did it set forth a minimum standard of family payments. These key issues were left to the states. However, the legislation (Title 4 of the Social Security Act) specifically authorized the payment of a federal percentage of AFDC costs (up to a specified level of allowance) *only* if needy children were living in a home with parents or relatives.

AFDC clearly was not designed as a DE program; rather it was set forth to help states deal with the massive problems associated with economic deprivation. By 1940 about 372,000 families were recipients of federal-state AFDC funds—compared to a 1931 estimate of 94,000 families receiving mothers' aid

(*Social Security Bulletin*, August 1980, p. 40; Bremner et al. 1971, vol. 2, p. 393). By 1950 the number reached 651,000 families.

State and county administrators were, of course, aware that public subsidies to dependent institutions and foster homes were not eligible for federal reimbursement, but that DE children, living at home or with relatives, could qualify as AFDC eligibles. From 1935 to 1961 state and county administration of public child welfare functioned under an unambiguous, federal "home care" policy. During this period DE occurred without federal government subsidies for alternative forms of institutional care and supervision. Subsequent amendments, in 1962 and 1967—permitting, for the first time, payments to private foster care homes *or* institutions—did not check the long-term decline of the traditional institutions; however, subsidized alternative institutionalization began to offset some of the decline.

The trend of the number of youth residing in dependent/neglected institutions is as follows: *1933*—140,350; *1950*—96,300; *1960*—73,300; *1970*—47,600; *1973*—37,800 (Adapted from U.S. Bureau of the Census Reports: 1933, 1950, 1960, 1970; and National Center for Health Statistics, Series 14, no. 16, 1976).

This substantial long-term decline occurred during a significant increase in the national youth population. Therefore, the institutional decline, as measured by rates per 100,000 population under 18, is even more pronounced than revealed by only the raw numbers. The resident rates are as follows: *1933*—340; *1950*—200; *1960*—114; *1970*—68; *1973*—55 (Based on Ibid.; U.S. Department of Health, Education, and Welfare, 1966, for 1933 and 1950 rates; and *Social Security Bulletin*, August 1980, p. 52, for 1960, 1970, and 1973 population figures).

The approaching demise of this institutional type is not only linked to the belated acceptance of a federal responsibility to subsidize home care for dependent children. It is also associated with the belief that "normal children" do not require the expensive care and supervision associated with traditional institutional programs. As a corollary, there is a belief that normal, traditional institutions for the dependent/neglected are no longer necessary. By the year 2000 it is quite likely that traditional dependent/neglected institutions will go the way of the almshouse—a historical relic of outdated public relief policies.

The Changing Population, and Uses of Child Welfare Institutions

In 1933 about 25 percent of youth in institutions for the dependent/neglected were 14 years and older; in 1950 the proportion was similar. But in the 1960 census that figure jumped to 32 percent, and by 1970, to 46 percent. If current child welfare placements in foster homes are compared to past institutional placements, the differences in age distribution are quite striking. A 1974 analysis of over 29,000 New York City foster children in placements provides information

TABLE 7–2

Percent Distribution of New York City Children in Placement, by Type and Age

Placement Types			Age		
Foster Homes	*Under 3*	*3–6*	*6–12*	*12+*	*Total*
Temporary foster home	42.2	20.0	26.7	11.1	(1,071)
Foster home/prospective adoption	9.3	22.3	51.3	17.1	(4,593)
Foster home/boarding home	8.8	17.3	35.5	38.4	(13,470)
Home, suspended payment	6.7	10.0	38.3	45.0	(1,428)
Group Care/Institutional Facilities					
Temp. group care	0	0	31.2	68.8	(381)
Group home	0	0	16.7	83.3	(1,571)
Group residence	0	0	4.8	95.2	(500)
Gen. institution	0	2.4	27.7	69.9	(3,951)
Residential treatment center Type A	0	2.7	35.1	62.2	(881)
Residential treatment center Type B	0	0	45.4	54.6	(262)
Institution for retarded	0	0	9.2	90.8	(262)
Secure detention/other	0	0	0	100.0	(452)
Awaiting placement	5.3	10.5	31.6	52.6	(904)

SOURCE: Bernstein, Snider, and Meezan, 1975, p. 203.

about age distributions for various types of foster homes, temporary group quarters, and traditional and nontraditional institutions.

The data reveal that unlike 1933, when 12.5 percent of the residents of institutions for the dependent/neglected were under 6 years of age, few of the group care/institution facilities house this age group. Child welfare institutional facilities, still under a variety of private secular and church auspices, are apparently now reserved for older children. Of particular interest is the "general institution"—the traditional institution *without* a specialized function (according to the authors of table 7–2). The authors define this type of facility, housing nearly a majority of group care/institutional youth (3,951 out of 8,560—or 46 percent) as follows: "A congregate care facility for more than 25; children cared for in such facilities may be from all categories, i.e., abused, neglected, dependent, in need of supervision, and emotionally disturbed" (Ibid., p. 253).

The description appears to fit the traditional dependent/neglected category. This type of institution contributed to the 140,000 institutional youth figure of 1933. Later, referring to the "general institution," the authors state that these "institutions for dependent and neglected children are not an appropriate resource since too much is provided for a *normal child* and too little is provided for the youngster needing intensive on-site *professional treatment*" (Ibid., p. 107; italics added). New York City no longer needs a general institution for normal children. According to the study, these youngsters should be redistributed to other "placement resources" on the list (including a possible return to home). Some general institutions have begun to add more treatment services and this should be encouraged. The study recommends that facilities that provide special services should "transform their facilities to residential treatment centers for the moderately or seriously disturbed children" (Ibid., p. 38).

The most-needed facility type is the child welfare version of the residential treatment center (RTC):

> We need *many more* residential treatment centers. We need them now and we are going to need them five and ten years from now. We need them to serve a group of disturbed, vulnerable children, *often truants or delinquents*, who, if they do not obtain the necessary residential treatment service, are likely to turn into miserable, unhappy adults prone to crime and other continuing serious emotional and behavioral problems." [Ibid., p. 38; italics added]

Experienced New York social work professionals, not unlike the child welfare workers in other states, perceive the majority of youngsters needing group care/institutional residence as those youth with differential degrees of "emotional and behavioral problems." Not unexpectedly, youth appear to exhibit these problems as they enter adolescence—the same age when youthful deviance and delinquency also increase. According to other data, it is clear that New York City youth deemed eligible for residential type of placement are those youth who presented a child problem—rather than a parent problem—at time of placement. In addition, these older youth present more current behavioral problems than younger foster home type children. Table 7–3 presents the data.

The New York City child welfare institutions appear to serve a population quite different from that residing in foster homes. The most temporary categories—"temporary foster home" and "temporary group"—are awaiting specific placement decisions. The projected foster home arrivals are perceived as candidates for a substitute family home because of their parental problems (87 percent); they also have a minority with 2+ problems, despite these parental problems. By contrast the temporary group care population has only half as many (47 percent) with parental problems as a reason for placement. Regardless of reason, 75 percent are classified as having 2+ behavioral problems.

In 1974, in New York City, unless youngsters were older and exhibited demonstrable behavioral problems, it was unlikely that they would become residents of a group care/residential type placement. In general, the old and new institutions are reserved for troublesome youth in need of social control—or in child welfare terms, varying degrees of a "structured style of living" (Ibid., p. 106). These youth, besides being in trouble, are also labeled by child welfare leaders as "emotionally disturbed."

TABLE 7–3

New York City Children in Foster Care: Type of Residence, Primary Reason
for Current Placement, and Number of Problems (in percent)

	Primary Reason for Placement			Current Behavioral Problems
Family Type	Parent Problem	Child Problem	AO	2+ Problems
Temporary foster home	(1,071) 87%	02%	11%	22%
Foster home	(13,470) 90	03	07	34
Foster home/prospective adoption	(4,593) 93	02	05	29
Home, suspended payment[a]	(1,428) 62	23	15	33
Residential Type				
Temporary group care	(381) 44	56	0	75
Group living	(2,071) 71	18	10	51
General institution	(3,951) 66	23	11	56
Residential treatment Type A	(881) 19	78	13	90
Residential treatment Type B	(262) 09	91	0	90
Institution for retarded[b]	(262) 18	82	0	91
Secure Detention/other	(452) 32	68	0	79
Residence Unclear				
Awaiting placement	(904) 50	50	0	63
Total	(29,726) 79%	14%	7%	42%

SOURCE: Bernstein, Snider, and Meezan 1975, pp. 180–89.
[a]Children sent home from placement because they are "AWOL" or "difficult or unmanageable" (p. 186).
[b]Children with IQs "from 30 to 80 whose retardation is generally accompanied by some degree of emotional disturbance" (p. 189).

Assessing Recent Child Welfare Institutional Trends

From 1933 until 1966, the federal agency primarily responsible for reporting child welfare data was the U.S. Children's Bureau. Until 1958, institutional placements only referred to facilities for dependent/neglected youth. In that year, the institutional category was broadened to include "child welfare institutions for neglected, dependent, and emotionally disturbed children" (U.S. Children's Bureau, 1966). Inasmuch as data were never reported by separate institutional types, it is difficult to chart the growth of this new type over a long period. The most recent reliable data about nonmedical facilities for emotionally disturbed persons and dependent/neglected facilities are released by the National Center for Health Statistics (NCHS).

Table 7–4 is a three-part presentation of the most recent available data by: (A) residence on a census date; (B) admissions during a year; and (C) custody/care/treatment episodes. The latter category refers to a one-day residence count *plus* admissions during a year, thereby producing a sum of all institutional episodes for the entire year; its meaning is similar to the NIMH "inpatient care episode" discussed in Chapter 5.

Table 7–4 indicates that within a three-year period, a sizable shift occurred between the distributions of youth residing in institutions for the dependent/neglected in 1970–71 compared to 1973 (61 percent vs. 51 percent). This shift is also true for admissions. Part C takes into account both basic institutional facts: how many are resident on an average *day*, and how many are admitted during a *year*. The sum of the two distinct institutional indicators provides insight into how many youth might utilize (or be forced to live in) such a facility during a one-year period. Because we cannot omit duplications of individuals within *and* between institutional types, the data do not refer to individuals, but rather to custody/care/treatment (CCT) episodes. This indicator suggests that some time between 1970–71 and 1973, the balance shifted between the traditional (i.e., dependent/neglected) and the modern alternative (i.e., emotionally disturbed), so that the child welfare field was no longer dominated by "general institutions" on a national scale.

From all that we have learned from other lines of evidence, we can infer that this shift is also accompanied by a shift in the age of residents and admissions, and in the presenting problems of youth; child-centered, rather than family-centered, problems and behaviors probably constitute the salient admissions characteristics of both types of facilities.

One other major shift has occurred: length of stay in an institution. In 1933 about 50 percent of the residents of institutions for the dependent/neglected lived there for three years or more, and only 21 percent lived there for under one year (U.S. Bureau of the Census, 1933, p. 36). By contrast, facilities for the emotionally disturbed tend to experience a turnover of the entire institutional population in a little less than a year (in that admissions/residence ratios are 1.28 instead of 1.0, as noted in table 7 4). Current traditional institutions turn over their population in about a year. By using length of stay to estimate the admissions/residence ratio of 1933 facilities at no more than .33, it is possible to compare the CCT episodes for the two time periods: in 1933 there were 186,668 episodes at a rate of 441 per 100,000 youth; in 1973 there were 155,208 episodes at a rate of 228 (sources include: U.S. Bureau of the Census, 1933, p. 36, table 8–3; U.S. Department of Health, Education, and Welfare, 1966, Social Security Bulletin, August, 1980; and NCHS, Series 14, nos. 4 and 16, 1973 and 1976).

Because of the difference in length of stay, the 1973 child welfare institutions can handle more youth in a year; therefore, the reduction in total CCT episodes is only about 17 percent. However, because the youth population has increased by a significant amount since 1933, the overall use of child welfare institutions, per 100,000 youth under 18, has decreased by about 48 percent.

TABLE 7–4

Recent Trends of Youth Living in Child Welfare Institutions: 1970, 1971, and 1973
(in percentages)

A. Resident Trends[a]

Child Welfare Type	1970/1971	%	1973	%
Dependent/Neglected	(43,867)	61	(36,876)	51
Emotionally Disturbed	(28,481)	39	(34,759)	49
N =	(72,348)		(71,635)	

B. Admissions Trends[b]

	1970/1971	%	1973	%
Dependent/Neglected	(46,499)	56	(39,089)	47
Emotionally Disturbed	(31,456)	44	(44,492)	53
N =	(82,955)		(83,581)	

C. Custody/Care/Treatment Episodes[c]

	1970/1971 (est.)	%	1973	%
Dependent/Neglected	(90,366)	58	(75,965)	49
Emotionally Disturbed	(64,937)	42	(79,243)	51
N =	(155,303)		(155,208)	

SOURCES: [a]*Dependent/Neglected* data for 1970–71 are from U.S. Bureau of the Census, 1973, p. 11; *Dependent/Neglected* data for 1973 are from NCHS, Series 14, no. 16, May 1976. *Emotionally Disturbed* data for 1970–71 and 1973 are from NCHS, Series 14, nos. 4 and 16, 1973 and 1976.

[b] Admissions data for juveniles are based on information about admissions and residents provided by NCHS to the author; 1973 number of admissions to residence ratios are computed to be 1.06:1 for dependent/neglected and 1.28:1 for emotionally disturbed. All 1971 estimates are based on these rates being multiplied by residence figures in Part A.

[c] Custody/care/treatment episodes refers to residence count plus admissions during year, thereby producing a sum of all "episodes" for that type for the year. Its meaning is similar to the NIMH "inpatient-care episode."

8 Juvenile Corrections and Mental Health: A New Youth-in-Trouble Institutional System

The systems of juvenile corrections and mental health did not exhibit institutional use patterns comparable to the long-term reductions of the facilities for dependent/neglected youth. Although traditional juvenile correctional facilities have experienced reductions in populations, these demographic trends have been offset by the expanded use of other institutional types. The mental health system has increased youth utilization rates in all types of facilities. These trends and the intersystem overlaps of all three juvenile systems are the focus of this chapter.

Assessing Recent Juvenile Correctional Trends

Unlike the field of child welfare, there was no sustained decrease in the use of traditional juvenile correctional facilities after 1933. Instead, census data revealed increases in the number of youth residing in detention and long-term facilities. Although from 1960 on, "community treatment" was discussed as an alternative to the training school, the 1970 census did not support a diminished reliance on traditional institutions (U.S. President's Commission, 1967; Lerman 1975). Finally in 1974, a survey conducted by the U.S. Bureau of the Census for the Law Enforcement Assistance Administration (LEAA), disclosed a marked decrease in the use of public correctional facilities. However, a companion survey of private correctional facilities (conducted systematically for the first time) produced a surprising result: the private sector's population easily offset the DE of the traditional system. The private sector, in turn, is linked to the child welfare system and performs multiple functions for all types of youth, regardless of the referral source.

Table 8–1 provides information basic to an understanding of recent trends in the juvenile correctional system (as defined by the U.S. Bureau of the Census and LEAA).

Data in Part A disclose that the total number of youth resident in detention and long-term facilities increased from close to 41,000 in 1950 to nearly 77,000 in 1970. Virtually all of the increase occurred in the public sector, as the proportion of youth living under private auspices declined from 20 to 11 percent. The 1974 census captured trends moving in an opposite direction: a marked decrease in the public sector and a sharp rise in the use of private facilities. The 1977 census, released as an advance report, indicates that the relative proportion of youth residing in a privately operated facility has stabilized at about 40 percent. If deten-

TABLE 8–1

Residents of Public and Private Juvenile Correctional Facilities:
1950, 1970, 1974, and 1977

A. *By Numbers and Percentage Distribution* (including detention)[a]

	1950		1970		1974		1977	
Auspice	Number	%	Number	%	Number	%	Number	%
Public	32,936	80	67,963	89	44,922	59	44,096	60
Private	7,934	20	8,766	11	31,749	41	29,400	40
Total	40,880		76,729		76,671		73,496	

B. *Resident Rates per 100,000 Youth under 18*[b]

	1950	1970	1974	1977
Public	70	98	65	69
Private	17	12	46	46
Total	87	110	111	115

SOURCES: [a]Correctional data are based on: U.S. Bureau of the Census, *Institutional Population, 1950*, vol. 4, pt. 2, chap. C, and *Persons in Institutions and Other Group Quarters, 1970*, vol. 4E, Pc(2); and Law Enforcement Assistance Administration, *Children in Custody, 1974* (SD-JD-5A). [b]Population data were obtained from U.S. Bureau of the Census, *Historical Statistics of the United States, Colonial Times to 1957*, and *Social Security Bulletin*, March 1980, p. 65.

tion/shelter facilities were to be excluded, then the proportion of 1974 youth residing in private, long-term facilities would rise to about 48 percent, as compared to a 1950 figure of 21 percent. Using estimates of admissions data, the private sector probably accounted for about 54 percent of all long-term admissions (see table 8–4 for sources and method of estimation).

If attention is focused only on the public sector, then data in Part B reveal that the 1977 rate per 100,000 youth was approximately equal to the 1950 rate (70 vs. 69). The private rate, of course, is sharply divergent. As a matter of fact, the increase in the total rate of institutionalization is entirely due to the increase in the private sector (from 17 to 46). Using the resident rates as an indicator, controlling for population reveals that there has been no DE of the public sector since 1950, only a diminution from the high of 1970. Instead, there has been an increase in total institutional rates: from 87 to 115, or about 32 percent.

The Emergence and "Discovery" of the Private Correctional Sector

Prior to 1974, the inventory of child welfare and correctional institutions was primarily based on the list of institutions maintained by the U.S. Children's Bu-

TABLE 8–2

Number of Juvenile Detention and Correctional Facilities, Classified by Auspice:
1969, 1971, and 1974

Auspice	(NCHS)[a] 1969	(NCHS)[b] 1971	LEAA[c] 1974
Government	620	659	829
Nonprofit	113	85	1,337
Proprietary	07	2	NA
Total	740	746	2,166

SOURCES: [a]National Center for Health Statistics, Series 14, no. 6, 1972, p. 43.
[b]Ibid., no. 12, 1974, p. 49.
[c]U.S. Law Enforcement Assistance Administration, *Children in Custody*, 1974, pp. 12, 62.

reau. This list was used both by the Census Bureau and the National Center for Health Statistics (NCHS). Using NCHS data, we can determine the pre-1974 number of surveyed facilities, classified by auspice. The NCHS surveys of 1969 and 1971, reported in Table 8–2, were conducted by the U.S. Bureau of the Census. The bureau also conducted the LEAA survey of 1974. The number of private facilities "discovered" indicates that a totally new list had been compiled and used as the basis of surveys of private correctional facilities.

It is most likely that the old listing had just not been kept up to date, for the sudden emergence of 1,337 nonprofit facilities is probably too great an increase for a three-year period. The old list indicated a downward trend from 1969 to 1971 (113 to 85), when in all likelihood, the number of nonprofit facilities was increasing. Besides the problem of "Master Facility Inventory" lists, there is also the likelihood that definitions of a private facility changed in 1974. According to the 1974 joint LEAA–Census Bureau definition: "For a private facility to be included, at least *10 percent of its population* had to have been adjudicated delinquent, declared in need of supervision, *voluntarily committed*, and/or pending disposition by court" (LEAA, *Children in Custody*, 1974, p. 7; italics added).

In an effort to limit this broad definition, the following were explicitly excluded: "Nonresidential facilities, facilities exclusively for drug abusers or for dependent and neglected children, foster homes" (Ibid.). The 1975 census attempted to specify the exclusions even further: "Excluded were facilities in which *more than 90 percent* of the residents were dependent and neglected or other nonoffenders" (LEAA, *Children in Custody*, 1975, p. 8; italics added). In addition, facilities exclusively for alcoholics, unwed mothers, the emotionally disturbed, or the mentally retarded were not to be included in the census (Ibid.).

On the basis of the available evidence, it appears that the virtual explosion of private correctional facilities in 1974 is partially a census artifact. An unknown—but sizable—proportion of the 1,337 facilities were probably operating in the late 1960s, and in all likelihood could have qualified as meeting the 1974 definition. From a historical perspective, these additional private facilities constitute nontraditional additions to the total juvenile correctional system.

Multiple Uses of Private Correctional Facilities

Private facilities, unlike public institutions, can take referrals for placement from a variety of sources, both public and private. The 1974 LEAA surveys found that 90 percent of the 1,337 private facilities obtained admissions referrals from the juvenile court. In addition, 82 percent reported referrals from welfare departments, and 50 percent from parents (LEAA, *Children in Custody*, 1974, p. 62). These large numbers of referrals from welfare departments indicate that these private facilities are closely linked to the child welfare system (as well as to the correctional system via the juvenile court referrals). Many youths are also voluntarily referred by parents or guardians, as well as by welfare agencies, without going through a formal commitment procedure. The survey data indicate that private facilities are much more likely than the public sector to house youth classified as "voluntary commitment" (see table 8–3).

Table 8–3 reveals that public facilities possess a much less diverse mixture of youth than does the private sector. Public institutional residents, in both 1974 and 1977, tended to be either "adjudicated delinquents" or in custody "pending disposition/transfer" (86–87 percent). By contrast only about 33 percent of private youth fit these classifications. The majority of private correctional residents are *not* official delinquents. They are voluntary commitments from social agencies

TABLE 8–3

Types of Youth Living in Public and Private Juvenile Correctional Facilities:
1974 and 1977 (in percentages)

	1974		1977
Types of Youth	*Private*	*Public*	*Public Only*
Adjudicated delinquent	31	70	86
Status offender	16	10	11
Pending disposition/transfer	2	17	Not used
Voluntary commitment	24	2	1
Dependent/neglected	22	1	2
Emotionally disturbed, mentally retarded, other	5	0	1
N =	(31,749)	(44,922)	(44,096)

Sources: U.S. Law Enforcement Assistance Administration, *Children in Custody, 1974*, pp. 18–19; and *Children in Custody, 1977*, p. 3.

or parents (24 percent), dependent/neglected youth (22 percent), status offenders (16 percent), or an assortment of other youth in trouble (5 percent)—a total of 65 percent.

The mixture of population types in private facilities would, in fact, be illegal if it occurred in public facilities in many states. For example, in 1974 a total of twenty-five states had created a special legal category for juvenile status offenders. Of these, eighteen placed restrictions on mixing status offenders and delinquents in long-term public facilities, and four required separate detention facilities. Even more stringent restrictions were placed on institutionalizing dependent/neglected youth with delinquents in public facilities (Levin and Sarri 1974, p. 12).

The Correctional Overlap with the Child Welfare System

LEAA and the U.S. Bureau of the Census have defined "private facilities" as "correctional" if at least 10 percent of the residents are adjudicated as delinquent or status offenders, are voluntarily committed, or are awaiting a court disposition. To avoid duplicating counts of youth, I have accepted this definition, and thus consider only those facilities for the dependent/neglected and emotionally disturbed as part of the child welfare system. But many state and/or county child welfare agencies do not bother to keep child welfare and correctional statistics separate. In practice, therefore, they define many of the 1,337 juvenile correctional facilities as "child welfare" placement resources.

Massachusetts offers an excellent example of the correctional overlap with the child welfare system. Considered one of the leading deinstitutionalized states because of the diminished reliance on public facilities, Massachusetts recently legislated that all children in need of supervision (CHINS) were to become the formal responsibility of the State Department of Public Welfare (DPW), instead of the state correctional agency, the Department of Youth Service (DYS). A study of actual placement practices in 1975–76 revealed that almost all of the new CHINS referrals were perceived as "emotionally disturbed," and that these referrals—together with other "emotionally disturbed" youth—were often placed in the same private facilities as those chosen by the state correctional agency. The report called the system "The Children's Puzzle":

> Each agency places children differently. They apply different selection criteria. Yet the children wind up in *the same facilities*. . . .
>
> DPW purchases group care for approximately 1,800 youngsters and defines them in three major categories: 1) mentally retarded (320); CHINS (129); and emotionally disturbed (1,091). . . .
>
> In 1975–76, there were 948 referrals to the group care unit. Of that number, 557 were emotionally disturbed and *348 were CHINS (341 of them were also labeled emotionally disturbed)*. . . .

[There is] harm caused by placing status offenders in the same facilities as juvenile offenders. In 1975–76, DYS spent 7 million dollars and DPW spent 10 million dollars *purchasing services from the same providers of care.*" [University of Massachusetts Institute for Governmental Services, February 1977, pp. 20–22, 28; italics added]

This overlap, whereby the two systems use the *same facilities*, is also occurring in other states. A site visit to Minneapolis, Minnesota, in 1977 disclosed that one private agency used its shelter facility to house juvenile court, child welfare, private agency, and family referrals. Its long-term facility housed a similar mix. The agency director perceived his agency as a family and child welfare organization, not a correctional agency, even though many youngsters were legally classified as juvenile delinquent. He perceived the agency's major service to be "residential treatment," applicable to all youth fulfilling the agency's intake criteria. Residential care, treatment, and supervision services were purchased from this private agency by both the county probation and welfare departments.

Another example of overlap is contained in a recent General Accounting Office report, *Children in Foster Care Institutions* (February 1977). The GAO complained to Congress that in eighteen facilities visited in four states—California, New York, Georgia, and New Jersey—"many juvenile delinquents are placed at foster care institutions rather than juvenile detention facilities, and their care is partially financed by the AFDC program" (Ibid., p. 4). According to Title 4 of the Social Security Act, as amended in 1962, only private, nonprofit organizations could qualify for federal reimbursement as foster "child care institutions" (sec. 408). GAO accountants found that the institutionalization of delinquents in child welfare institutions was technically compatible with the new AFDC–foster care program. They might have been surprised to learn that nonwelfare agencies of the government (LEAA and the Bureau of the Census) were probably classifying many of the eighteen institutions as "private juvenile correctional facilities."

One last example of the overlap between the correctional and child welfare systems is perhaps the most interesting: the setting of child care residence financial rates by a probation officers' organization. By law every California county welfare agency is supposed to pay the same board rate when it places a child in an institution. However, county probation departments and private child-caring agencies are not included in this requirement; they can negotiate higher and lower rates than those paid by welfare agencies—for the *same facilities*. In the San Francisco Bay Area, seventeen counties have formed a Bay Area Placement Committee (BAPC) to reduce competition over rates and placement resources. The BAPC negotiates jointly with *all* institutions used by the two systems. Technically, the BAPC is "an arm of the Association of Child Probation Officers," an unusual organization to be setting rates for child welfare facilities (Pers 1974, p. 504).

Juvenile Admissions to Correctional Facilities:
A Fifty-Year Perspective

Until now the analysis of changes in the correctional system has referred primarily to one-day residence counts. Following this approach the trend data revealed a continued reliance on institutions, controlling for changes in the youth population (see table 8–1). Adding admissions figures to the analysis discloses that one-day counts underestimate the extent to which institutional use has increased. As a matter of fact it is estimated that over a fifty-year period, youthful admissions to *all* types of correctional facilities have increased over ten times, while one-day resident counts increased about two and a half times, and the youth population (under 18 years of age) less than doubled. The evidence supporting this conclusion is presented in Table 8–4, where resident and admissions data are presented for 1923 and 1974.

In 1923 the U.S. Bureau of the Census attempted to collect data about children received and resident in all correctional institutions. Table 8–4 lists all the correctional types of organizations included in the census survey. Of the six types, the local jail and workhouse facilities were the major source of underreporting, in that only committed persons were counted in the census. The exclusion of jailed youth awaiting trial or a dispositional decision is an important omission from the table, but there is no basis for estimating the number of youth involved on a census day or during the year. The other correctional types appear, in the main, to be fully reported.

In 1923 institutions varied widely according to the frequency with which they were used. Detention homes, for example, reported fewer than 1,500 residents, but received over 33,000 admissions during the year—a ratio of more than 22 admissions to every youth counted on a census day (see table 8–4, ratios of admissions/residence column). By contrast, special public and private institutions for delinquents had a much lower rate of turnover—about .62 in 1923. In effect, this meant that youth stayed about 19.4 months in a long-term juvenile correctional facility in 1923, as compared to a stay of about 16 days in a detention home (i.e., 12 months divided by .62, and 365 days divided by 22.20). It is interesting to note that youth in state prisons stayed under 11 months, much shorter than the stays of reformatory youth.

Using admissions as well as resident data, one can calculate the number of custody/care/treatment (CCT) episodes for each 1923 correctional type. CCT episodes are, of course, not equivalent to number of persons, but this indicator of institutional use does provide an approximation of the total number of youth who might be subject to an institutional stay during a census year. Controlling for population yields a CCT rate of 244 per 100,000 youth under 18 years of age— as compared to a resident rate of 92 and an admissions rate of 152.

The data for 1974 provide strong evidence that each correctional type comparable with one in 1923 has increased the ratios of admissions per residence.

TABLE 8–4

Comparison of Resident and Admissions Data of All Correctional Facilities for
Juveniles under 18 Years of Age: 1923 and 1974

1923 Correctional Types	Number of Residents[a]	Number of Admissions[b]	Ratios of Admissions to Residents	Total Custody/ Care/Treatment Episodes
1. Jails/workhouses	580	4,890	8.43	5,470
2. Detention homes	1,489	33,056	22.20	34,545
3. Prisons and reformatories	1,650	1,890	1.15	3,540
4. Private institutions for delinquents	715	} 18,640	.62	48,740
5. Special institutions for delinquents	29,385			
6. Institutions for women and girls	2,233	1,384	.62	3,617
N =	36,052	59,860	1.66	95,912
Rate/100,000 under 18 years.[c]	92	152	———	244

1974 Correctional Types	Number of Residents[d]	Number of Admissions[e]	Ratios of Admissions to Residents	Total Custody/ Care/Treatment Episodes
1. Jails/workhouses (1970)[f]	7,800	258,818	33.18	266,618
2. Detention Centers	11,175	469,462	42.01	480,637
3. Shelters	812	21,851	26.91	22,663
4. Diagnostic/reception centers	1,376	17,709	12.87	19,085
5. Prisons/reformatories (1973)	1,970	2,266	1.15	4,236
6. Training schools	29,475	58,655	1.99	88,130
7. Ranches/forestry camps/ farms/school	22,187	60,571	2.73	82,758
8. Group homes/ halfway houses	11,646	30,745	2.64	42,391
N =	86,441	920,077	10.64	1,006,518
Rate/100,000 under 18 years[g]	129	1,369	———	1,497

SOURCES: [a]*1923 Residence Data* are from U.S. Bureau of the Census, *Children under Institutional Care, 1923*, Tables 1 and 79; Jails/workhouses figures refer only to sentenced youth and do not include those awaiting trial.

[b]*1923 Admissions Data* are from Ibid., Tables 42 and 79; data for Table 42 were for six months and multiplied by 2, whereas data for Table 79 were for three months and multiplied by 4. From the text it appeared that "institutions for delinquents" excluded "institutions for delinquent women and girls," and the latter's admissions were estimated by using the admission/resident ratio for the comparable facilities.

This means that lengths of stay are shorter for all facility types where data are available for both time periods. Instead of staying in a special institution for an average of 19.4 months, 1974 youths lived in a training school for about 6 months; instead of being held in detention for 16 days, 1974 youths lived in detention for under 9 days.

A comparison of the two census years reveals a modest increase in the total resident rate per 100,000 youth (from 92 to 129), but an explosive increase in the admissions rate (from 152 to 1,369). Even if jails and workhouses were omitted from the calculations, the striking disparity in rates would remain (140 to 984). It is quite apparent that many more 1974 youth experienced an institutional stay than did 1923 youth. It is also apparent that the dominant correctional type is the short-term facility, for over 75 percent of all 1974 CCT episodes occurred in detention centers, jails, shelters, or diagnostic centers.

Except for shelters, short-term facilities are primarily under public auspices. The traditional training school is also primarily a public facility. The private sector is represented by the less traditional facility type. About 70 percent of all ranch/forestry admissions are private, as are 85 percent of the group home admissions (see sources, table 8–4). This means that the private sector is beginning to dominate the nontraditional, long-term sector, leaving the public sector to operate the short-term lockups and the long-term traditional training school. This conclusion is based on the fact that "short-term" now means an average stay of about 9 days, and "long-term" means about 6 months in a training school and 4–5 months in a group home.

The Mental Health System and Youth in Trouble

Since the end of World War II there has been a growing utilization by youth of inpatient psychiatric facilities. Between 1950 and 1970 the resident psychiatric

c *1923 Population Data* on which rates are based were estimated by combining the population of ages 10–17, from Ibid., Table 39, and the 1920 under-10 population from U.S. Bureau of the Census, *Historical Statistics of the United States, Colonial Times to 1957*, Series A71–85.

d *1974 Residence Data* are from LEAA, *Children in Custody, 1974*, except for jails/workhouses data and prisons/reformatories; latest jail data are from LEAA, *National Jail Census, 1970*; latest prison data are from LEAA, *National Prisoner Statistics, 1973*.

e *1974 Admissions Data* were obtained by using admissions/residence ratios computed for latest data available in LEAA, *Children in Custody, 1971*; private institutions were classified by correctional type and included with public institutions; for jail source see no. *f*, below; prison data unavailable, and 1923 ratios are used to estimate probable 1974 admissions.

f *Jail/Workhouse Admissions Data* are based on the combined average length of stay for nuisance offenses (9 days) and lesser violent and property crimes (13 days) for all persons held prior to trial, as adapted from LEAA survey data reported in Hindelang et al., *Sourcebook of Criminal Statistics—1976*, Table 6.12, p. 647.

g *1974 Population Data* can be found in *Social Security Bulletin*, March 1980, p. 65.

institutional rates for youth under 20 more than doubled—from about 22 per 100,000 in 1950, to 28 in 1960, to 46 in 1970 (Kramer 1977, p. 63). This is a remarkable achievement, in that all other age groups exhibit resident rate decreases during this time (see data reported in Chapter 5).

In addition to data on resident rates, there is also information about first admissions from 1946 to 1975 for the traditional institutions: state and county mental hospitals.

Table 8–5 reports on the trends of first admissions, as controlled for the number of persons categorized by specific age groups. The age breakdowns of the data reflect traditional groupings dating back to the 1920s, and therefore cannot provide an accurate image of the juvenile population. However, by focusing on the two youngest age groups, it is possible to gain insights into the trends of the past thirty years. The bottom row, for all ages, indicates that admissions continued to gain until 1969, then decreased in 1972, and are now below the 1946 rate (57 to 69). In contrast, the youngest group is the only age group to have steadily increased in every time period; the rate has more than quintupled, from 3 to 16. The 15–24 and 25–34 age groups are the only other groups to display any gain between 1946 and 1975. These gains, however, appear to have leveled off at a rate lower than the peak year of 1969.

Types of Diagnoses Associated with Current Admissions

Perhaps the most intriguing data are the reasons provided for admissions to the inpatient units of the state/county hospitals and general hospitals. Table 8–6 presents data regarding "primary diagnosis" for all admissions (first and readmissions), classified according to age, for two major MI facilities.

The data in Table 8–6 are presented using the diagnostic types provided by NIMH. These types are grouped under two major headings (not used by NIMH): "classical symptoms" and "general/behavioral" disorders. The former includes the diagnoses traditionally associated with psychiatric hospitalization. Even when the aged comprised a major population group in the state hospital, disorders of senility would have been categorized within one of the classical symptom types. The "general/behavioral" category is much less specific, even vague, encompassing behaviors that are clearly not psychotic or neurotic. Here one is able to find a variety of "acting out" or deviant behaviors or symptoms that are not classical signs of psychiatric disturbance.

The classification is useful in distinguishing the major reasons why juveniles were hospitalized in a psychiatric facility in 1975. Almost three-fourths (74 percent) of all ages were admitted to specialized general hospital units for classical symptoms—but only 42 percent of the juveniles were admitted. Instead, juveniles were hospitalized for imprecise disorders like personality, childhood, transient situational, or "other." Drug disorders are more specific, but this, too, is hardly a classical psychiatric illness.

TABLE 8–5

First Admissions to State/County Mental Hospitals, by Age: 1946–75
(age-specific rates per 100,000 persons)[a]

Age Group	1946	1955	1962	1969	1972	1975
Under 15	03	04	06	11	14	16
15–24	48	62	77	114	95	92
25–34	69	92	105	111	104	92
35–44	86	96	96	134	107	75
45–54	84	94	91	107	83	55
55–64	100	95	82	100	63	53
65+	240	236	164	101	69	37
Total	69	75	11	82	68	57

[a] Rounded to nearest whole number.
SOURCES: Years 1946 and 1955 are from Kramer 1977, p. 81; all other years are from National Institute of Mental Health, *Statistical Note*, no. 145, March 1978, p. 9.

TABLE 8–6

Comparison of Primary Diagnosis of Admissions or Discharges to Psychiatric Inpatient
Units of State/County Hospitals and Nonfederal General Hospitals, by Age: 1975
(in percentages)

Primary Diagnosis	General Hospital Psychiatric Units[a]		State/County Mental Hospitals[b]	
	Under 18	All ages	Under 18	All ages
A. *Classical Symptoms*	42.0%	74.0%	27.0%	53.1%
1. Organic brain	too small	3.7	2.8	5.3
2. Depressive	17.7	37.8	2.7	11.7
3. Schizophrenia	16.4	24.1	17.7	33.7
4. Other psychoses	0.9	2.2	too small	0.9
5. Neuroses	7.0	6.2	3.8	1.5
B. *General/Behavioral*	57.2%	26.0%	71.8%	46.9%
1. Personality disorder	8.0	5.8	10.4	6.8
2. Childhood disorder	10.8	0.9	54.0	4.9
3. Transitional situational disorders	26.7	5.1	NA	NA
4. Other[c]	6.0	3.7	6.2	3.8
5. Alcohol disorders	too small	7.0	too small	27.7
6. Drug disorders	5.7	3.5	1.2	3.7
N =	(42,690)	(515,537)	(25,252)	(385,237)

SOURCES: [a] NIMH, *Statistical Note*, no. 137, August 1977, p. 19.
[b] Ibid., no. 138, p. 11.
[c] For general hospital is undifferentiated; for state/county hospital, "other" is for under-18 mental retardation (5.0%) and undifferentiated (1.2); for state/county all ages, "other" is mental retardation (1.9%) and undifferentiated (1.9).

The disparity between the two age groups also exists at the state hospital level. However, at this longer-term facility there are fewer classical patients of both age groups. Only a little more than 27 percent of juveniles conform to a "sickness" image. At the state level, apparently there are far fewer "affective and depressive" cases (which include many suicidal persons) for both age groups than at the general hospital level. Table 8–6 also reveals that more juveniles with "transient and situational" and "childhood" disorders can be found at the state level; and more adults with drinking problems are admitted to state hospitals.

It appears that the increase of juveniles in the mental health subsystem has been accompanied by a distinct utilization pattern. The state hospitals, in particular, are probably admitting many youth who may be engaging in deviant behaviors, but who are not mentally ill in a classical sense. This indicates that the mental health system has probably broadened its definitional boundaries to include a heterogeneous array of behaviors that evoke official and adult concerns. This type of usage was noted over ten years ago in Nebraska. There a psychiatrist and a social worker teamed up to assess clinical evidence about the post-World War II trend of "psychologizing problems of living in our society, to assign psychological causes to many of the ills of our culture" (Miller and Kenney 1966, p. 38).

Robert Miller and Emmet Kenney undertook a three-year study of admissions of adolescent patients to the inpatient service of a state mental hospital. They concluded that for a clear majority of the adolescents admitted (175 out of 247), "the primary symptom of mental illness—and the major concern of the community—was socially deviant behavior" (Ibid.). Examples of deviant behavior included *"truancy, vandalism, robbery, sexual offenses,* and *other violations* of law and social moral codes" (Ibid.; italics added). The authors concluded their 1966 study as follows:

> Is there a difference between social-moral and medical-psychiatric problems? No statistics anywhere answer this question. In practice, there appears to be no distinction, and perhaps there should be none. Perhaps the psychiatric hospital is becoming more sociological than medical in its therapeutic approach. Nevertheless, the treatment of behavior disorders, particularly those of adolescents remains an elusive problem. After all, how does a hospital treat *delinquency* and *other deviations* from social norms? [Ibid., pp. 52–53; italics added]

Evidently Miller and Kenney would not be surprised at the data reported in Table 8–6. They found that in 1966, 71 percent of youth referrals were sent to a state hospital for "socially deviant behavior"; Table 8–6 reports a figure of 71.8 percent for youth sent to state hospitals in 1975. Their 1966 findings, and their queries, appear to be unusually prophetic.

The Utilization of Psychiatric Facilities: A Fifty-Year Perspective

To better understand the utilization of psychiatric facilities by juveniles, a more detailed historical perspective is necessary. Table 8–7 compares information on residence, admissions, ratios of admission per residence, and total inpatient-care episodes, by types of psychiatric facilities, for two time periods: 1922–23 and 1971. Except for the community mental health centers (CMHC), the types of facilities compared are quite similar. CMHC inpatient facilities are usually associated with a general hospital (about 87 percent), but the NIMH has chosen to report all CMHC statistics separately. Omitted from Table 8–7 are data on residential treatment centers, classified by NIMH as psychiatric facilities. The reason for the exclusion is that the NCHS statistics, used in the analysis of facilities for the "emotionally disturbed" include NIMH residential treatment center information. The overlap of the mental health and child welfare systems will be discussed in the next section.

In 1922–23, very few juveniles utilized a psychiatric facility. Actually, the custom of collecting information about youth under 15, and from 15 to 19 years of age, precluded obtaining data on persons under 18. Therefore, the rates are generous estimates of psychiatric utilization by youth in the early 1920s. Compared to 1971, the most significant differences are the increase in total inpatient-care episodes and the relatively higher rate of bed use in psychiatric facilities. The inpatient-care episodes have increased about eight times (from 23 to 160), and the ratio of admissions to residence has increased from 1.39 to 4.80. Meanwhile, resident rates increased at a lower pace (from 10 to 23).

The Overlap of the Mental Health and Child Welfare Systems

In 1966 a University of Chicago survey team conducted a detailed census of *Children's Residential Institutions in the United States*, sponsored by the U.S. Children's Bureau (Pappenport et al. 1970, 7 vols.). They found that 307 out of the 2,318 institutions designated their "current primary function" as a facility for "emotionally disturbed children" (Ibid., vol. 1, p. 41). Significantly, about 64 percent of these self-designated institutions for emotionally disturbed were started many years earlier, when their original function had been as an institution for dependent/neglected youth; 6 percent began as a "pre-delinquent" institution; 4 percent as another children's facility; and only 26 percent began as a facility for emotionally disturbed children (Ibid., vol. 1, table 31, p. 41). In 1972 two child welfare scholars, reviewing the literature on residential treatment for emotionally disturbed children, concluded that "a majority of today's residential treatment facilities emerged from sectarian institutions, whose original goals were shelter, care, and training" (Maluccio and Marlow 1972, p. 23).

Between 1958 and 1971 three different agencies claimed they were counting *nonmedical* treatment facilities for emotionally disturbed youth: (1) the U.S. Children's Bureau included them in their total count of "children under care" in a child welfare institution; (2) the National Institute of Mental Health (NIMH) reported youth living in "residential treatment centers" as of 1966; and (3) the National Center for Health Statistics (NCHS) began counting nonhospital facili-

TABLE 8–7

Comparison of Resident and Admissions Data of All Inpatient Psychiatric Facilities
Used for Youth: 1922–23 and 1971

1922–23 (under 20)

Facility Type	Number of Residents[a]	Number of Admissions[b]	Ratio of Admissions/ Residents	Total Inpatient-Care Episodes
State/county				
Private institutions	4,144	4,303	1.04	8,447
General hospital-				
psychiatric wards[c]	102	1,605	15.74	1,707
N =	4,246	5,908	1.39	10,154
Rate/100,000 youth under 20 yrs.[d]	10	13	———	23

1971 (under 18)

Facility Type	Number of Residents[e]	Number of Admissions[e]	Ratio of Admissions/ Residents	Total Inpatient-Care Episodes[e]
State/county	12,844	26,352	2.05	39,196
Private hospital	1,248	6,420	5.14	6,668
General hospital-				
psychiatric wards	1,935	44,135	22.81	46,065
CMHC[f]	NA	NA	NA	18,092
N =	16,027	76,907	4.80	111,021
Rate/100,000 youth under 18 yrs.[g]	23	111	———	160

Sources: [a]*1923 Resident Data* are from U.S. Bureau of the Census, *Patients in Hospitals for Mental Disease, 1923*, Tables 2, 15, and 120. Private are included in State/county total.

[b]*1922 Admissions Data* are based on adding actual first admissions and estimated readmissions from Ibid., Tables 16, 63, and 120; estimated readmissions are based on using same percent of persons under 20 for first admissions: 4.8 percent. Private are included in State/county total.

[c]*1922–23 General Hospital–Psychiatric Ward* data were not broken down by age; therefore all figures are estimates based on resident and admissions proportions found for other facilities in Ibid.: 1.5 percent for resident, and 4.8 percent for admissions.

[d]*1922 population data* are based on U.S. Bureau of the Census, *Historical Statistics of the United States, Colonial Times to 1957*, Series A22-33; actual figures for persons under 14 were added to estimated figures for 14 to 20 year olds comprising the 14–20 age category used by the census in 1922.

[e]*All 1971 admissions and inpatient care episodes* of persons under 18 are actual figures from National Institute of Mental Health, Series B, no. 5, 1973, Tables 14 and 20; resident figures were obtained by subtracting admissions from inpatient-care episodes for facility type.

[f]*CMHC data* are for persons under 20 only, from Ibid., Table 20; separate admissions data not available (N.A.).

[g]*1971 population data* for persons under 18 are in *Social Security Bulletin*, March 1980, p. 65.

ties for the "emotionally disturbed" in 1971 (U.S. Department of Health, Education, and Welfare, 1966; NIMH, Series B, no. 1, 1968; NCHS, Series 14, no. 3, 1971).

Of the three attempts to count facilities for the emotionally disturbed (ED), the most complete surveys are those of the NCHS. Inasmuch as these surveys are conducted for NCHS by the U.S. Bureau of the Census, it is probable that ED statistics are not only more accurate, but also are actually mutually exclusive of other census surveys (e.g., the LEAA survey of juvenile correctional facilities). The most recent available data have been summarized in Table 7–4.

Historically, the child welfare field believes that *its* system—not the mental health system—pioneered the development of these nontraditional institutions. A 1974 statement by Joseph H. Reid, past executive director of the Child Welfare League (the private sector's major national organization), expressed his system's perception about ED facilities as follows:

> The history of the field of child welfare, the first field to deinstitutionalize—gives clear evidence of the necessity to plan alternatives clearly before burning down existing structures. . . .
>
> Although some of this history is marked by an anti-institutional climate, in the main there was careful planning of alternatives. The development of foster homes, group homes, the substitution of decentralized community-based small group settings over huge centralized institutions marked the change. And *most importantly*, the development of the small residential treatment centers for emotionally disturbed children, appropriately cared for in group settings, came out of the closing of the harmful custodial institutions. [Child Welfare League, 1974, pp. 1, 8; italics added]

Although Reid may be overly optimistic in his belief that DE has been completed in the child welfare system, it is clear that he believed that developing ED facilities was "most important" for child welfare. He would have been displeased to learn that a NIMH count for 1973 would have missed about half of the under-18 residents of nonmedical ED facilities (NIMH, Series A, no. 4, 1974; Ibid., *Statistical Note*, no. 135, July 1977; NCHS, Series 14, nos. 3, 4, 16). A statistical as well as a substantive overlap exists between the systems—although the precise counting of residents, admissions, and CCT episodes may be confusing to unwary readers.

Overview of Total Youth-in-Trouble System: A Fifty-Year Perspective

A useful way to summarize long-term trends for all three systems dealing with youth in trouble is to display all of the data together in a summary fashion. Table 8–8 provides this comparative summary by adapting the data provided in earlier tables (tables 7–4, 8–4, and 8–7). This summary, of course, can only approximate fifty-year trends, for all of the reasons cited in the footnotes of the tables.

Except for the child welfare system, the data in Parts A, B, and C of Table 8–8 depend upon whether the facilities are short term or long term. It is clear

TABLE 8–8

Summary Comparison of Long-Term Trends of Custody/Care/Treatment Episodes
for Three Youth-in-Trouble Systems:
1920s and 1970s

	1920s		1970s	
	Total CCT Episodes	Rates/ 100,000	Total CCT Episodes	Rates/ 100,000
A. *Child Welfare*				
Dep./neglect.	186,668	441	75,965	112
Emotionally disturbed	——	——	79,243	116
Total =	186,668	441	155,208	228
B. *Juvenile Corrections Only*				
Short-term[a]	34,545	88	522,385	777
Long-term[b]	52,357	133	213,279	317
Total =	86,902	221	735,664	1,094
C. *Mental Health*				
Short-term[c]	1,707	04	78,880[e]	119
Long-term[d]	8,447	19	51,020[e]	77
Total =	10,154	23	129,900[e]	196
D. *Combined Systems*				
Child welfare	186,668	441	155,208	228
Juv. corrections	86,902	221	735,664	1,094
Mental health	10,154	23	129,900	196
Total =	283,724	685	1,020,772	1,518
E. *Combined Systems by Length of Stay*				
Short-term	36,252	92	601,265	896
Long-term	247,472	593	419,507	622
Total =	283,724	685	1,020,772	1,518

SOURCES: Adaptations of Tables 7–4, 8–4, and 8–7, except for *e*.

[a] *Short-term corrections* refers to detention, shelter, and diagnostic.

[b] *Long-term 1923 corrections* refers to private and special institutions for delinquents, and institutions for women/girls. *Long-term 1974 corrections* refers to training schools, ranches/camps/schools, and group homes/halfway houses.

[c] *Short-term* refers to general hospital–psychiatric and CMHC.

[d] *Long-term* refers to state/county and private institutions.

[e] These figures are estimates for 1975 for all facilities, except CMHC; I used 1971 admissions/ residence ratios to approximate the 1975 figure; 1975 CMHC data are based on 1971 youth proportion of all CMHC inpatient-care episodes (or 13.9 percent). Sources used for these estimates include: NIMH, Statistical Note, nos. 137–39, 1977 and 146 (1978); NIMH Series A, no. 18, 1977; and President's Commission on Mental Health, vol. 2, 1978, p. 101. Population data are for 1975, *Social Security Bulletin*, March 1980, p. 65.

that the child welfare system is the only system exhibiting a sustained institutional reduction, even though a new long-term facility—for the emotionally disturbed—has offset about one-fourth of the reduction. The other two systems had far more institutional usage (i.e., CCT episodes) in the 1970s than in the 1920s. The increase is particularly marked in the short-term facilities.

Part D of Table 8–8 provides insight into the dominance of each system during the two decades under consideration. In the 1920s the child welfare system was clearly dominant, while the mental health system was only of minimal importance. In the 1970s the juvenile correctional system was clearly dominant (particularly because of the increased use of detention), while child welfare was only slightly ahead of the mental health system (228 vs. 196). However, due to the close ideological and professional links of the facilities for the emotionally disturbed with those of the mental health system, it is reasonable to infer that the traditional child welfare system actually ranks third in use.

In Part E, system boundaries are set aside so that the relative dominance of short-term and long-term facilities can be assessed. There is little doubt that short-term facilities are the primary source of the total gain in CCT episodes. There is only a slight difference for long-term facilities (593 vs. 622), but a substantial difference for short-term facilities (92 vs. 826). In addition, the relative proportion of CCT episodes accounted for by short-term facilities changed from 13 percent of the total episodes in the 1920s to 59 percent of the 1,518 episodes of the 1970s.

Regarding long-term facilities, an intersystem perspective reveals that the fifty-year reduction in the use of institutions for the dependent/neglected has been completely offset by the gains of the correctional and mental health systems (593 vs. 622). It is quite likely that these gains occurred among youth 12 to 17 years old, particularly in the use of private correctional facilities and state/county and private mental hospitals.

Assessing DE from a Federal Normative Perspective

This chapter's approach to DE of youth assumes that any reductions in institutional use in one system could be offset by gains in related systems. This approach is quite different from the narrow definition associated with the Juvenile Justice and Delinquency Prevention Act of 1974 and the Juvenile Justice Amendments of 1977 (U.S. Senate Committee on the Judiciary, May 1977).

According to this act, as amended, youths who had committed criminal offenses (i.e., delinquents) were not to be "detained or confined" with adults; status offenders and "such nonoffenders as dependent or neglected children, shall not be placed in juvenile detention or correctional facilities" (Ibid., sec. 223[a] [12] [13]). According to the administering agency—the Office of Juvenile Justice and Delinquent Prevention (OJJDP)—the "least restrictive" environments were to be sought in lieu of detention or correctional facilities. In defining compliance with the standard of least restrictive environment, OJJDP guidelines set forth five institutional characteristics: size (under 21, except for certain cases); distance from home; degree of security; restricted populations mix; and community programming (U.S. Office of Federal Register, 16 August 1978, pp. 36402–10).

For the purpose of further analysis, these ideal standards can be used to assess *all* juvenile facilities, not only correctional institutions. Although no systematic surveys have been conducted, a variety of sources can help estimate relative progress in meeting these federal norms of DE. Regarding population mix, it is generally agreed that ending the commingling of delinquent with noncriminal youths is difficult for many private facilities. As was noted earlier, the confinement of various types of youth in trouble in a single facility is a salient characteristic of the emergent youth-in-trouble system (see, for example, table 8–3).

If the OJJDP definition of "secure facility" is used, then most residences for nondelinquents that classify themselves as "open" would not meet the official interpretation of the security standard: "If exit points are open, but residents authoritatively prohibited from leaving at any time without approval, it would be a secure facility" (Ibid.). In addition, many psychiatric units for adolescents within general and state hospitals contain locked wards, and youths are free neither to move inside the facility nor to leave at will.

Many facilities would also be hard pressed to meet the standard of proximity to a youth's home and family. Whereas short-term facilities would usually be able to comply with this standard, many long-term facilities built before 1970 were deliberately located away from urban centers. Only by arbitrarily defining "near" as "within a day's drive" could a sizable number of facilities be described as community-based.

Many facilities that pride themselves on providing a "structured setting," "milieu therapy," "residential treatment," or a "therapeutic environment" employ or supervise their own teachers and recreation leaders, and would consequently be unable to yield evidence of community programming. For example, a recent study of eighteen facilities used as foster care institutions for children with "mental and delinquent problems" found that in only four did childen attend community public schools exclusively (GAO, April 1975).

Children in Foster Care Institutions

Restricted size is also a criterion that all types of facilities could have difficulty meeting. The standard for size—fewer than 21—cited by OJJDP regulations hardly conveys an image of a small facility. The only new type of institution that appears to come close to meeting this criterion is the group home. LEAA data indicate that in 1974 and 1975 public and private group homes averaged about 10 to 12 youths per facility; ranches, forestry camps, and schools averaged 43 to 49 each; and training schools averaged 67 residents per private and 137 per public facility (LEAA, *Children in Custody, 1974*, and *Children in Custody, 1975*). However, only about 20 percent of all long-term correctional placements in 1974 were in group homes (computed from LEAA, *Children in Custody, 1974*).

More precise data on size are available for the two types of child welfare facilities: those for dependent/neglected youngsters and those for emotionally disturbed youths. The older child welfare institution confined only 3 percent of its charges in 1973 in residences with fewer than 15 youths, and an additional 5 percent in facilities with less than 25—amounting to a total of 8 percent of youths in living arrangements close to the OJJDP standard. Emotionally disturbed youths fared somewhat better, but not much, in that in 1973 only 12 percent were living in facilities with less than 25 residents. If a less stringent standard of 50 residents is used, then 74 percent of dependent/neglected youths and 72 percent of emotionally disturbed youths lived in facilities housing *more* than that number. In fact, 42–44 percent lived with 100 or more youths (based on special computer runs provided to the author, on request, by staff of the National Center for Health Statistics).

This brief review—using one national set of standards for assessing juvenile facilities—indicates that a majority of youths in trouble who are not officially adjudicated, but who are living in an out-of-home placement with 5 or more unrelated youths, are probably living in a facility that is not the least restrictive choice. As this analysis discloses, even if the most controversial standard—commingling of delinquent, nonoffender, and status youths—were set aside, a majority of placed youths would still be situated in less-than-ideal living arrangements. Many environments might not be as confining as detention homes, traditional training schools, or locked hospital wards, but it is likely that they are not the least restrictive alternative possible.

Aside from the problems of finding least restrictive environments, OJJDP regulations are troublesome regarding the narrow approach to population statistics. A state can be deemed in compliance with regulations if it can provide evidence that the requisite reductions in institutionalization are occurring in traditional correctional facilities. In effect, regulations based on this narrow definition of DE do not address the alternative use of institutions clearly classified as child welfare or mental facilities. The overall rate of institutionalization may remain unchanged, or even increase (from a base year), yet a state can still be judged to be in compliance with OJJDP regultions if the traditional correctional system displays the appropriate rate reductions.

Federal Funding of Alternative Institutional Placement

The national shift toward using the private, rather than the public, correctional sector was first demonstrated with the assistance of the 1974 LEAA survey.

However, available evidence indicates that this shift, as well as the increased utilization of the mental health system, began prior to 1974. To account for the changes in institutionalization patterns and the emergence of a broad youth-in-trouble system, it helps to understand the role of federal funds in shaping the results presented in Table 8–8 (the summary comparison of long-term trends in custody/care/treatment episodes).

Prior to 1960 no federal funds from the Social Security Act were permitted to subsidize youth residing in institutions. Beginning with the 1961 Social Security amendments, the following sources of federal funds were made available for reimbursing part or all of the costs of private or medical institutional placements—costs that had traditionally been paid for by state and/or local funds: AFDC Foster Care (Title 4, amendments of 1961, 1962, and 1967); Child Welfare Services (Titles 4, 5, and 20, amendments of 1962, 1967, and 1975); Medicaid (Title 19, amendments of 1965 and 1972; and Supplementary Security Income or SSI (Title 16, amendment of 1972). (These and other federal programs having a direct or indirect impact on children in "vulnerable situations" are briefly described in the final report of the Children's Defense Funds, *Children without Homes*, 1978, pp. 105–50.) On the basis of current information, it appears that the changes in AFDC and child welfare services made the greatest contribution in altering traditional institutional utilization patterns.

In 1961 the federal policy of home care—first adopted in 1935—was changed to permit the payment of maintenance funds to foster homes for those AFDC children removed from homes "contrary" to their welfare, "as a result of a judicial determination" (U.S. Senate, 1963, sec. 408 [a]). This amendment was originally passed to assist states in subsidizing substitute care for AFDC children determined to be living in an "unsuitable home" (Pers 1974, p. 462). In 1962 the definition of foster care was broadened to include placement in an institution, providing it was a private "nonprofit child care institution" (sec. 408 [a]). When the legislation was first passed, it was expected that not many AFDC children would be directly affected. This assumption was borne out for the first few years. But between 1965 and 1972 the AFDC–Foster Care Program (AFDC-FC) experienced a very sharp expansion. This growth in AFDC-FC is summarized as follows: *1961*—600; *1965*—5,779; *1972*—79,527; *1973*—86,000; *1975*—100,000; *1976*—115,000 (Pers 1974, p. 462; U.S. General Accounting Office, 1977).

HEW has never had a complete statistical reporting of how many AFDC-FC youth were living in foster homes or institutions. In 1976 the GAO attempted to audit the program's functioning. GAO staff estimated that about 29,000—or 25 percent—of all AFDC-FC youth in March 1976 were residing in a foster care institution (U.S. General Accounting Office report on *Children in Foster-Care Institutions*, 1977). The GAO estimated that about $138 million had been expended by the federal government in 1975 for AFDC-FC (for maintenance purposes). Of this amount about 40 percent—or slightly more than $55 million—

was spent for eligible AFDC youth residing in child care institutions (Ibid., p. 2). The GAO complained that the program, originally designed for needy children, had changed drastically from the early 1960s: "According to state officials, the Program's scope has changed to include children placed *primarily* because of mental or delinquency problems" (Ibid., p. iii; italics added). This change in the program's scope appeared to puzzle GAO staff. However, if they had paid closer attention to the 1967 Social Security amendments, subsequent legislative modifications, and regulations, the change would not have been as surprising. These statutory and regulatory changes can be briefly summarized:

1. In 1967 *all* state costs for public assistance categories (Titles 1, 10, 14, and 16, as well as Title 4-A) were declared eligible for reimbursement at a federal matching rate that used "the federal medical assistance percentage (as defined in Section 1905), instead of the percentages" formerly used in the past (U.S. House of Representatives, 1973, Title 11, sec. 1118). The Medicaid percentage matching rate was set at a minimum of 50 percent and a maximum of 83 percent (according to a state's relative affluence), "without regard to any maximum on the dollar amounts per recipient which may be counted" (Ibid.). All states were virtually guaranteed to do better, in that the "federal share" percentage, under Title 4-A (AFDC), has ranged between 33.3 percent and 66.6 percent of the first $100 spent per child by a state (Ibid.; Pers 1974, p. 475). States choosing to participate in the AFDC-FC program could receive a higher federal share of mainte nance care costs, regardless of the cost of the foster care placement.

2. As of 1 July 1969, all states were mandated to include foster care as an integral part of their state plan (U.S. House of Representatives, 1973, Title 4, sec. 402 [a]). Compliance was eased by the higher federal matching rates possible from Title 11 (sec. 1118).

3. Eligibility for inclusion in the AFDC-FC program was expanded to include children not currently on state AFDC rolls, providing they "would have received such aid in or for such a month *if application* had been made therefore" (Ibid., sec. 408; italics added).

4. All needy children could receive social services (distinct from maintenance-care payments), reimbursable by a new 75 percent federal matching rate. Service eligiblity was expanded beyond the definition applicable for maintenance payments. Needy children included current AFDC recipients and relatives in the home, or "any child or relative who is *applying* for aid to families with dependent children or who, within such period or periods as the secretary may prescribe, *has been* or *is likely to become* an applicant of such aid" (Ibid., sec. 403 [a] [3] [A]); italics added).

HEW regulations defined a "former client" as an AFDC recipient within the past two years, and a "potential client" as a likely AFDC recipient within five years (Mott 1976, p. 27). Services were broadly defined as including child welfare services which "supplement, or *substitute for parental care*, and supervision," for the purpose of "remedying, preventing, or assisting" in dealing with problems that "may result in neglect, abuse, exploitation, or *delinquency* of children"; or "protecting and caring for homeless dependent, or neglected children" (Ibid., Title 4, sec. 425; italics added).

5. Public child welfare agencies were permitted, for the first time, to purchase social services from nonpublic sources. These included child welfare, family planning, and general family services (Title 4, sec. 403). This amendment, coupled with the other changes, permitted states to be reimbursed for purchasing allowable "placement services" at a 75 percent matching rate, and maintenance care costs at a 50–83 percent matching rate. States varied in how they "packaged" placement costs, as well as how extensively they chose to be involved in a combined state AFDC-FC and AFDC Social Service Program.

In 1975 HEW estimated that the federal government spent about $265 million for social services linked to the AFDC-FC program (U.S. Senate Committee on Labor and Public Welfare, 1975, p. 312). These service expenditures could include payments for the federal share of child welfare salaries for foster care activities and administrative expenses allocated to AFDC-FC programs. In addition, these services could also include professional treatment salaries for staff inside a residential treatment center for emotionally disturbed youth, a group home, or any other nontraditional facility. If the costs of services to institutionalized youth were comparable to the proportionate costs of maintenance care, then federal funding for institutional programs for youth could have amounted to an additional $106 million in 1975 (i.e., 40 percent of $265 million). If added to the 1975 AFDC-FC costs estimated by the GAO, the total federal share for institutional care and services could amount to $161 million. Considering that in 1975, LEAA could only have spent a maximum of $41 million for juvenile "rehabilitation" purposes and $8.5 million for deinstitutionalization of status offender programs, it is clear that welfare programs probably spent much more for alternatives to detention and public correctional facilities—$161 million to $49.5 million (for LEAA data see U.S. Senate Subcommittee to Investigate Delinquency, 17 March 1975, p. 89).

In 1975 the funding authority for AFDC-Social Services was transferred to the generic Social Services Title 20. Because of the $2.5 billion "cap" on all social services (for all ages), there was also a dollar limit placed on federal reimbursement for child care "placement services." Although the definition of social service is currently left to the discretion of each state, within fairly broad statutory language, the federal government has retained control over the meaning of "maintenance care" of the AFDC-FC program. This program still has no ceiling (in contrast to Title 20), and is therefore potentially more attractive to the states as a placement funding resource. A recent interpretation of federal regulations indicates that established policy is to provide for an extremely broad approach toward defining the "federally reimbursable cost items" for child care placements. According to the statute, "only those items which are included in such term in the case of foster care in the foster family home of an individual" can be included in setting foster care rates (U.S. Senate Committee on Finance, 1978, sec. 408 [a]). According to a "program interpretation," institutional rates can include, besides shelter, food, clothing, and personal care items, the following "federally reimbursable cost items":

1. EDUCATION COSTS. Includes school supplies, fees, transportation, daily living skills programs, and specialized education.

2. CARE COSTS. All child care staff, social workers, and supervisor salaries, fringe benefits, staff development, in-service training, conferences, memberships, and subscriptions to professional associations, and administrative, clerical, and support services.

3. TRANSPORTATION. All costs that are "an integral part of the 24-hour program of care."

4. HEALTH COSTS. Physical examination, medical care and treatment, psychological testing, psychiatric examination and treatment, dental care, and eye glasses if these are not provided under a state's Medicaid program (U.S. Department of Health, Education, and Welfare, 19 May 1978).

Given the discretionary interpretation of reimbursable cost items, it is not surprising that the children's defense fund estimated that by July 1977, about 47 percent of the AFDC-FC federal maintenance funds were spent on institutional care. However, the number of children living in such facilities was still approximately 25 percent (Children's Defense Fund, 1978, pp. 130, 276).

Summary and Conclusions

There have been three major types of DE of youth over a 150-year period. The first type was the removal of youth from adult facilities and the construction of new age-specialized facilities for dependent/neglected and wayward/delinquent/status offender youth. The second type of DE was the relocation of dependent/neglected youth into foster homes or to their own homes (subsidized by outdoor relief, mothers' aid, or aid to families of dependent children). The third type was the diminished use of both long-term traditional correctional facilities and the remaining dependent/neglected institutions, and their replacement with nontraditional youth facilities: facilities for the emotionally disturbed; group homes and other private correctional facilities; and mental health institutions. Only the second type of DE resulted in an actual decrease in institutional use; the first and third types have been associated with an increase in the variety and use of institutions.

The removal of youth from adult facilities was associated with the emergence of two youth-oriented systems: child welfare and juvenile corrections. Private charities were dominant in child welfare, whereas juvenile corrections were sponsored by city, county, and state authorities. The influence of private charities in child welfare and public relief policies varied by state. In states like Massachusetts—where a strong state leadership was established quite early (in the 1860s), and where the policy ideal of "institutions as a last resort" was cautiously but consistently supported by a purposeful, entrepreneurial allocation of public funds—the second type of DE was in evidence by 1910. In many other states where the interests of private charities were dominant, institutionalization could be defended as a justifiable response to homes characterized by poverty and/or "inefficiency and immorality." Public welfare programs were actively fought. Not until the passage of the Social Security Act, and until the provision of AFDC was made widely available, did the country witness reduced reliance on privately operated institutions for dependent/neglected youth.

The third type of DE has involved shifts away from certain kinds of long-term institutions, but any population reductions have been matched, and even surpassed, by increases in other types of institutionalization. There have been increases in the use of private correctional facilities, residential treatment associated with child welfare, and psychiatric units of general and state hospitals. In effect, there has recently emerged a new youth-in-trouble institutional system that includes old and new institutions from all three fields: juvenile corrections, child welfare, and mental health. A significant implicit assumption of this broader system is that the behaviors resulting in short- and long-term placement decisions could, under statutes in all fifty states, bring youths into conflict with the juvenile laws of their jurisdiction—if the enforcement and judicial systems took official note of their "acting out" behaviors.

The reasons for the emergence of this youth-in-trouble system are provisionally set forth as follows:

1. There has been a *shift in the balance between the public and private sector*. The custody, care, and treatment of delinquent and status offender youth has been increasingly shared by the public sector and private organizations (mainly nonprofit, but also some proprietary). An informal division of labor—whereby private organizations concentrated on younger children and youths classified as dependent, neglected, or mildly deviant—emerged in the latter half of the nineteenth century and continued for the first half of the twentieth. However, that situation has changed. Recent LEAA data reveal that between 43 and 48 percent of all youth resident in nondetention correctional facilities are living under private auspices. Secondary analysis of recent data reveals that private facilities providing long-term care accounted for approximately 54 percent of all juvenile correctional admissions.

2. The *increase in voluntary commitments* has contributed to the nonjudicial use of private institutions. Private organizations, unlike public institutions, can take referrals for placement from a variety of sources, both public and private. Recent data from the LEAA-sponsored surveys indicate that private juvenile correctional facilities receive 22–24 percent of their residents from such commitments. Although the circumstances contributing to these voluntary commitments remain unknown, one might infer that these youths could otherwise be adjudicated as delinquent, officially labeled as persons in need of supervision, or clas-

sified as dependent/neglected. In practice, a voluntary commitment can be synonymous with diversion from the official enforcement or judicial systems.

3. The increased reliance on private institutions permits a *mixing of official and diagnostic labels* that is much broader than can occur in public facilities. Private agencies' official papers of legal incorporation rarely restrict them to housing only youths subject to specific labels. Thus, the mix of youths confined within the same facilities, revealed in LEAA surveys, probably cannot be attacked as violating any of the states' statutes. Although the recent federal guidelines (promulgated in August 1978) on commingling of various youth populations could change this diverse population mix, available evidence indicates that monitoring of private facilities is not systematic. A 1978 GAO report revealed that only four states bothered to monitor private facilities containing any juvenile delinquents.

4. The movement to take status offenders out of public correctional institutions has often been accompanied by a *transfer of legal responsibility from probation and correctional authorities to public child welfare officials.* Historically, public welfare officials have made extensive use of private child welfare agencies; many public child welfare authorities were originally organized to take children from almshouses and place them into "benevolent" child care institutions or foster homes. State and county public welfare authorities have been purchasing care services from private institutions since the post–Civil War period. This pattern has continued into the twentieth century. Past and recent surveys indicate that over 80 percent of all residents of child welfare organizations are under private auspices. Various types of youths in trouble receiving "protective services" from state or county welfare authorities are, therefore, most likely to be placed in private foster care institutions—some of these classified as correctional and others categorized as child welfare facilities.

5. Since the emergence of the child guidance clinics in the 1920s, there has been an increasing tendency to *redefine delinquent-type behaviors as "acting out"* or as symptoms of an emotional disturbance. Both public and private child welfare agencies tend to concur in these diagnostic assessments; since the early 1960s, the placement of delinquents has been theoretically linked to a presumed need for "residential treatment in a structured setting." Although residential treatment facilities for emotionally disturbed youth are usually classified as mental health or child-caring institutions, not as correctional facilities, the residents are also described as requiring a "high level of structure."

6. Recently the *mental health profession has extended its services* beyond patients hospitalized with obvious psychiatric disturbances to persons not usually cared for in a hospital: alcoholics, drug users, and adolescents with a variety of "transient" behavioral problems. The latter have been admitted into state and county mental hospitals, psychiatric units of general hospitals, and private hospitals, as well as specialized children's psychiatric facilities. Instead of being admitted because of classic psychiatric symptoms, the majority of juveniles have been admitted because of general behavioral disorders: transient situational dis-

orders, childhood disorders, personality disorders, and drug disorders. These nonclassical diagnoses often indicate behaviors that could result in court adjudications or other formal dispositions.

7. Finally, *since 1962, federal funding has been available to subsidize out-of-home placements*, providing they are not in a traditional public correctional institution. Federal funds for placement of children have been permissible under the following titles in the Social Security Act: Aid to Families with Dependent Children (AFDC) (Title 4); Child Welfare Services (Title 4); Social Services (Title 20); Medicaid (Title 19); and Supplemental Security Income (SSI) (Title 16). The AFDC-FC and Social Services funds have been particularly important in encouraging the growth of private facilities. These institutions can compete with one another for 100 percent occupancy of beds for children and youth referred by probation, child welfare, mental health, private doctors and lawyers, and other voluntary sources. In practice, this also means that diverse placement agencies can compete with one another for the use of the same private facilities.

In Massachusetts, for example, the Division of Youth Services—the state correctional agency associated with closing down the state training schools—spent $7 million, and the state child welfare agency spent $10 million purchasing services from the *same* providers of residential care and treatment. Inasmuch as placements in a traditional training school would rarely qualify for maintenance service or medical payments, according to federal statutes or regulations, there is an increasing incentive to redefine youths in trouble according to diagnostic categories that will legitimate placement in facilities deemed appropriate for reimbursement. The perception that a youth has an emotional problem—apart from the fact that he or she may be in trouble with local or state officials—can provide the rationale for reimbursements in nontraditional placements.

PART III

The Least Restrictive Doctrine and the Welfare State

Normative Ideals and the Search for a Federal Policy Agenda

The fields of mental health, mental retardation, child welfare, delinquency, and the aging are replete with criticisms about problems associated with DE. Complaints have been expressed about child abuse in alternative foster care institutions, profiteering and unloving care in nursing homes, fire hazards and starvation diets in board-and-care homes, the creation of psychiatric ghettos in communities, the theft of SSI checks by shelter-care proprietors, or the lack of adequate follow-up by social service and mental health agencies. Although each problem could become an item on a federal policy agenda, it would be cumbersome to deal with them on a separate basis. In addition to having an unwieldy list of problems, it would also be difficult to judge which problems to include, and in what order.

The difficulty in defining a policy agenda is compounded by the diverse interests and preferences of those who participate in the process, or who have a stake in the outcome. Differences of opinion are often based on explicit or implicit normative ideals and standards. However, because these ideals are usually fewer in number than specific program goals, it may be more useful to discuss major ideals and concerns in the fields of mental health and mental retardation, as well as recent judicial rulings and legislation that pertain to both fields.

A distinctive normative orientation has developed during the past decade that contrasts with earlier pragmatic justifications for depopulating state hospitals: too many people are admitted and stay too long when they could be helped to live in the community. In recent years the goals of "normalization," "least restrictive conditions," and "balanced care systems" have emerged. After assessing these newer DE ideals, I will offer an analysis of a recent conflict between the GAO and officials in HEW (now Health and Human Services, or HHS) over what constitutes the federal definition of the major policy problem. Such an analysis will highlight the potential implications of choosing between competing ideals.

Normative Approaches in the Mental Health Field

In 1975 Dr. Bertram Brown, former head of NIMH, cited three "essential" components as necessary for DE in the field of mental health:

1. The prevention of inappropriate mental hospital admissions through the provision of community alternatives for treatment;

2. Release to the community of all patients that have been given adequate preparation for such a change; and

3. The establishment and maintenance of community support systems for non-institutionalized persons receiving mental health services in the community. [Bachrach 1976, p. 1]

Using this tripartite normative definition, with emphases on treatment alternatives, adequate preparations, and support systems, L. Bachrach reviewed over 400 citations in the mental illness (MI) literature, in order to assess issues associated with DE. She developed eight broad categories to summarize issues of concern in the MI field. It is evident that the concerns would not be manifest without the normative emphases. Briefly the issues pertain to:

1. THE SELECTION OF PATIENTS FOR COMMUNITY CARE. The "needs of chronically ill patients" have been ignored; discharged patients have not been adequately prepared to learn "the practical skills needed to function in an ordinary community"; disadvantaged and minority groups have been less able to utilize community-based services and these "tend to be irrelevant" to their needs.

2. THE TREATMENT COURSE FOR PATIENTS IN THE COMMUNITY. There is an "inadequate range of treatment services" readily available to ex-patients, except for psychotropic drugs; local mental health services are "lacking in centralized administration and this results in fragmented responsibility"; community services are often "less accessible" because of limited business hours, distance, transportation, or costs of travel; the quality of care is open to "serious doubt" and there is a "disproportionate heavy reliance on psychoactive drugs."

3. THE QUALITY OF LIFE OF PATIENTS IN THE COMMUNITY. Inadequate attention and provision of "community support systems," the development of friendship networks, employment opportunities, transportation, and leisure and social activities; residential facilities and living arrangements, "on a widespread basis," have been found to be below acceptable standards associated with a humane environment.

4. THE RECEPTIVITY OF THE GREATER COMMUNITY. There has been widespread resistance and opposition to mentally ill individuals; there has been a concentration of facilities in certain neighborhoods to a point of possible "community saturation," and there are problems of local "absorption of deviants"; there have been ecological impacts on the life and economy of communities dependent on hospitals, as well as specific impacts on hospital staff affected by closing of wards, "cottages," or total institutions; families often have to contend with new problems of caring for relatives, and this may create "crises" and induce severe emotional and social strain on other family members.

5. FINANCIAL AND FISCAL PROBLEMS. Knowledge required to make accurate cost-benefit comparisons between community- and hospital-based care is unavailable; there has been a "transfer of major fiscal responsibility" from the mental health system to the local welfare agencies, police, courts, and emergency rooms.

6. LEGAL AND QUASI-LEGAL PROBLEMS. The concern about patient rights within an institution has followed discharged persons as they have reentered the community; there are conflicting reports on the dangerousness of released patients or potential hospital patients and debate over whether professionals are capable of making accurate predictions.

7. INFORMATIONAL NEEDS AND ACCOUNTABILITY. There has been a lag in effective and conclusive research; the inability to locate individuals for follow-up studies is a reflection of the inability to locate them for treatment purposes; there is lack of knowledge about what actually happens to released hospital patients.

8. THE PROCESS OF DE CREATES PROBLEMS. DE has often been accomplished with "precipitate implementation" and "in haste," thereby undermining any rational planning; patients' views about hospital or community preferences have not been taken into account; there are problems in maintaining the hospitals according to acceptable standards while they are being "phased out"; there is failure to establish liaison between hospitals and community-based programs, facilities, and personnel; the dissolution of traditional arrangements gives rise to "role-blurring" of mental health professionals; there exists a resistance to change because of disenchantment with the failure to establish the requisite network of community services before the discharge of thousands of patients (Bachrach 1976, pp. 10–17).

Bachrach believes that these issues have emerged because "functional alternatives" to the traditional hospital have not been created. She argues that mental hospitals have always had "primary functions" demanded by a society, but that these have often been different from the publicly proclaimed ideal purposes and goals of the managers of traditional institutions. According to Bachrach, "the deinstitutionalization movement in the United States represents a search for functional alternatives to the mental hospital" (Ibid., p. 19). Primary functions have included: (1) Public safety and removal from society of "socially disruptive" individuals, and (2) custodial care for persons unable to care for themselves. Treatment and rehabilitation have always been, therefore, "secondary functions." A strict functionalist position would argue, therefore, that "mental hospitals must not and cannot be eliminated until alternatives for the functions of asylum and custodial care have been provided" (Ibid., p. 19).

In effect, Bachrach appears to be suggesting that any normative approach would first have to take into account care and social-control functions, because treatment functions are secondary. Although treatment considerations may not always have to be secondary, it is important to emphasize Bachrach's proposal that care and social-control functions should be accorded priority in any realistic DE policy discussion. If they are not dealt with explicitly, it is likely that critics like Bachrach (and the many authors she cites) would continually scrutinize living arrangements according to unspecified normative standards pertaining to the type, degree, duration, and scheduling of care and custody/supervision, as well as the presence or absence of "appropriate treatment."

A 1978 panel of MI leaders, comprising the President's Commission on Mental Health, responded to these concerns by proposing a modified ideal mental health policy. This normative approach is influenced by recent judicial decisions in federal courts (see later sections of this chapter): "A responsive mental health service system should provide the most appropriate care in the least restrictive setting. Whenever possible, people should live at home and receive outpatient treatment in the community. When they cannot, the facility in which they are treated should offer the maximum possible independence" (President's Commission on Mental Health, 1978, vol. 1, p. 16).

By emphasizing the ideals of "appropriate care," "least restrictive setting," and "maximum possible independence," the commission has attempted to go beyond the phrase, "community alternatives for treatment" (proposed by Brown). Despite their vagueness and the problems of specifying "appropriate," "least restrictive," and "maximum possible independence," the ideals could provide a basis for formulating standards to deal with the problems of care, social control, and treatment outside of traditional institutions. However, it appears that the commission assumes that inpatient settings must include treatment. This inference is supported by reviewing the commission's recommendations for community-based facilities. The only nonhospital setting proposed for priority funding is an Intermediate Care Facility–Mental Health (ICF-MH)—a type of nursing home adapted for mental patients. This image of "smaller, home-like facilities" (p. 24), with nurses and quasi-hospital routines, is quite different from the ideals set forth by leaders in the mental retardation field. In this field, deliberate attempts are made to exclude nurses and quasi-hospital routines from being considered part of the community-residential facility; they are excluded because they are not "normal."

Normative Approaches in the Mental Retardation Field

Instead of viewing living arrangements as sites for treatment, many MR leaders stress the need for environments providing normalized care. As defined by an HEW spokesperson, G. O'Connor, DE is "an aspect of the normalization concept for persons who are handicapped" (1976, p. vi). O'Connor summarized the importance and meaning of this idealistic concept as follows:

> Normalization of the quality of life for developmentally disabled persons is a goal toward which many strive. The movement receives its energy not only from the labor of concerned professionals and parents, but also from court mandates, legislative enactment, and presidential directive.
>
> The current zeitgeist of changing services for the retarded is reflected in the emphasis placed on the "normalization principle" by the President's Committee on Mental Retardation in 1969. Bengt Nirje (1970) defined normalization as "making available to the mentally subnormal, patterns and conditions of everyday life which are as close as possible to the norms and patterns of the mainstream of society" (p. 62). More recently, Wolfensberger (1972) refined the definition as follows: "uti-

lization of means which are as culturally normative as possible in order to establish and/or maintain personal behaviors and characteristics which are as culturally normative as possible (p. 28). [Ibid., p. 2]

The proposed normalization ideal is based on humanitarian and democratic values, and on a technical means for establishing or maintaining appropriate behaviors. Nirje's definition stresses the ideal of having MR persons live like others in a society, and striving to make this "mainstream," everyday life available to all. Implicit in this humanistic approach is the assumption that normalized living arrangements should be provided even if personal behaviors and skills are not improved. For C. Edward Meyers, another MR leader, normalization is an "idea whose time has come [for] fellow citizens":

> Under the philosophy of normalization the resident should be entitled to something more like home living in a smaller place, with some personal space and the right to have lots of his own things, the choice of his own clothes instead of communal clothing, and the dignity of not being herded like a prisoner from bedroom to toilet to eating hall. In theory, the community residential facility should provide qualities of life more like family living with personalized attention, fewer caretaker faces in a week's time, and some private and maybe secret places for one's own treasures. Above all, it should be a place which has no need for the routines required to manage large numbers of people. [Ibid., p. vi]

Many advocates of normalization may find that it is easier to base their proposals for DE on humanistic value preferences for "home living," "own things," "choice," "dignity," "quality of life," and "no need for routines" than to use effectiveness as a basis for their actions. From a purely technical perspective, a review of the literature indicates "that the data base is far too scanty at this time to construct a social policy based on empirical evidence" (Balla 1976, p. 123). A summary of the evidence available around 1976 concluded:

> From the studies concerned with what may be called the quality of life dimension, care is more adequate in smaller community-based institutions, especially in those under 100 population. However, there also seems to be considerable variation in quality of life among small community-based facilities. There is very little evidence to suggest that the behavioral functioning of residents is different in institutions of different sizes. There are essentially no data on the issue of whether smaller institutions are more adequate than larger ones in terms of returning their residents to the community. There is minimal evidence to suggest that parental and community involvement may be enhanced in community-based facilities. [Ibid., p. 122]

It appears that the strongest evidence supporting nontraditional institutions relates to improved quality of life, rather than improved behavioral functioning. Nirje, Meyers, and others might be satisfied with this result, in that improved quality of living conforms with normalization ideals and requires no further justification. However, some professional workers and evaluational researchers are less certain about embracing normalization on its own merits, since their primary interest lies in improved behavioral functioning. Balla, for example, in his re-

view of the literature on institution size and quality of care, approvingly provides
the following quote from a fellow researcher at Yale:

> Research takes on added importance at this particularly critical juncture in construct-
> ing social policy for the retarded. At the social policy level, the mental retardation
> field is in a state of flux and disarray. Some years ago, experts convinced decision-
> makers that special education was the solution to the problem of training the re-
> tarded. This view is now suspect and decision-makers are committing themselves to
> such concepts as normalization and deinstitutionalization. I join with those many se-
> nior workers in the field who view these concepts as little more than slogans that are
> badly in need of an empirical data base. We have little knowledge about what is the
> best type of classroom or the optimal institutional setting for the retarded. [Ibid.,
> p. 123]

In contrast to this position, O'Connor was interested in finding the type of
community placement that "can provide excellent opportunities for our handicapped citizens" (1976, p. 68). Instead of assessing behavioral functioning, she
attempted to operationalize the normalization concept per se, so that a national
sample of community residences could be examined and compared. She was not
dissuaded from this task by the finding that only 611 out of 3,582 nominated
community residential facilities (CRFs) fit her conception of a community residence, while 2,714 clearly did not (from 1972 to 1974). Facilities were screened
out if: (1) Reference was made to nursing home or convalescent hospital in response to a query about a term generally used to describe the facility; (2) The
staff titles list included nursing positions; (3) Less than one-fourth of the total
number of residents were developmentally disabled; and (4) Facilities reported
over fifty residents and did not contain evidence of smaller units within the administrative structure (Ibid., p. 8).

O'Connor defined a CRF as one that "provides services" and operates 24
hours a day for a "small group of mentally retarded and/or otherwise developmentally disabled persons who are presently capable of functioning in the community with some degree of independence" (Ibid., p. 6). Facilities were assessed
according to the following normalization criteria: (1) residential location and
type of building in which facility is located; (2) absence of security features,
such as high fences, barred windows, and locked areas; (3) existence of personalized effects in the area around residents' beds; (4) amount of privacy provided
each resident in bathrooms and bedrooms; (5) type of homelike furnishings; and
(6) interviewer's impressions of the "general atmosphere," management, and
physical layout of the residence.

Clearly, none of the criteria refer to treatment or habilitation services. The
findings indicated that facilities housing fewer than 10 or from 11 to 20 persons
were the highest in normalization (86 and 81 percent, respectively), whereas
only 36 percent of CRFs with over 20 residents rated as highly. Because Balla's
review of American, English, and Scandinavian findings focused on "resident-
oriented care practices," not normalization criteria, it is possible that size is
more critical than the general literature revealed. It appears that CRFs with 20 or

fewer residents are more likely to provide a normalized living environment for MR persons.

Although MI facilities were not explicitly included in the O'Connor study, some residents were "emotionally disturbed" (Ibid., p. 48). It is possible, therefore, that if similar criteria were applied to CRFs housing MI persons, comparable results might be obtained; all of the criteria are nonspecific to a disability, and therefore could be applied to all types of CRFs. This type of classification would only make sense, however, if normalized living were valued independently of its impact on emotional, behavioral, or interpersonal functioning.

Legal Approach to Institutionalization: The Least Restrictive Environment Standard

Normative ideals have also become the focus of recent official government policy, primarily via judicial channels. Since 1972 numerous federal courts have formulated and attempted to specify a constitutional doctrine to serve persons in the "least restrictive environment," if they have been involuntarily committed, or are in danger of being committed, to state institutions. Unlike the other normative ideals, this principle has the moral and legal support of significant court rulings. As a result, from 1972 on, deinstitutionalization could legitimately be perceived from a legal, as well as an operational, analytic, and normative perspective.

The principle of least restrictive handling of governmental interests was first set forth by the Supreme Court in a noninstitutional context, in *Shelton* v. *Tucker*, 364 U.S. 449 (1960). In that case the Supreme Court upheld the general constitutional principle that "even though the government purpose be legitimate and substantial, that purpose cannot be pursued by means that broadly stifle fundamental personal liberties when the end can be more narrowly achieved" (cited in President's Commission on Mental Health, Task Force Reports, 1978, vol. 4, p. 1,427).

Following this precedent, legal experts in the fields of mental health and retardation argued that the state has an affirmative obligation to search for alternatives to commitment that are less restrictive than a state hospital, whenever the state's purposes could be carried out "as well or better" (Ibid., p. 1428). In addition, a state had a duty "to limit confinement to the least restrictive institutional setting and to discharge the committed patient outright, or to less restrictive community alternatives, once continued institutionalization could no longer be therapeutic" (Ibid., p. 1428).

The first attempt to define precisely the meaning associated with the constitutional principle of "least restrictive conditions" was enunciated in an Alabama federal district court by Judge Frank M. Johnson. In 1971 he argued that "to deprive any citizen of his or her liberty upon the altruistic theory that the confinement is for humane therapeutic reasons and then fail to provide adequate treatment violates the very fundamentals of due process" (*Wyatt* v. *Stickney*, 325 Federal Supplement, 785 M.D. Alabama, 1971). In 1972 Judge Johnson set forth the judicial order, "Minimum Constitutional Standards for Adequate Treatment." Under the first standard, a "humane psychological and physical environment," the court listed the following nineteen items:

1. Patients have a right to privacy and dignity.

2. Patients have a right to the least restrictive conditions necessary to achieve the purposes of commitment.

3. No person shall be deemed incompetent to manage his affairs, to contact, to hold professional or occupational or vehicle operator's licenses, to marry and obtain a divorce, to register and vote, or to make a will *solely* by reason of his admission or commitment to the hospital.

4. Patients shall have the same rights to visitation and telephone communications as patients at other public hospitals. . . . Patients shall have an unrestricted right to visitation with attorneys and with private physicians and other health professionals.

5. Patients shall have an unrestricted right to send sealed mail. Patients shall have an unrestricted right to receive sealed mail from their attorneys, private physicians, and other mental health professionals, from courts, and government officials.

6. Patients have a right to be free from unnecessary or excessive medication. . . . Medication shall not be used as punishment, for the convenience of staff, as a substitute for program, or in quantities that interfere with the patient's treatment program.

7. Patients have a right to be free from physical restraint and isolation. Except for emergency situations, in which it is likely that patients could harm themselves or others and in which less restrictive means of restraint are not feasible, patients may be physically restrained or placed in isolation on a qualified mental health professional's written order which explains the rationale for such action.

8. Patients shall have a right not to be subjected to experimental research without the express and informed consent of the patient.

9. Patients have a right not to be subjected to treatment procedures such as lobotomy, electroconvulsive treatment, adversive reinforcement conditioning or other unusual or hazardous treatment procedures without their express and informed consent after consultation with counsel or interested party of the patient's choice.

10. Patients have a right to receive prompt and adequate medical treatment for any physical ailments.

11. Patients have a right to wear their own clothes and to keep and use their own personal possessions.

12. The hospital has an obligation to supply an adequate allowance of clothing.

13. The hospital shall make provision for the laundering of patient clothing.

14. Patients have a right to regular physical exercise several times a week.

15. Patients have a right to be outdoors at regular and frequent intervals, in the absence of medical considerations.

16. The right to religious worship shall be accorded to each patient who desires such opportunities.

17. The institution shall provide, with adequate supervision, suitable opportunities for the patient's interaction with members of the opposite sex.

18. Rules shall govern patient labor.

19. A patient has a right to a humane psychological and physical environment within the hospital facilities. These facilities shall be designed to afford patients with comfort and safety, promote dignity and ensure privacy. The facilities shall be designed to make a positive contribution to the efficient attainment of the treatment goals of the hospital. [Ibid., 344 Federal Supplement 373, Appendix A.M.D., Alabama, 1972]

Besides being deficient in providing a "humane and psychological environment," the state failed to provide two other "fundamental areas": qualified staff in numbers sufficient to administer adequate treatment, and individualized treatment plans specifying "the least restrictive treatment conditions necessary to achieve the purposes of commitment." At a subsequent hearing the order containing the "fundamental conditions" of adequate and effective treatment was extended to the state's institutionalized retarded population (Ibid., 344 Federal Supplement 387, M.D., Alabama, 1972).

One can reasonably infer that by including nontreatment rights, the judicial conditions associated with a least restrictive doctrine are quite compatible with normalization ideals. The order includes rights to privacy and dignity; patients wearing their own clothes; keeping and using their own personal possessions; laundering patients' clothing; religious worship; and granting opportunities for interaction with the opposite sex. It is also reasonable to infer that ex-patients placed in community residential facilities would also possess rights to privacy and dignity and other "least restrictive conditions."

In 1974 Judge Johnson's judicial policy was contested in a U.S. Court of Appeals. The appeals court noted that the defendants did not contest the specific details of the order, but rather contested the district court's decision on other grounds. In fact, the state's governor and mental health officials "conceded that if there is a constitutional right to treatment enforceable by a suit for injunctive relief in federal courts those standards accurately reflect what would be required to ensure the provision of adequate treatment" (*Wyatt* v. *Aderholdt*, U.S. Court of Appeals, Fifth Circuit, 503 F. 2d, 1305, 1974).

To examine the major arguments advanced by Alabama state officials, the appeals court abided by the following definition of "treatment" and "habilitation":

Treatment means care provided by mental health professionals and others that is adequate and appropriate for the needs of the mentally impaired inmate. Treatment *also encompasses a humane and psychological environment.* . . . For convenience, in this opinion we group "habilitation" and "treatment" under the single term "treatment," and to include those instances where rehabilitation is impossible in which event the requirement is minimally adequate habilitation, and care, beyond the subsistence level custodial care that would be provided in a penitentiary. [Ibid., n. 1; italics added]

State officials provided two major arguments against the *Wyatt* v. *Stickney* decision. First, the Constitution does not guarantee a right to treatment for persons civilly committed to state mental institutions. Second, the state's justification for civilly committing persons is not that they need treatment, but that there is a "need for care." The mentally ill and retarded chosen for commitment are unable to care for themselves. In effect, the state of Alabama argued that the primary function of civil commitment is to "relieve the burden imposed upon the families and friends of the mentally disabled." The families and friends of the disabled—rather than the mentally disabled themselves—constituted the "true clients" of the system of institutionalization of treatment. This second type of argument is reminiscent of the historical practice of using institutions as a site of indoor relief, in order to save the counties and the families the costs of caring for "dependent and defective persons" (see Chapter 2).

The appeals court disposed of the denial of responsibility for the provision of treatment by citing the court's 1974 decision in *Donaldson* v. *O'Connor* (493 F. 2d, 507, 1974). In that case, the court held that the "only permissible justifications for civil commitment, and for the massive abridgements of constitutionally protected liberties entailed, were the danger posed by the individual committed to himself or to others, or the individual's need for treatment and care." Even when persons were institutionalized because of danger to self or other, treatment had to be provided as society's *quid pro quo* for the extra safety "derived from denial of liberty" (*Wyatt* v. *Aderholdt*, 503 F. 2d, 1305, 1974).

The appeals court responded to the "need for care" (without treatment) argument in two ways. First, even if the court conceded that a need for care is a constitutionally adequate justification, the state would have an "affirmative obligation" to provide a "certain minimum quality of care." In fact, many of the standards required for a "humane and psychological environment" might have to be adhered to by the state. The appeals court argued that

> at least where the right to a "humane environment" is concerned, then it is irrelevant whether the right be viewed as a facet of a "right to treatment," or a "right to care." It is likewise irrelevant for those purposes whether state interest imputed to the civil commitment system be called the need to "treat" the mentally ill, or the need "to care" for them. [Ibid.]

The court further argued that social and economic relief for families, friends, or guardians bearing the burden of providing care was an insufficient constitutional justification for civil commitment. Civil commitments provide too many "massive curtailments" of individual liberty to offset the state's interest in assisting families and friends, whose interests are "trivial" when balanced against the deprivation of liberty involved.

Since the first *Wyatt* v. *Stickney* case, other district and appeals courts have upheld the "least restrictive" and "humane environment" doctrine. A recent GAO report summarized federal court rulings that require that residents move from:

> (1) more to less structured living, (2) larger to smaller facilities, (3) larger to smaller living units, (4) group to individual residences, (5) places segregated from the community to places integrated with community living and programming, and (6) depen-

dent to independent living. The standards imposed in New York went further in requiring that, with certain exceptions, community placements be a noninstitutional residence in the community of 15 or fewer beds for mildly retarded adults and 10 or fewer beds for all others coupled with a program adequate to meet the residents' individual needs. [GAO, January 1977, p. 16]

As of December 1979, the federal courts were utilizing newly developed constitutional standards to assess institutional treatment and care in at least half of the states (President's Commission on Mental Retardation, 1978, pp. 22–40; 1979, pp. 12–22). Although the U.S. Supreme Court has not yet formally ruled on the least restrictive doctrine, it is clear that since 1972, judicial involvement in formulating and implementing DE policies has become extensive. In addition, recent federal statutes have begun to explicitly incorporate the least restrictive and humane environment doctrine. Besides the Developmentally Disabled Assistance and Bill of Rights Act (Pub. Law no. 94-103) and the Education for all Handicapped Children Act (Pub. Law no. 94-142), the Juvenile Justice and Delinquency Prevention Act of 1974 (amended in 1977 as Pub. Law no. 95-115) makes explicit reference to the "deinstitutionalization of juveniles" and the use of "least restrictive alternatives appropriate to the needs of the child" (sec. 223 [a] [12] [B]).

In an effort to comply with the "deinstitutionalization of juveniles" mandate, federal officials have relied on five characteristics to identify least restrictive alternatives: (1) size of residence (under 21 persons, except for certain cases); (2) distance from home; (3) degree of physical security; (4) restricted population mix; and (5) community-based programming (U.S. Office of Federal Register, 16 August 1978; see also Chapter 8).

The Developmentally Disabled Assistance and Bill of Rights Act codifies many of the humane environment rights found in the initial *Wyatt* v. *Stickney* order. The statute asserts that Congress finds that: (1) there exists "a right to appropriate treatment, services, and habilitation for developmental disabilities"; (2) treatment, services, and habilitation should be designed to maximize developmental potential and "be provided in the setting that is least restrictive of the person's personal liberty"; (3) the federal government and the states have an "obligation to assure that public funds are not provided to any institutional or residential program" that does not provide these rights and meet "minimum standards" (42 U.S.C. sec. 6010, 1976). The Pennsylvania U.S. Court of Appeals used this statute in a recent case to conclude that "institutionalization is a disfavored approach to habilitation," and, therefore, there exists a "presumption" that current residents and future admissions to a state facility (Pennhurst) should be placed in community living arrangements (CLAs) rather than in a traditional institution. Pennhurst can only be used for those who cannot be treated in any less restrictive environment and only if that institution is "improved" to meet "statutory requirements" (originally, *Halderman* v. *Pennhurst*, 446 F. Supp. 1295, E.D. Pa., 1977; U.S. Court of Appeals, 3d Circuit, nos. 78-1490, 78-1564, 78-1602, December 1979).

Although the pre-1972 movement of mentally ill and retarded persons out of state institutions was not guided by a least restrictive judicial or statutory doctrine, it is evident that all future policy actions could employ ideal legal standards. Insofar as this doctrine pertains to rights to a humane and psychological environment and least restrictive care and treatment, the doctrine can be used to scrutinize all nonfamilial living arrangements—regardless of size and location— subsidized by public funds. As a matter of fact, the appeals court in *Halderman* v. *Pennhurst* asserted that a court-appointed master had a responsibility to determine that "program deficiencies which were found at Pennhurst are not duplicated on a smaller scale in the CLAs" used as residential alternatives (Ibid.).

While Pennsylvania and other states could follow this policy, they are not obliged to do so on federal statutory grounds according to a U.S. Supreme Court decision of 8 April 1981 (*Pennhurst State School* v. *Halderman*, 67 Legal Edition 2d 694, 101 Sup. Court). By a 6 to 3 vote the justices ruled that section 6010 of the Developmentally Disabled Assistance and Bill of Rights Act "did not create in favor of the mentally retarded any substantive rights to 'appropriate treatment' in the least restrictive environment." Rather, the court held that section 6010 "did no more than express a congressional preference for certain kinds of treatment" (Ibid.). It is now up to each state to interpret and implement this "preference"—rather than "substantive rights" granted by existing federal statute.

Combined Normative-Legal Approach: The GAO Report

A current definition of DE, one that builds on normative and legal approaches, has been proposed in the GAO report on the mentally disabled (i.e., mentally ill and/or retarded):

> Deinstitutionalization . . . can be defined as the process of 1) preventing both unnecessary admission to and retention in institutions, 2) finding and developing appropriate alternatives in the community for housing, treatment, training, education, and rehabilitation of the mentally disabled who do not need to be in institutions, and 3) improving conditions, care, and treatment for those who need institutional care. This approach is based on the principle that mentally disabled persons are entitled to live in the least restrictive environment necessary and lead their lives as normally and independently as they can. [GAO, January 1977, p. 1]

It appears that the GAO report has amalgamated the recommendations of Brown, Bachrach, O'Connor, and judicial rulings. Couched in prescriptive terms, DE strives to achieve the multiple goals of: preventing institutional admissions; providing early discharge of residents; developing nontraditional alternatives; promoting residence in the least restrictive environment; and encouraging normalization and independent living. In addition, the GAO stresses one other goal as intrinsic to DE: the upgrading of traditional institutional care. Including this characteristic indicates that development *within* the traditional institutional sphere, as well as events outside, are of concern, so long as the focus deals with mentally disabled persons. The GAO definition of DE also assumes that all of these major "processes" (i.e., major goals) are compatible, but it is not difficult to hypothesize that financing the upgrading of institutional care can readily conflict with funding and developing alternatives to traditional institutions (see Chapter 10).

The GAO report documented that the federal role in DE had grown so substantially since 1963 "that the amount and types of financial assistance provided; the requirements, standards, and restrictions imposed; and the policies of federal agencies have significantly influenced both the progress made and problems encountered by the states in their efforts" (Ibid., p. 4). The study revealed that 135 federal programs, operated by 11 major departments and agencies, impact directly or indirectly, and estimated that 89 of the programs are operated by HEW. Other federal agencies include HUD, Labor, Justice, and Action. Under these programs, "almost every type of service needed by mentally disabled persons residing in communities can be financed wholly or partly with federal funds." However, the varied direct income maintenance, indirect subsidies, and service programs each have eligibility requirements (such as age, income, and degree of disability) and state limitations that yield a great deal of variability and inconsistency.

After reviewing problems at the national and state level (in Maryland, Massachusetts, Michigan, Nebraska, and Oregon), the GAO tried to identify critical factors contributing to DE problems at a state and federal level. At the state level, investigators found that administrative responsibility for ex-institutional patients was "generally fragmented and unclear." Ex-patients have a variety of needs: education, mental health services, habilitation, social services, medical and dental services, vocational rehabilitation and training, income support, housing, transportation, and employment. However, state and local agencies have not yet "clearly defined, understood, or accepted" the distinctive roles and responsibilities required to address these needs. In addition, "full and well-coordinated support" has not been forthcoming. This lack of support has led to difficulties in financing DE and a lack of, or lack of access to, appropriate facilities and services.

The GAO also pointed out that state mental health and retardation agencies were still devoting "the bulk of their resources to institutional care." Therefore, they must "rely on other agencies for community placement efforts" (Ibid., p. 24). This lack of funds earmarked specifically for DE "has forced states to use whatever funds they could and to maximize federal reimbursement"; the incentive of using federal funds to replace state funds has often resulted in many disabled persons "being shifted from public institutions" to nursing and board-and-care homes—even though the choices may not have constituted "the most appropriate setting" (Ibid., p. 174).

At a federal level, the GAO charged that HEW and other departments have not been sufficiently helpful to states and local communities:

> There has been no clear, comprehensive, consistent federal strategy for helping state and local governments. . . . Such questions as what constitutes acceptable community-based care and who should be treated in various settings have not been answered. In some cases, federal courts have dictated procedures for answering such questions.
>
> In addition, roles, responsibilities, resource commitments, and specific actions to be taken by federal agencies have not been determined. As a result, federal agencies, including HEW, have not addressed deinstitutionalization comprehensively or systematically or given needed attention to it. Federal agency officials and staff administering programs that can or do greatly affect deinstitutionalization have not viewed these programs as affecting it and have not made such an effect an objective. [Ibid., p. 175]

The Federal Conflict over Setting the Policy Agenda: GAO versus HEW

The GAO report on DE was sharply critical of many federal agencies, but particularly of HEW. The GAO charged that there had been a clear "lack of a planned, well-managed, coordinated, and systematic approach to deinstitutionalization" by HEW leaders (Ibid., p. 25). In effect, the GAO charged that HEW lacked both a DE policy and an implementation plan. What the GAO did not realize until it received the HEW response to its criticisms was that HEW and the GAO did not share a common set of assumptions in their definition of the problem. This lack of agreement indicates that defining the critical problems cannot be taken for granted.

On 26 August 1977, HEW responded to the GAO report. Because the response was from officials purportedly representing the views of the newly formed Carter Administration, it could have been written nondefensively, blaming the previous administration for "leadership deficiencies." The HEW authors chose not to do this. On the first page of the response, after deferentially noting the usefulness of the GAO report, the HEW leadership supported the following position:

> We take issue with the Report, however, on the following points:
>
> While we realize that this Report is an effort to find suitable or appropriate settings for individuals whether in institutions or in family or community settings, we believe that the term "deinstitutionalization" is a misnomer. In fact, the most appropriate setting for some individuals at a given point in their lives may well be an institution. The purpose of this effort is to focus attention on the most appropriate means to assist this constituency. For this and other reasons, departmental initiative in this area will avoid conceptualizing goals in terms of deinstitutionalization per se, and instead will be concerned with developing a balanced system of care, making use of a range of facilities and services with emphasis on upgrading and expanding community-based care.

The GAO Report ignores the extremely important issue of recruitment, training and appropriate utilization of the personnel needed for a community-based system of care. This issue is crucial to an effective deinstitutionalization program. [HEW "Comments," August 1977, p. 1]

This direct challenge to the GAO's conception of the problem indicates that HEW's leadership felt very strongly about how the problem was to be conceptualized. The statement openly asserts that "deinstitutionalization is a misnomer" and that the department will "avoid conceptualizing" *any* policy goals within a GAO definition of the problem. This means that HEW will disregard the GAO's emphases on least restrictive environments, least restrictive habilitation/treatment procedures, and normalized care. These emphases are, according to HEW, misplaced, in that the *real problem* is one of "developing a balanced system of care."

At issue here is more than a disagreement about words or concepts. It is a conflict about the substance of HEW's policy focus and direction, allocation of resources, responsibilities, and implementation follow-through. HEW's statement appears to recognize that giving priority to a "least restrictive" policy conceptualization would be at odds with—and probably upset—their conception of a "balanced system." A pro-deinstitutionalization policy is, in fact, likely to be opposed to the status quo arrangements for financing and administering federal welfare programs. A least restrictive policy, for example, could change the current balanced system by requiring that as of a specific date, all resident persons subsidized by federal funds—currently living in any type of facility (regardless of name), under any auspice (public or private), and in any location (in or out of the "community")—should be individually assessed. This assessment would be based on a presumption that the least restrictive environment is preferred. In addition, all proposed admissions to any facility could be assessed with a comparable presumption in favor of the least restrictive doctrine.

The HEW conception of "balance" is never specified. However, the number of persons admitted to, and resident in, traditional institutions is an intrinsic part of defining a "balanced system of care." In the case of one school for the retarded (Willowbrook), for example, there were about 5,200 residents at the time that a class action was filed in the New York Federal District Court in Brooklyn. By the time the case was completed, there were 3,000 residents. The order ratifying a consent decree between the parties projected a 1981 population of 250 (GAO, 1977, p. 220). Was the system "balanced" at 5,200? At 3,000? Or would it be at 250? The HEW position offered no guidelines.

In addition, HEW leaders concerned about balance were unable to provide guidelines regarding who and how many should be admitted to a traditional state institution. In 1962, for example, the first admission rates for state/county mental hospitals of persons 65 years and older was 164 per 100,000 age-specific persons; in 1972 it was 69; and in 1975 it was 37 (see table 8–5). California proposes to reduce the rate to 0 by 1985. At what point would first admissions of aged persons into a state hospital system be in "balance" for aged persons: 164 or 0? And should the rates of nursing home admissions continue to rise to create a new balance of institutionalization?

It is possible that in specifying the initial responses to the GAO, the HEW authors could modify the department's approach to institutions and systems of care. On 17 October 1977, the secretary of HEW set up a task force on deinstitutionalization. After engaging in a series of preliminary meetings and literature searches, the task force issued a departmental paper outlining its "background and purpose," views on a "need for a coordinated effort," and "task force organization." The internal statement of 2 March 1978 was a paraphrase of its earlier response to the GAO as follows:

> In general HEW viewed the GAO Report as especially helpful in pointing out the need for a central federal locus of responsibility for deinstitutionalization and the need for coordination with other federal agencies. . . . However, the term "deinstitutionalization" may be a misnomer. While early proponents of deinstitutionalization refuted the utility and need for institutionalized care, the current meaning of deinstitutionalization based on a decade of implementation, is less dogmatic and rigid. It is now recognized that the need is for a continuum of long and short term institutional and community-based care settings to meet both the mental health and supportive needs of persons who are handicapped by chronic mental disabilities.
>
>   . . . HEW departmental initiatives in this area have attempted to avoid conceptualizing goals in terms of deinstitutionalization per se, and instead are concerned with developing a balanced system of care which makes use of a range of facilities and services, with emphasis on upgrading and expanding community-based care. The ultimate goal is to assure "least restrictive care environments" and "least obtrusive treatment" along a spectrum ranging from community-based programs to quality institutions. [HEW, 2 March 1978]

It appears that the 1977 position has been maintained, but has been slightly toned down. Deinstitutionalization "may be"—not "is"—a "misnomer"; approval of "institutions" as an "appropriate setting" has been omitted, and references to "quality institutions" and "care settings" have been inserted. A major addition is a new sentence about striving to achieve the "ultimate goal" of "least restrictive care environments" and "least obtrusive treatment," but this is linked to the original position of a "balanced system of care" by referring to a "spectrum."

This potential softening of the HEW position suggests that a conflict regarding the definition of the problem may also exist within HEW. There is another indication that a definition of the problem sympathetic to a least restrictive conceptualization exists within HEW. In a background paper prepared for the task force on DE, an HEW official presented a formulation quite different from that proposed in March 1978. The HEW response to the GAO could have been formulated according to this minority view:

> Clearly, the major issue in the care of the mentally disabled is not whether they should be cared for in the community-based settings rather than in institutions or

vice versa but rather, based on federal legislation and court decisions, how the mentally disabled should be cared for in a manner appropriate to their individual needs in the least restrictive environment with the least obtrusive treatment and in a manner which is most cost effective. [HEW, November 1977, p. 14]

This HEW official is willing to set a priority that the earlier department position wanted to avoid. However, the reference to "cost effective" indicates that cost effectiveness can have equal priority—within HEW—as a value in weighing policy preferences. The GAO seems to have anticipated this kind of argument, and formulated a position that appears to differ:

We did not compare the cost of institutional care with community-based care because the relative costs of institutional and community care have not been the criterion for placement under Federal law or court decisions. . . . HEW believes that the state of the art of determining the costs in alternative long-term care settings is still in the early stage of development. In view of Federal legislation and court decisions, however, the most important question appears to be how to most cost effectively serve mentally disabled persons in the least restrictive environment appropriate to their needs. [GAO, 1977, p. 6]

Technically, the difference is between the words "in" and "and." The HEW formulation could imply that cost effectiveness should be considered in addition to other criteria for making a placement decision (or a policy choice); the GAO position implies that placement decisions (and policy decisions) should be based on the "least restrictive" criterion first. Within comparable levels of least restrictiveness, according to the GAO, it is appropriate to consider cost effectiveness (assuming that the "state of the art" permits comparisons). It appears, therefore, that even when HEW officials, in advisory positions, are willing to conceptualize the major issue as providing "least restrictive environments with the least obtrusive treatment," they also provide equal parity to cost effectiveness.

Summary and Conclusions

Understanding the meaning and uses of DE definitions is a necessary first step in assessing trends and issues. It is difficult to engage in empirical or disciplined analyses of trends and issues without establishing the boundaries and defining the basic terms. This is particularly necessary when there are differences of opinion concerning the basic terms. Even if one accepts my contention that there are at least three types of meanings associated with DE—operational, analytical, and normative (with and without legal support)—further scrutiny reveals that there are even differences of opinion within the normative type of meaning.

Utilizing an analytic definition can provide insights into trends, and even confront such issues as characterizing differences between traditional and nontraditional facilities, types and ages of persons living away from home, and relative costs per facility. However, a technical approach cannot assess degrees of "normalization," "least restrictive," or "balanced care" without paying attention to the ideals and rationales related to these normative terms. Nor can an analytical stance per se provide a basis for choosing whether a good community residential facility must exclude nurses and a nursing-type management (e.g., an intermediate care facility) to qualify as a nontraditional type worth including in a national survey (O'Connor 1976).

Normative meanings rely on value preferences and beliefs about people, places, and organizations. Although empirical investigations can sometimes distinguish between reasonable beliefs and values, if relevant data are available (e.g., size of facility and degree of congruence with indicators of normalization), on many occasions choices must be made on the basis of nonscientific criteria. With clearly specified meanings, one can determine how empirical facts can help assess the degree of congruence between ideals and reality, or when judgments and qualitative assessments involve the beliefs and values of policy analysts. For example, on what basis shall we decide whether the achievement of normalized environments is justified, even if it is not yet possible to demonstrate that CRFs with fewer than twenty beds improve the behavioral functioning of MR residents (as indicated by Balla's research review)? It is evident that value choices are involved in accepting normalized living without demonstrated improvement as an "advance" in the treatment/habilitation of MR persons.

Because value choices are buttressed by a growing body of legal opinion and/or legislative policy, it is less controversial for an analyst to make a choice for which official legitimation has been provided. Although normalization per se does not yet appear to have as solid a legal basis of legitimation as least restrictive conditions and humane psychological and physical environment standards, it is reasonable to suggest that minimizing social control, maximizing personal choice, and providing privacy and dignity are quite compatible with the criteria of normalization provided by O'Connor. These criteria specified: location and type of facility; absence of security features; personalized belongings; privacy; homelike furnishings; and noncoercive general atmosphere, management, and physical layout.

If we provisionally accept the normalization standards that are readily congruent with the constitutional position of the least restrictive and humane environment, then a legitimate approach to a federal DE policy could "presumptively" rank preferred living "environments." For adults this policy would favor, in descending order: (1) independent living; (2) living with family, relatives, or friends; (3) supervised apartment living; (4) community residential facilities with fewer than sixteen beds; (5) larger facilities integrated with community living and programs; and (6) small living units within larger facilities. This policy would also favor the reexamination of all federal programs—beginning with the Department of Health and Human Services (formerly HEW)—to determine how to remove impediments and provide incentives to implement this rank order of least restrictive living arrangements.

Whereas many leaders in the fields of MR (and aging) would readily accept these standards, it is uncertain whether MI spokespersons would be willing to substitute an ideal nursing home, ICF-MH type of facility (of unspecified size) for a CRF that is more normalized and less restrictive. The final report of the President's Commission on Mental Health indicates that the leadership is not yet ready to give up its prototype of an ideal community-based facility (i.e., ICF-MH); if so, then this field's definition of DE diverges from the normative-legal one discussed above.

There is greater certainty that as of 1978, the leadership of HEW (now HHS) is unwilling to make a clear choice in favor of a primary valuation of the least restrictive/humane psychological and physical environment doctrine. Rather, they view this proposed policy approach as an ultimate goal. They also seem to be at least as interested, perhaps more, in developing a balanced system and striving for cost effectiveness. The GAO is not disinterested in cost effectiveness; as an accounting agency it could hardly be. But it is curious that accountants emphasize least restrictive environments for the disabled, while leaders of the nation's welfare agency value this ideal on a par with cost effectiveness and balanced systems.

10

Modifying Health and Welfare
Policies and Programs

Until recently DE developed as an expedient policy under the aegis of state leaders taking advantage of opportunities created by expanded health and welfare programs in the 1960s. The policy was guided primarily by an antipathy to institutional living and disenchantment with the institution as a site of treatment or habilitation. Entrepreneurial leaders favored available, or easily developed, community alternatives, funded primarily by categorical grant programs authorized by one or more of the twenty titles contained in the Social Security Act. Each title was originally created for purposes other than DE. From a federal perspective it therefore seems appropriate to view DE as an emergent policy, rather than as the product of a national course of action implemented via federal legislation, regulations, and leadership.

There now exists a firm statutory and constitutional basis for a clear DE policy entailing the modification of all government programs, but particularly of strategic titles comprising the mainstay of DE—the Social Security Act. This purposive policy could be guided by the presumption that all health and welfare programs and funds be administered and allocated on behalf of a least restrictive doctrine, which favors humane and normalized living arrangements for all recipients covered by the Social Security titles. It also includes delivery of treatment/habilitation and supportive services in the least intensive, normalized manner.

Evidence indicates that strategically located HEW (now HHS) leaders appear opposed to implementing this type of policy direction (see Chapter 9). Even more astute officials, who recognize the judicial and statutory bases of a least restrictive policy, imply that "cost effectiveness" must be demonstrated prior to HEW approval of alternatives presumptively less restrictive. Current HHS leaders appear to have adapted and accommodated to the DE levels that have occurred without any national leadership from Washington, D.C. Health and welfare officials seem interested in administering their programs as part of the new "balanced care system." B. C. Vladeck believes that the current leadership is interested in "fine tuning" the current array of unplanned, ad hoc programs (1980, p. 258). Therefore, implementing a purposive DE policy could be extremely difficult without a concomitant change in strategic positions of federal health and welfare leadership, or without interest group pressures, congressional oversight activities, and other forms of political influence.

Aside from the problems of executive and program leadership at the national level, there are statutory, regulatory, and implementation barriers to modifying and redirecting the operations of the Social Security Act. The following discussion aims to identify significant areas that currently impede a more purposive federal initiative on behalf of realizing legitimate policy goals. One strategic impediment is the apparent reluctance of pro-DE advocates to address directly the conflict between financing the upgrading of traditional institutions and promoting alternative living arrangements and programs. In the absence of preferential regulatory guidelines and active monitoring, discretionary federal programs are disproportionately biased in favor of traditional and quasi-traditional institutions (e.g., nursing homes). A second problem involves the failure to deal directly with the inadequate income-maintenance payments and living standards of former and potential institutional residents. Other problems are related to redesigning the proinstitutional bias of Medicare and Medicaid, and addressing the conflicting aims of the nation's major social service program, Title 20. A study of the youth-in-trouble system indicates that the AFDC-Foster Care program (Title 4) is fiscally biased in favor of residential institutions.

Conflict between Upgrading Institutions and Creating Alternatives

The HHS leadership has expressed an interest in "upgrading and expanding community-based care," but this emphasis is balanced by a desire to develop "quality institutions." HHS leaders are not alone in placing a dual emphasis on both community and institutional improvements. The GAO definition of DE favored community living, but also explicitly referred to "improving conditions, care, and treatment of those who may need institutional care." Even judicial rulings, often cited as "lead" cases in expressing the least restrictive doctrine, have this dual thrust.

In *Wyatt* v. *Stickney*, for example, the court ordered staffing and physical improvements, as well as individualized plans to move mentally disabled persons into less restrictive living arrangements. According to the *Wall Street Journal* (18 December 1973), the 1972 order in Wyatt had the effect of raising Alabama's annual expenditures on mental institutions from $14 million in 1971 to $58 million in 1973—a sizable increase in the allocation of state dollars on behalf of traditional institutional programs (Cohen 1980, p. 503).

Besides being costly, it is likely that implementing a judicial policy that includes upgrading can divert scarce resources away from less traditional, more independent, living arrangements and supportive programs and services. In addition, upgrading the traditional institutional system can sustain its legitimacy, as well as reinforce the economic stake of diverse building, service, and professional occupational groups in the maintenance of large, isolated facilities. In general, upgrading is likely to reduce the impact of a DE strategy based on the ideal policy of promoting least restrictive and normalized environments.

A recent nonjudicial effort to upgrade MR facilities and simultaneously move residents into the community provides insight into how a dual emphasis operates as part of the Medicaid program for retarded residents of state schools. In the MR field, since 1972, Title 19 Medicaid funds can be used to reimburse states for housing residents in traditional facilities, providing that the buildings, living spaces, and programs meet hospital-oriented regulatory standards, adapted for a skilled or intermediate care facility for MR persons (SNF/MR and ICF/MR). The regulatory standards for ICF/MR—the category that fits the bulk of MR residents—were to become officially enforceable in January 1977. However, state officials complained vigorously about the cost of upgrading existing facilities to meet ICF-MR standards; they were particularly concerned about the cost of converting existing buildings into four-bed living units, and meeting the associated space and Life Safety Code requirements per resident (State of California Department of Mental Health, 1976). To make the changes required to meet these standards, the State of California estimated it would have to increase spending capital funds over projected levels by $31 to $77 million—depending on the resident population reductions achievable by January 1977 (State of California, DMH 1976, p. 4).

National enforcement of the ICF/MR regulations was delayed for a year, until January 1978. More recently, enforcement was postponed until 18 July 1980— and in special waiver cases until 1982—to correct deficiencies (President's Commission on Mental Health, 1978, vol. 4, p. 1,414). Meanwhile, states that agreed to make the upgrading effort, and that offered visible indicators of building and staffing compliance, could receive Medicaid federal reimbursement *as if they were in full compliance*. This meant that states could receive at least 50 percent of their institutional per diem costs from the federal treasury, and theoretically use the other 50 percent to upgrade institutional facilities to meet ICF/MR standards. Allowable costs that can be used in computing a reimbursable Medicaid rate include: all operating expenses; retirement and other personnel fringe benefits; administrative and supervisory expenses at an institutional and divisional level; and *all* capital improvement costs associated with each bed in a "qualifying building" (State of New Jersey Division of Mental Retardation, June 1978). Between 1973 and September 1978, the Federal Treasury paid out over $3.5 billion for the ICF/MR Program (*Health Care Financing Review*, Winter 1980, p. 107), mostly to state institutions.

A recent plan to upgrade the existing facilities of the New Jersey State Schools for the Retarded into ICF/MR facilities offers further insights into the operation of Medicaid. The plan estimated that Medicaid would allow reimbursement at a rate of $35 per diem for each MR resident living in ICF/MR beds located in "qualifying buildings." Noncomplying beds, located in buildings which could not be renovated to meet ICF/MR regulatory standards, would, therefore, not be Medicaid-reimbursable; in 1980 it was estimated that they would cost the state $30 per diem (State of New Jersey, Division of Mental Retardation, 1978). This means that Medicaid-eligible facilities could cost New Jersey, in 1980, only $17.50 per diem for each resident, rather than the $30 rate generated by ineligible buildings. The differential of $12.50 per diem permits the State of New

Jersey to capture a difference of about $65,000 per diem in 1980 for the eligible persons residing in qualifying buildings—even though the buildings will not be in full compliance until 1982. In 1980 this can result in an annual rate of "new" money (from the federal portion of Medicaid) amounting to about $23,725,000; a comparable amount could be generated in 1981. But the state's new money cannot be used to implement an ideal DE strategy for three major reasons: (1) The New Jersey ICF/MR plan relies on actually converting into "qualifying residences" the buildings containing the eligible residents; (2) the specified capital construction costs and staffing increases must be completed by the waiver deadline of 1982; and (3) by the end of 1982, only a portion of the original total beds will actually qualify for ICF Medicaid reimbursement, thereby reducing the amount of federal funds paid to New Jersey. By relying on the ICF/MR standards of four persons per bedroom unit, requisite square footage, and institutional Life Safety Code requirements, the ideal institutional population size is significantly influenced by the maximum number of beds that can be converted to comply with federal regulations. Out of an original 7,750 beds in 1977, about 2,050 cannot be included in qualifying buildings. Out of the 5,700 qualifying beds, only 3,200 can be generated to meet ICF/MR standards; the remaining 500 beds already meet SNF/MR standards. This could result in a 1982 size dictated by the eligible existing physical plant—3,200 ICF/MR and 500 SNF/MR beds.

Although an institutional reduction to 3,700 persons (from 7,750) could be significant, it is, of course, not the result of a rigorous individual examination of *persons*, aimed at assessing their potential for living in a more normal community setting. Nor is it based on an assessment of recent and potential admissions to estimate future demand. But upgrading is not only influenced by physical plant potential for conversion; it is also influenced by the incentive to "increase Medicaid collections" (Ibid., p. 8). The plan also calls for adding 1,100 "replacement beds" in new buildings. These beds can provide sufficient space to maintain high eligible case-load levels while residents are displaced by renovation. They can also insure that a high level of Medicaid collections will continue after 1982. The planners, therefore, project a total *state* institutional capacity of about 4,800 state beds—rather than 3,700. They also project an increase in subsidized *private* facilities' usage, from 700 to 1,100. This means that the traditional private sector can also upgrade by receiving Medicaid-reimbursable residents, while the state can remain in compliance and obtain its maximum level of federal funding. Both components of the traditional system can benefit.

By 1987, the State of New Jersey expects to reduce the combined public/private traditional institutional system, supported by federal and state Medicaid funds, from 8,450 beds to 5,900 ICF/MR and SNF/MR supported beds—a reduction of 2,550. This is undoubtedly much less than might be expected under an ideal DE policy, inasmuch as the state planners admit that "a large number of our clients were placed in state schools not because of the nature of their disabilities, but, rather, because no other resource was available" (Ibid., p. 22). If New

Jersey followed the earlier DE examples of Minnesota or Nebraska, it might project a resident decrease of about 50 percent over a ten-year period, rather than 30 percent—or a decrease of 4,225, rather than 2,500 persons (see Chapter 5 for examples). If it followed the New York Willowbrook example, the reduction would be much higher (see Chapter 9).

There is strong evidence that New Jersey's upgrading plan reduces the impact of an ideal DE policy. Decisions are primarily influenced by Medicaid collections and building considerations, rather than by individual potential for residing in a more normal environment. New sources of federal funds are mainly diverted toward the segregated public/private traditional institution, rather than the more dispersed, smaller living environments that could be located throughout New Jersey's twenty-one counties. In practice, the dual emphasis of DE and upgrading results in a distinct "presumption" toward the traditional system—or 5,950 MR persons living in upgraded traditional institutions versus 2,500 living in dispersed community residential facilities (by 1987). Although the bedroom units will be smaller in the seven public institutions, average facility size will be reduced from about 1,100 to 525—hardly ideal sites or sizes for realizing normalization values.

It is possible that other states relying on the ICF/MR Medicaid funding mechanism for upgrading might not duplicate the results to be achieved by the New Jersey plan. However, it appears that the number of convertible building units and the maximization of Medicaid collections will continue to be potent influences in states relying on ICF/MR to implement the dual emphasis proposed by HHS, GAO, and the courts.

Whereas this line of analysis appears reasonable, citizen groups and civil liberty advocates in favor of a least restrictive DE policy behave as if they are unaware of the proinstitutional bias of upgrading facilities. They continue to pursue the immediate and full implementation of the 1977 ICF/MR regulations (e.g., President's Commission 1978, pp. 1,410, 1,414, 2,049). They argue that the postponement has "encouraged continued federal support for substandard institutional care." They charge that instead of promoting "quality institutions" in the MR field, HEW officials have permitted MR residents to continue to live in facilities similar to ICF/general nursing homes—twelve persons to a room instead of four. Citizen groups oppose this because they believe that hospital standards are antithetical to living in a "normalized" environment. But ICF-approved hospital units are presumptively less normal than fifteen-bed group homes. This type can also be financed via the ICF/MR program, but only a few states have developed this option on a large scale (see Chapter 3).

The problem of combining upgrading and DE is also posed in the MI field. State mental hospitals receiving Medicaid funds for persons under 22 and over 65 years of age are required to meet hospital-type standards. These are not as stringent as the ICF/MR standards, but substantial upgrading of buildings and staffing ratios in mental hospitals has been required for units housing these age groups (Mulhearn 1974). Besides improving staffing and facilities, states have also been asked to upgrade programs. A recent President's Commission on Mental Health urged institutions to continue to upgrade their "service quality" as part of an overall plan to improve mental health services in the nation. They recommended that:

> the Department of Health, Education, and Welfare, in consultation with state and local governments, develop a national plan for: a) the continued phasing down and where appropriate closing of large state mental hospitals; b) upgrading service quality in those state hospitals that remain; and c) allocating increased resources for the development of comprehensive, integrated systems of care which include community-based services and the remaining smaller hospitals. [President's Commission 1978, vol. 1, p. 22]

To accomplish this plan, it is proposed that the states and the federal government sign formal "performance contracts" to define the goals, responsibilities, and resources required to meet the goals. The contract could provide "a mechanism for consolidating federal funds," and these funds could be augmented with new money. The commission recommends that HEW seek authorization from Congress for "up to 50 million new dollars for each of the next five years." In essence, the commission is proposing only $50 million of new annual money for its ambitious proposal.

Even if such legislation for new funds passed in Congress, it is unlikely that many states would rush to sign up. There are no funds mentioned for the staff, time, and resources required to formulate the plan, write up the contract, negotiate with the federal government, and monitor the performance. In addition, it is proposed that federal funding terminate after five years, leaving the states with unknown regulations and obligations that may have financial consequences for years. States with entrepreneurial leaders are unlikely to be enticed by such a fiscal proposal.

In addition to these problems, there is the issue of insufficient funds. The commission proposes only $50 million for the dual emphasis. Besides the problem of future phasing down and upgrading, the $50 million must compete with the needs of persons who have left the phased down institutions. In light of recent experiences, this effort also requires funding and special attention. For example, the commission depicted the following problems of ex-patients already released:

> Time and again we have learned—from testimony, from inquiries, and from the reports of special task panels—of people with chronic disabilities who have been released from hospitals, but who do not have the basic necessities of life. They lack adequate food, clothing, or shelter. We have heard of woefully inadequate follow-up mental health and general medical care. [Ibid., p. 5]

The commission appears painfully aware of the problems of ex-patients living without the basic necessities. Yet there are no recommendations for increases in the level of income-maintenance programs (see next section). The commission also appears to have learned that follow-up has generally been "woefully inadequate." But there are no extra funds proposed to subsidize the follow-up for expatients. It appears that $50 million of new money is to pay for contracts to overcome *all* of the problems identified by the commission: phasing down existing facilities; upgrading service quality in the remaining facilities; allocating increased resources for community-based services; providing patients with the basic necessities of life; and delivering follow-up services.

Because $50 million obviously is not enough to accomplish these goals simultaneously, it is instructive to read other recommendations to discern priority preferences. The only hints we are offered are the other recommendations requesting new funds: $75 million for new community mental health centers in "underserved areas"; $48 million for research projects; $6 million for research training; and $10 million to continue support of "old" community mental health centers. Inasmuch as old and new community mental health centers are the only other programs noted with specific dollar recommendations, it is reasonable to infer that the commission favors community-based services. However, the historical record indicates that there is a minimal, inconsistent relationship between community mental health centers and DE. Thus, it cannot be assumed that these funds will be of much help to former or potential patients lacking basic necessities or receiving "woefully inadequate follow-up" (see Chapter 6).

In 1980 Congress addressed the proposals set forth by the Mental Health Commission, by passing the Mental Health Systems Act (PL 96-398). Section 202 of the Systems Act authorized the following amount of funds for "services for chronically mentally ill individuals": $45 million of $184 million in fiscal 1982; $50 million of $210 million in 1983; and $60 million of $243 million in 1984. At a minimum, funded projects must include assisting chronically mentally ill persons "to function outside of inpatient institutions to the maximum extent of their capabilities" (sec. 202 [a] [1] [B]). Since no funds were authorized to upgrade state facilities, it is clear that Congress favored a DE policy. Despite this legislative preference the Systems Act has not yet been funded at any level. The budget-cutting actions and block-grant proposals of the Reagan administration offer scant hope that the Systems Act will be implemented on schedule—or in the near future.

Another way to establish a preferential policy on behalf of a general least restrictive doctrine—and away from an institutional bias—is to amend directly the Social Security Act. Instead of amending each title, this goal could be accomplished by inserting a policy obligation in Title 7—dealing with "administration" of the act—and Title 11, providing definitions for "General Provisions and Professional Standards Review." Section 702 of Title 7 orders the secretary of HEW "to perform the duties imposed upon him by the Act," as well as "studying and making recommendations regarding effective methods, legislations, and administrative policy." Section 702 could, for example, be amended to include the following wording (with suggested amendments italicized):

Duties of the Secretary

Sec. 702. The Secretary of Health, Education and Welfare shall perform *and imple-ment* the duties imposed upon him by this Act *in a manner that is least restrictive to each beneficiary for each title*, shall also have the duty of studying and making rec-ommendations as to . . . [U.S. Senate, April 1978, p. 273]

Title 11, section 1101, sets forth definitions applicable to all titles in the Social Security Act. Section 1101 could be amended to include the following definition of "least restrictive," as an addition to other definitions:

Sec. 1101 (a) When used in this Act—

. . . (9) The term "least restrictive" means a 24-hour or long-term living environ-ment and/or program setting that is least restrictive of each beneficiary's personal liberty and provides a humane psychological and physical environment that is as nor-mal as possible, and presumptively favors, in order of preference—

(A) independent living or living with family, relatives, or friends in a home or multiple household dwelling;

(B) supervised apartment living;

(C) free-standing community residential facilities with under 16 beds;

(D) multiple unit facilities, with distinct units of 15 beds or under near or easily accessible to a normal range of religious, shopping, social, and other community facilities that residents are permitted to use;

(E) bedroom units that comfortably sleep 4 persons within larger facilities not near or easily accessible to a normal range of community facilities;

(F) all other temporary or long-term living arrangements."

These amendments, if enacted, would apply to all twenty titles, as well as any subsequent ones. Of course, they would still require actual implementation. In the event that the secretary and "such offices and employees . . . as may be nec-essary for carrying out his functions under this Act" (sec. 703) were deemed lax in implementing an amended section 702, interested parties would have statutory leverage to readily promote compliance. For example, the New Jersey ICF/MR plan (discussed earlier) could be legally attacked in a federal court on the statu-tory grounds that the state plan and its acceptance by HEW officials was illegal because the plan did not provide for the least restrictive living for "each benefi-ciary." According to the suggested amendments, the secretary and his employees would be required to demonstrate that the proposed options of section 1101 (a) (9) (A), (B), (C), and (D) were not possible for *each* one of the beneficiaries of Medicaid funding (Title 19), before authorizing federal payments for (F) until 1982 and (E) after 1982. This type of legal challenge would have a strong chance of success, in that statutory grounds for an attack are generally preferred over constitutional ones (see Chapter 9, *Halderman* v. *Pennhurst* discussion).

Income-Maintenance Problems

Historically, states used Old Age Assistance (OAA) and Aid to Permanently and Totally Disabled (APTD) as primary income-maintenance mechanisms for preventing and reducing the retention of public institutional residents, particularly after 1962. The current replacement for these two grant-in-aid programs is Supplementary Security Income for the Aged, Blind, and Disabled (SSI). Under SSI (Title 16), the federal government for the first time provided a national standard of minimum payments to eligible persons fully funded by the federal treasury. In addition, SSI included a child under 18 as a disabled recipient "if he suffers from any medically determinable physical or mental impairment of comparable severity" to that of an adult (U.S. Senate Committee on Finance, April 1978, sec. 1614 [a] [3] [A]).

Besides setting forth eligibility requirements for a minimum national standard of federal payments, states were mandated to retain prior levels of payment for "old" APTD recipients if the federal SSI payment fell below their earlier income (as of December 1973). States were also permitted discretion to award "optional supplements" to the minimum federal grant for all old and/or new recipients, or they could provide optional supplementation for designated categories of persons or living arrangements. The states had freedom to decide how much these payments would be, and to whom they would be given. By the end of 1978, seven states still provided only a mandatory supplement, twenty-seven states provided limited optional supplementation, and sixteen provided a broad optional supplementation (Hawkins 1980, pp. 23–28).

Originally the SSI program prohibited food-stamp participation, but this was remedied when the next session of Congress extended food-stamp eligibility to most SSI recipients. However, by the end of 1978 California and Massachusetts could not provide this extra benefit, "because their state supplementary payments included the cash equivalent of the food-stamp bonus" (Ibid., p. 22). As of July 1975, automatic cost-of-living increases in federal SSI benefits became part of the program; these increases were coordinated with Old Age Security and Disability Insurance (OASDI) cost-of-living increases, so recipients eligible for funds from both programs would not receive a double inflation rate increase. Some states chose to maintain the level of their prior optional supplement payments and did not pass along these federal SSI cost-of-living increases. Mandatory supplement payments were also reduced or eliminated in some states. In an effort to deal with the reduced standard of living for many SSI recipients, an amendment was passed to require states to pass along the cost of living increases, as of June 1977. However, states were considered in compliance if they could demonstrate that they expended the same or higher state payments in a 12-month period as had occurred during the preceding 12-month period. States with limited or "broad" optional supplementation did not have to keep up with inflation; mandatory supplement states were not affected because their payments were keyed to December 1973 (Ibid., p. 22).

Besides the continued federal-state complexity of public assistance for the aged, blind, and disabled, two major impediments are associated with the current legislation: payments are too low, and payments are reduced by one-third if SSI recipients reside "in the household of another" (if the household is considered noninstitutional).

Alternatives to institutions must, at a minimum, provide food, shelter, clothing, and basic amenities. The President's Commission on Mental Health recognized this fact, but failed to address the issue (see last section). For an unknown number of SSI recipients, attaining an independent living arrangement that can provide a minimum quality of life standard is beyond their financial capability. Aviram and Segal illustrate this point with the following summary based on an interview with a former mental patient, residing in one of the board-and-care homes in their 1976 California sample:

> Jane is in her mid 40s. She was hospitalized for two years. She will have lived in this board-and-care home for two years this February. She likes it better than the hospital as one is *free to come and go as one pleases*. She didn't like the state hospital and feels freer now. When asked about what she does, it seems TV is a major activity. She sometimes goes to a nearby coffee shop that a lot of board-and-care residents frequent, as one can get as much coffee as one wants for $0.20—some stay there a good part of the day. She also goes to a pizza parlor. Sometimes she walks in the neighborhood and occasionally goes out to a shopping center. When asked about wanting to move to an independent living situation, she said *she couldn't afford it with rent, food, utilities*, and *probably needing a car to get around*. She seemed to feel living in the community was fine, except it got "boring sometimes." [Segal and Aviram 1978, p. 271; italics added]

For Jane, and for over 90 percent of the residents of shelter-care facilities in California, support came totally or in part from welfare grants; 75 percent received their income solely from federally supported SSI. As Segal and Aviram note, "to a large extent consumptive patterns in this population are determined by factors external to their control—the policies of their benefactors" (Ibid., p. 137). In March 1976, the maximum combined monthly federal and state SSI payment for disabled persons living in California out-of-home placements (or in their own home) was about $306. At that time the federal maximum was $157, and the maximum California supplement was about $149—one of the highest supplements in the nation. Inasmuch as both of these amounts are conditional on having no other countable unearned or earned income or resource—and living in one's own household or a "supervised living arrangement"—the average combined payment in California was less than $306; it was actually about $247 per month (Kochhar 1977).

By April 1980, the average combined federal and state SSI payment for disabled persons in California amounted to $250—a gain of only $3 per month since 1976. Meanwhile, the Consumer Price Index (CPI) during this four-year period rose from 170.5 to 242.6—or a cost-of-living increase of about 41 percent (*Social Security Bulletin*, August 1980, pp. 36, 53). As a result, California is now paying its disabled SSI recipients at a standard of living level about 40 percent below what recipients received in 1976. Evidently, California is attempting to restrict state increases in supplementary payments, while complying with the law's requirement that it maintain a minimum level of supplementary effort. Other states that in 1974 started from a lower level of optional supplementation appear to be behaving in a comparable fashion. For example, in January 1974— the starting date of SSI—and September 1979, other industrialized states (classified as providing "broad optional supplementation," except for Ohio) provided *state* SSI grants to disabled persons, as shown in table 10–1.

During the same time period the CPI increased from 147.7 to 223.7—an inflation rate of over 51 percent. None of the industrialized states came close to matching this inflation rate, except Pennsylvania; however, Pennsylvania started with such a low supplement that it was still far from California's state grant of $119.

Federal SSI payments for the disabled increased nationally from $106 to $144 from January 1974 to September 1979—a gain of 36 percent. This increase did not match the inflation rate because SSI was amended to provide federal cost-of-living increases as of July 1975—but not retroactively to compensate recipients for the January 1974 to July 1975 rate of inflation. Aside from the real income loss occurring with state supplements (mandatory and/or optional), SSI federal payments also had a real income loss since 1974. Because fewer than half of the nation's disabled SSI recipients qualify for Social Security or receive other forms of income, it is not surprising that the president's commission discovered former mental patients "who do not have the basic necessities of life." In the absence of a fair and reasonable SSI income-maintenance standard, many former and potential institutional residents live in circumstances below the poverty threshold.

Not surprisingly, many SSI recipients choose to remain in board-and-care homes, even though they offer poor environments and are often criticized by journalists, state investigation commissions, and the Senate Committees on Long-Term Care (see Chapter 3). Given their levels of income, SSI recipients receive what they can afford. If an SSI recipient were "living in another person's household and receiving support and maintenance in kind from such person," the federal payment would be reduced by one-third (sec. 1612 [a] [2] [D]). This restriction on living with a family member, relatives, or a friend does *not* apply to a residential facility. This statutory policy discourages persons from pooling meager resources and living with a friend or relatives. Paradoxically, living in a board-and-care home can qualify one for an added supplement in most states (Kochhar 1977).

To encourage disabled persons to live with relatives or friends in shared and semiindependent living arrangements, it would seem fair and reasonable to remove the one-third reduction restriction. If this were done, it might be possible for the least restrictive residence—independent and semiindependent living—to compete more fairly with the higher optional payments associated with board-

TABLE 10-1

Comparison of State SSI Grants to Disabled Persons (per month)

State	1974	1979	Percent Difference
California	$110	$119	8%
Massachusetts	91	85	− 7
Michigan	51	66	23
New Jersey	48	34	−29
New York	74	57	−23
Ohio	44	30	−32
Pennsylvania	24	33	38
Total U.S.	73	79	8%

SOURCES: Hawkins, March 1980, p. 91; Callison, June 1974, p. 8.

and-care or nursing home facilities in many states. It is unlikely that a DE policy can be implemented without paying attention to this and other strategic income-maintenance problems (for further proposals, see National Association for Retarded Citizens, 18 March 1977).

A reasonable national solution to the twin problems of inadequate benefits and "living in the household of another" would require federalizing the total grant necessary to guarantee all SSI recipients the right to a decent standard of living. This is necessary to overcome the sharp discrepancies in supplementation between the states. Federalization of the entire SSI program could, of course, mean a potential windfall to the states. In 1979–80, the annual level of state funds spent on state supplementation (whether federal- or state-administered) was about $1.9 billion for all categories of SSI recipients (*Social Security Bulletin*, August 1980, pp. 34, 37).

The legislation federalizing SSI could be drafted to require states to use windfall funds to finance mortgages for the construction or rehabilitation of buildings compatible with a least restrictive doctrine—particularly nonprofit group homes with fifteen or fewer beds, and multiple-unit apartment buildings (with and without space for congregate-type dining rooms). Each unit utilizing these funds could also become eligible for public housing rental subsidies, thereby ensuring that the special housing constructed for the aged, blind, and physically and mentally disabled would be affordable.

The windfall SSI legislation could refer to an initial five-year period of state funding for community housing alternatives. At that time the results of the construction and/or rehabilitation of such alternatives could be assessed. By that time, too, states would have amassed about $10 billion of a variety of mortgages. The portion of rental funds allocated to mortgage repayments could help the original funds "turn over" and be used for other projects. State mortgage financing agencies might be the most likely administrative agencies to operate a national program directly earmarked to provide the "seed" money for community alternatives, money that until now was unavailable for this purpose (GAO, 7 January 1977 and 30 September 1980).

HHS leaders might want to raise the issue of cost effectiveness. But it is difficult to fathom how they would compare living above a poverty threshold with living without "the basic necessities of life." Although the existing policy is certainly cheaper, low cost and cost effectiveness are not equivalent concepts. In theory, cost effectiveness analysis would include a comparison of alternatives designed to accomplish *similar* goals. However, the policy of a federally guaranteed minimum income level, funded at a minimum level of decency, is quite unlike the current system of substandard federal-state SSI payments. Therefore, the issue is not one of comparing the relative costs of equally desirable outcomes; it is whether the nation wishes to subsidize adequate or substandard levels of living. Adequacy of living levels and economic efficiency are distinct evaluative concepts that should not be confused.

The Medicaid Bias toward Institutional Care

In 1977 Medicaid expenditures for direct mental health services were estimated to total $4.1 billion (President's Commission on Mental Health 1978, vol. 2, p. 520). In Table 10–2 the distribution categorized by site of services discloses an unusual bias toward institutional-based mental health services.

The preponderance of funding in the institutional sector is striking. However, not all of these funds are actually used for remediation efforts. Medicaid does not publish any separate breakdowns for: personal and social care functions; food, shelter, and basic amenities; supervision and custodial functions; clinical treatment; drugs; and supportive and social services. It is also important to note that MI fiscal accountants classify ICF/MR facilities as "mental health services." Eliminating this type of facility would reduce Medicaid funding for MI institutions to about $2.9 billion, and the total amount to $3.4 billion. Excluding ICF/MR funds, these sites account for about 65 percent of all estimated Medicaid funds associated with direct mental health services (or $2.2 billion out of $3.4 billion).

Medicaid's institutional bias is also evident if all types of medical services are assessed for any reimbursable problems. In 1972 about $6.3 billion in Medicaid vendor payments were recorded. Of this amount about 41 percent was paid to general hospitals, 23 percent to nursing homes, and about 2 percent to state mental hospitals—a total of 66 percent. In 1976 Medicaid payments increased to a total of $14.1 billion. Of this amount, general hospital decreased to 28 percent, nursing homes increased to 33 percent, 4 percent went to state mental hospitals, and 4 percent to the new SNF/MR and ICF/MR hospital programs—a total of 69 percent. Two years later (1978) the public treasuries—federal and state—spent

TABLE 10–2

Estimated Expenditures of 1977 Medicaid Funds for Mental Health
Services (in millions of dollars)

	Estimated
Institutional MI Services	*Expenditures*
Nursing homes (SNF and ICF)	$2,189
ICF/MR	702
State, county, and private hospitals	558
Residential treatment centers	110
Subtotal	$3,559
Mixed Institutional/Outpatient	
General hospital – inpatient and outpatient	185
Outpatient MI Services	
Drugs	110
CMHCs	100
Physicians and other practitioners	82
Private free-standing clinic	25
Total	$4,061

SOURCE: President's Commission on Mental Health, 1978, vol. 2, p. 520.

about $18.1 billion. Nursing homes continued to be the largest service purchased—34 percent. General hospitals received 28 percent, institutions for the retarded increased to 7 percent, and state mental hospitals received 3 percent. Institutions now receive about 72 percent of all Medicaid funding. By contrast, only $211 million, or 1 percent of all Medicaid payments, was earmarked for "home health" care services (*Health Care Financing Review*, Winter 1980, p. 107).

Home Care versus Institutional Care for the Elderly

Whether viewed from a mental health or a general health services perspective, it is clear that public funds designed for the medically needy are primarily funding institutional programs. Within this general funding priority nursing homes have become the fastest growing and largest health care category (Ibid.). Because nursing homes (excluding SNF/MR and ICF/MR) are primarily populated by persons 65 years and over, this growth is related to the increasing reliance on Medicaid as a means of funding within an institutional context the varied medical, social, and personal problems of old age. This is not by design, but because

Medicare limits the nursing home–care benefit to only 100 days of skilled nursing care per benefit period, that must follow at least three days of hospitalization (Social Security Act, Title 18, sec. 1812 [a] [2]).

Recent studies of demonstration projects suggest that many elderly persons currently residing in nursing homes could receive medical, personal, and social services in a noninstitutional context (GAO, 26 November 1979, Chapter 5; Vladeck 1980, Chapter 10; U.S. Congressional Budget Office, 1977). One of the more comprehensive demonstration projects, in Monroe County, New York, has focused on assessing elderly candidates for nursing care prior to placement. Both Medicaid and non-Medicaid clients have been included. Each of the 3,750 elderly persons receiving a comprehensive assessment of problems was classified as needing one of the following levels of care: skilled nursing facility level care (SNF); intermediate care facility level care (ICF); or domiciliary level care. The project demonstrated that 54 percent of the SNF, 74 percent of the ICF, and 76 percent of the domiciliary care clients remained in the community by being assisted with a "package" of services, which could include one or more of the following: medical; home nursing; home health aide; homemaker; personal care; chore/home repair; home-delivered meals; shopping assistance; transportation; adult day care; housing assistance; congregate housing; day hospital; social/recreational; legal and financial; information and referral (GAO, 26 November 1979, pp. 74, 133).

Data on Monroe County, one of the few demonstration projects to include non-Medicaid patients, provided information about two significant variables that distinguished whether elderly nominees for out-of-home care could be kept out of a facility. First, there was a sharp difference between Medicaid and non-Medicaid patients: 66 percent of Medicaid SNF clients remained in the community, but only 44 percent of the non-Medicaid clients were cared for outside of a facility. Second, there was an even greater difference in source of referral: 86 percent of community-referred SNF and only 31 percent of hospital-referred SNF clients remained in the community; and 86 percent of community-referred ICF versus 45 percent hospital-referred ICF clients remained in the community. Before concluding that the more affluent prefer institutional facilities, and that hospital referral agents have a greater ideological affinity toward medical-type living arrangements, it may be prudent to consider other explanations offered by project staff. A non-Medicaid person may be admitted to a nursing home much more rapidly than a Medicaid patient because the "private rate" is higher. In addition, non-Medicaid persons would have to pay for noninstitutional services, but third-party payments—primarily via Medicare—would pay primarily for nursing home or hospital care (Ibid., p. 136).

Projects like Monroe County suggest the diversionary potential of comprehensive assessments of both nonmedical and medical problems of the elderly. However, none has been conducted under such stringent conditions that it is certain that all of the assessed clients would, in fact, have been placed in a facility. Because of this possibility, a number of analysts have suggested that expanded home care programs could become "add ons" to the existing system, rather than substitutes for institutional care (U.S. Congressional Budget Office, 1977; GAO, 26 November 1979; Vladeck 1980). If this occurred, the Medicaid cost would continue to increase without any compensating benefits. In HEW terms, it would not be "cost-effective." Although nursing home care has yet to be proven cost-effective, the current debate accepts this form of care as part of the existing system and treats the least restrictive options as add ons.

It could be argued that add ons are still socially useful because most impaired elderly persons are cared for by families, not nursing homes. A 1977 Congressional Budget Office (CBO) study estimated that the current ratio of non-institutionalized personal care services to institutional services is approximately 1½:1 (CBO, 1977). However, a recent report by an HEW Long-Term Care Task Force estimates that the ratio could easily be between 2 and 4:1 (Callahan et al. 1980, p. 35). A recent review of family assistance to disabled or impaired persons concludes that the family directly assists between 60 to 85 percent of all impaired elderly persons (Ibid.). If the nonreimbursable care provided by family members were to diminish by even a small percentage, the demands for long-term institutional care could, of course, increase accordingly. Policy designs, therefore, have begun to consider family assistance and "incentives" in order to support the tradition of families caring for their elderly members (Ibid.; Moroney 1976).

Although many legislators and HEW leaders might express sympathetic sentiments about the plight of the impaired and their families, their major concern appears to be influenced by the soaring costs for nursing home care. The problem, according to this view, is to reduce the annual rate of increased costs of the SNF and ICF programs. HEW is interested in continuing the demonstration projects on a limited scale to find the most cost-effective approaches to nursing home care (see HEW response to GAO report on *Entering a Nursing Home—Costly Implications of Medicaid and the Elderly*, 26 November 1979, App. 1). GAO analysts propose that Congress enact legislation to authorize community-wide demonstration projects on a long-term basis in several areas, "to obtain more information on costs, people who could be served, service utilization and total system effects" (Ibid., p. 164). The proposals of the two agencies differ on the length of the demonstration and its geographical breadth. However, the GAO's proposed demonstration is more focused, in that their proposal would create a new mechanism to rule on the admissions of all nursing home applicants whose care would be reimbursed by Medicaid or Medicare.

The mandated intervention proposed by the GAO would occur as part of a strategy to reduce "avoidable institutionalization." This plan would employ the following strategic concepts: (1) a nursing home gate-keeping mechanism to keep people out; (2) a comprehensive needs assessment of nonmedical, as well as medical, factors; (3) a mechanism for planning, coordinating, and monitoring community-based services; (4) a single, comprehensive source of funding to replace fragmented dollar sources; and (5) controls over costs and utilization. The

GAO proposal would legislate mandatory comprehensive needs assessments for all applicants claiming reimbursement by Medicaid or Medicare (Ibid., pp. 123, 162). Although it would not include private patients and persons reimbursed by nongovernmental third-party payments, the proposal could affect a significant proportion of nursing home residents. In 1978, public funds (i.e., primarily Medicaid and/or Medicare) paid for about $8.4 billion out of $15.8 billion expended for all nursing home care—about 53 percent. By 1985 the projected cost of nursing home care is estimated to rise to $42 billion, with the public sector funding about 52 percent of the cost (Freeland et al. 1980, p. 17).

The proportion of elderly nursing home residents relying on public funding— and, therefore, eligible for screening—could be higher than 52 to 53 percent, inasmuch as many persons start out as private payers; after exhausting personal or insurance resources as well as Medicare, they "spend down" and become eligible for Medicaid funding. A 1976 survey of institutionalized persons in nursing homes found that over 70 percent of the sample had a record of mixed or total public funding (Liv and Mossey 1980, p. 54). Under the GAO proposal, an unknown portion of these residents would receive mandated screening only after they had first been admitted as private payers (and then applied for public funding).

To promote the broadest voluntary compliance and mandated coverage of the medical-social needs assessment, the GAO proposes that this assessment service be included as an additional benefit under both Parts A and B of Medicare (without a co-insurance requirement). However, the GAO proposes that the actual in-home or community-based service be financed as a welfare program, out of general revenues; the costs would be shared with states, as in the Medicaid program. Control over costs and utilization of services would be achieved by limiting reimbursement to a fixed percentage of the cost of the "appropriate level of institutional care." Because total program costs are unknown, the GAO suggests that the service part of the plan be implemented on a demonstration basis.

Although the costs of the GAO proposal are not set forth, estimates have been projected for an expansion of services to the elderly. The Congressional Budget Office prepared the following estimates of the costs for a broadened Medicare insurance plan that would include "universal coverage for nonpsychiatric long-term care through an entitlement program for all aged and disabled" (CBO, 1977, p. 40). Determinations of need would be made through local community long-term care centers (similar to the GAO proposal). But services of all types would be provided: skilled and intermediate care facilities; personal care homes; congregate housing, foster care; liberalized home health care; home care (homemaker, personal care, social and nutrition service); and adult day care. Projected costs for 1980, 1982, and 1985 were generated on the basis of the projected elderly population, estimates of impairment, and probable service supply growth. Table 10–3 presents these projections by service categories and the expected incremental (i.e., "add on") federal costs.

These projected incremental federal costs are lower than the total projected

TABLE 10-3

Distribution of Total Incremental Federal Costs of Medicare Long-Term Care Insurance
Programs, by Fiscal Years 1980, 1982, and 1985 (in billions of dollars)

Service	1980	1982	1985
Institutional care	$9.6	$13.7	$20.2
Sheltered living and congregate housing	0.1–1.7	0.3–3.1	1.5–6.4
Home-based services	1.0–1.9	2.1–5.5	5.9–22.5
Administration	0.3	0.4–0.6	0.7–1.2
Total	$11.0–14.0	17.0–23.0	28.0–50.0

SOURCE: U.S. Congressional Budget Office, August 1977, pp. 43, 44.

costs because the expanded insurance program would replace Medicaid and some
Medicare and VA spending for the specified population groups. CBO analysts
estimate that the total incremental federal costs could be $11 billion–$14 billion
in 1980, and $28 billion–$50 billion in 1985. The largest costs in the CBO estimate are for out-of-home care costs. If the expanded insurance coverage were
limited *only* to home-based services, the incidental costs could be much less for
each projected year: $1.7 billion–$1.9 billion in 1980; $2.1–$5.5 billion in
1982; and $5.9 billion–$22.5 billion in 1985. Administration costs would be reduced accordingly, but these would be modest reductions.

A third proposal concentrates on drastically reducing the nursing home population in a five-year period. Vladeck proposes to use these former institutional
funds for home care and other alternative arrangements and services. He is less
concerned with the governmental funding mechanism than with accomplishing a
one-third reduction in nursing home beds. Vladeck's proposals are based on his
assessment that the nursing home population consists of three distinct categories.
Group I contains elderly persons who stay only a short time (less than 6 months);
these early discharges include persons recuperating from acute illnesses (with
homes to return to) and those who are fatally ill; they utilize 10 percent of the
current nursing home days and could be better served in local general hospitals.
Group II contains persons chronically and socially ill, but not entirely helpless;
this group utilizes about 40 percent of the current nursing home days. Group III
contains those persons who actually need "round-the-clock custodial care," due
to "moderate to severe senility or other severe psychiatric or physical disability
(e.g., entirely bedfast)"; this group utilizes the remaining 50 percent of the current home days (Vladeck 1980, p. 222). Based on this assessment, Vladeck proposes the following "maximalist program for reform of nursing home and long-
term care services":

> 1. A reduction of existing nursing-home capacity by one-third over a five year pe-
> riod, with a target average occupancy of 75 percent in 1985 (with unused beds
> "stockpiled" to be put back into services as the over-seventy-five population and the

number of extremely disabled grows). That reduction should be achieved by closing nursing homes of the lowest quality.

2. Conversion of 100,000 to 125,000 currently unused or under-used acute-care hospital beds to extended-care facility beds, admission to which would be contingent on expectation of death or discharge home within six months, and reimbursement for which would be on the basis of these incremental costs to the hospital (which would be in the range of current rates for high quality SNFs).

3. Creation of 250,000 or so additional units of congregate housing—in existing buildings to the extent possible.

4. A substantial expansion of services in the home, directed by local gatekeeping agencies, financed at least initially on a block-grant or capitation basis with the funds saved from closing nursing home beds, combined with existing funds for categorical services. Those services should be provided on an abililty-to-pay basis. There probably won't be enough to go around.

5. A redoubling of regulatory and other quality control mechanisms in nursing homes, abandoning the methodology of rehabilitation and concentrating on basic personal care, food, and protective services to ensure that an increasingly sicker nursing home population does not suffer the consequences of complete desertion by society." [Ibid., pp. 240–41]

Vladeck believes that this plan can be accomplished a "little bit at a time." The only "indispensable element" is that "the supply of nursing home beds must be tightly controlled and admissions to scarce beds must be limited to those for whom there simply aren't any other alternatives." Relative to this requirement, the "exact balance" between varied services or living arrangements, the "details" of gatekeeping operations, or the "precise specification" of the physical characteristics of extended care facilities are "just not very important" (Ibid., p. 241).

Unlike the CBO or GAO proposals, Vladeck concentrates primarily on reducing existing bed capacity. If his approach were combined with a mandated screening mechanism, then critical discretionary decisions about nursing home use could be much more tightly controlled. However, Vladeck and the GAO are unwilling to propose an adequate, stable array of alternative home care services to accompany the control of nursing home utilization. In the absence of noninstitutional services, it is quite likely that the proprietary board-and-care industry would expand.

The recent history of DE in the mental health field indicates that the impaired elderly not placed in nursing homes would be disproportionately placed in board-and-care homes; they would be ignored at best or abused at worst. Rather than repeating old mistakes, it would be politically and morally prudent to create enough alternative services to replace Vladeck's Group II nursing home placements. It appears evident, therefore, that a consistent least restrictive policy for the aged would insist on creating actual services prior to, and simultaneously with, the reduction in nursing home admissions. The service would only be provided to eligible persons approved by a medical and nonmedical screening team—comparable to the 1962 Geriatric Screening Project in California (see

Chapter 6) and recent demonstration projects. These services would be provided to persons residing in apartments, homes, public housing, board-and-care homes, and congregate-type facilities—but only after a mandated screening.

Medicare, as a nationally accepted adjunct of Social Security insurance, would be the logical financial and organizational mechanism to fund and administer a universal program for the elderly (and insured disabled from OASDHI). The funding could come from the general revenues, added Social Security taxes, or a combination of the two. A new Medicare program—Part C, as an amendment to Parts A and B—could be the conduit for funding the necessary short- and long-term home care services, as well as the combined medical and social assessment of impaired functioning. The choice of gatekeeping, service delivery, and delivery mechanism could be adapted to local needs, interests, and personnel resources. For ineligible elderly persons, Part C could be subsidized by Medicaid funds.

According to the CBO estimate of this universal provision of services to eligible elderly and disabled insured persons, the projected incremental cost would be between $5.9 billion and $22.5 billion by 1985. Inasmuch as the coverage for institutional care would not be expanded, and the sheltered living and congregate housing *not* included as a new service, these incremented costs would be absent. Part of the incremental costs for home care could be offset if nursing home utilization were stabilized at 1980 levels. A greater amount of the costs could be offset if reductions in nursing home days occurred.

According to the latest projections by technical staff of the Health Care Financing Administration (HCFA), nursing home costs paid by the public sector are expected to rise by 93.8 percent from 1980 to 1985—from $11.3 billion to $21.9 billion, if recent patterns of use and inflation continue (Callahan et al. 1980, table 5). However, if only the inflation rate predicted for the consumer price index projection is used, and if utilization is stabilized at a 1980 rate, then it can be estimated that nursing home costs might only increase by 35.1 percent—from $11.3 billion to $15.3 billion (Ibid., based on table 2). This projected savings of about $6.9 billion (i.e., $21.9 billion vs. $15.3 billion) could occur if the proposed screening program met the minimal goal of eliminating any increases in nursing home days by 1985. If the lowest CBO home care cost estimate were realized, then the nursing home stabilization benefit could more than offset any increased cost ($6.9 billion–$5.9 billion). If the higher CBO figure occurred, based on the highest estimate of demand and the fastest rate of supply growth, then the insurance program would, of course, not be cost effective by HEW standards.

However, if Vladeck's estimate of 40 percent inappropriate nursing home placements is correct (i.e., Group II, "chronically ill and socially isolated, but not helpless"), the cost of nursing home days could be reduced by 40 percent by 1985. This could mean that estimated nursing home costs would be $9.2 billion in 1985, rather than $21.9 billion. The potential saving of $12.7 billion would provide a substantial benefit to balance against the projected CBO home care insurance cost of $5.9 billion–$22.5 billion. If attention were given to "fine tuning" the proposed Medicare home care proposal so it would not cost more than $12.7 billion by 1985, it is possible that targeted goals could be set up at a national, state, and local level to achieve nursing home reductions *and* home care service growth.

Achieving these goals might require an expanded housing program, as suggested by Vladeck. The states would provide the funds out of the proposed federalization of SSI (see earlier section on SSI). In addition, realizing these goals might require an essential human ingredient: qualified leaders committed to DE goals and the noninstitutional welfare of the elderly and disabled. If leaders interested in achieving a 40 percent nursing home reduction and the creation of home care services were appointed to strategic leadership positions, it is still possible that all of the targeted goals might not be achieved by 1985. From the perspective of a least restrictive policy, rather than the position of economic efficiency, the risk of add on costs for increasing the welfare of the impaired elderly and insured disabled might be accepted as a necessary price to pay for realizing DE ideals. It may, in fact, cost "add on" dollars for five, ten, or fifteen years in order to undo the policy mistakes of the past two decades associated with the disproportionate reinstitutionalization of the elderly into nursing homes. The experience of DE in California indicates that a lengthy time-frame may be necessary to realize the fiscal benefits of new policies (see Chapter 6).

Consumer and Cross-National Perspectives on Home Care

From a consumer perspective, available data indicate that elderly persons, by a wide margin, prefer living and receiving services in their own homes, as opposed to a nursing or board-and-care home (GAO, 26 November 1979, pp. 8–9; Callahan et al. 1980; and CBO, 1977). Survey data also reveal that older people, as consumers, are selective about the services they prefer. These preferences should be taken into account in the design of a nationally funded, but locally administered, home care service program.

In a recent survey of elderly in Cleveland, where people were classified according to their objective need for home help—according to the types of impairment reported—it is clear that home help services were readily acceptable. Over 75 percent of the people surveyed responded affirmatively to the need for the following types of home help services: personal care to dress, eat, groom, and bathe; homemaker to perform necessary housework and prepare meals; and administrative and legal expertise to handle money problems (GAO, April 1977, p. 25). Evidently home help is acceptable from strangers, as well as from family and friends.

By contrast, of those impaired economically, 52 percent expressed a need for more financial aid or food stamps. Only 21 percent of those impaired in social functioning expressed a need for social/recreational services. Of those judged to

TABLE 10-4

International Comparisons of Use of Home Care: 1973 and 1976
(per 100,000 population)

Country	1973 Home Helpers/ 100,000 Population	1976 Home Helpers/ 100,000 Population
United States	15	29
West Germany	19	22
Great Britain	138	265
Netherlands	405	599
Norway	577	840
Sweden	825	923

Source: Little 1978, p. 284.

be impaired in mental health, only 8 percent expressed a need for psychiatric services; however, 35 percent said they need psychoactive drugs.

The need and willingness to accept home help is not unique in America. In Sweden one out of three aged persons receiving a pension is a recipient of home help services. In Stockholm these services include: personal care, shopping, cooking, care of clothes, foot care, and housekeeping. Additional services are also available through the "home help organizer." In fact, "clients are urged to talk to their home helpers about any personal practical problems, so a good deal of informal counseling as well as reduction in social isolation takes place" (Little 1978, p. 285).

Compared to other nations of the world, the United States has lagged far behind in the provision of home care. An International Council on Home-Help Services, based in Utrecht, Netherlands, has gathered information for selected countries, for the periods of May 1973, and December 1976, as shown in table 10-4.

It is clear that a number of countries have made an extensive investment in providing this kind of new personal service. In the absence of a Medicare provision for home care services, the major federal funding source in the United States, since 1974, is Title 20 of the Social Security Act. Additional funds are also available via the Older Americans Act of 1965. Because Title 20 is also the primary source of social services for other interest groups, it is important to understand how these funds can promote or impede an ideal DE policy.

Social Services under Title 20

Between 1935 and 1956 the federal government did not reimburse states for providing any social services to recipients of public-assistance grants. In 1962 the federal reimbursement rate was changed from 50 to 75 percent; purchase of care was permitted, and former and potential recipients were included in order to emphasize the prevention and rehabilitation of economic and social dependency. However, the boundaries of the key term—"social services"—were not specified in legislation or in the regulations (Derthick 1975). The 1967 amendments permitted greater federal subsidization of social services by further easing the eligibility standards and by legitimating the purchase of services between government agencies.

Because these legislative provisions were primarily permissive rather than mandatory, not all states took full advantage of these service and fiscal opportunities. By 1971, an entrepreneurial state like California had been able to capture "over one-third of the federal service money expended the previous year" (Mott 1976, p. 11). As other states finally discovered the open-ended potential of the social service amendments, claims for federal reimbursement soared from $746 million in 1971 to an estimated $4.7 billion for fiscal 1973. In October 1972, Congress set a cap of $2.5 billion for all social-service reimbursements, to be divided among the states according to a set formula. In October 1975, Title 20 was added to the Social Security Act, setting forth new ground rules specifying how states could apply for and spend the capped federal funds for social services (Mott 1976; Derthick 1975).

Instead of being subject to precise requirements for carefully defined services for specific types of eligible persons, states are relatively free to: define the services to be offered; choose the services actually offered; and decide where, how, and to whom they want to provide the services. States are expected to direct their efforts at meeting five legislative goals: (1) achieving or maintaining economic *self-support* to prevent, reduce, or eliminate dependency; (2) achieving or maintaining *self-sufficiency*, including reduction or prevention of dependency; (3) preventing or remedying *neglect, abuse, or exploitation* of children and adults unable to protect their own interests, or preserving, rehabilitating, or reuniting families; (4) preventing or *reducing inappropriate institutional care* by providing for community-based care, home-based care, or other forms of less intensive care; or (5) securing referral or admission *for institutional care* when other forms of care are not appropriate, or providing services to individuals in institutions. (Social Security Act, April 1978, sec. 2001; italics added)

It is clear that goals 4 and 5 are in potential competition for funds, just as upgrading also competed with ideal DE goals. This potential conflict is not softened by other service conditions. States are obliged to offer one service (defined in state terms) that is directed at one of the five goals. Regardless of the stated goal, at least three services must be provided to SSI recipients. In addition, at least half of the federal funds must be spent for services to recipients of SSI, Medicaid, or Aid to Families with Dependent Children (AFDC). Support for medical or remedial care or room and board is not eligible for reimbursement "*unless* it is an integral but subordinate part of a reimbursable service" (sec. 2002 [a] [7]; italics added).

To the extent that services are used on behalf of goal 5, federal dollars are being used to subsidize institutional living. This subsidy could reinforce or augment existing state practices with MI or MR persons, inasmuch as the states already "devote most of their budgets to institutional care" (GAO, January 1977, p. 174). Data on how social services are actually spent would be useful for understanding what proportion of Title 20 funds are used to subsidize institutional programs.

National data about social services are, however, quite deficient. Definitions of services vary by state. For example, "foster care" can mean services to children or adults in a family-type home (with five or fewer persons), or services to persons living in facilities for the emotionally disturbed or developmentally disabled (with capacities often exceeding 100 beds). Services can also be offered to persons residing in restrictive institutions and be classified as meeting any of the four other goals. For example, the State of Minnesota, in its 1975–76 Comprehensive Annual Service Program Plan, defined homemaking as: "Provision of surrogate care in the absence or disability of the caretaker, providing for the personal care of ill or disabled individuals as well as instruction on more effective methods of home management, the development and maintenance of self-care and social skills" (State of Minnesota, October 1975).

Although the definition does not specify the site of "surrogate care," one can assume that it would occur in homelike, noninstitutional settings. However, the final Title 20 plan stipulates that $248,260 out of $5,429,469 designated as "homemaking" will be spent for goal number 5, "in order to enable recipients of service to receive maximum benefit from institutional care" (Ibid., p. 101). Out of 22 listed services, the Minnesota plan provides evidence that the institutional goal is to be supported by 19 of the designated services. Some of these institutional, goal-related services are counseling, protection, family planning, foster care, health, information and referral, and residential treatment.

In addition to this mode of service conceptualization, "residential treatment" —obviously referring to institutional care, custody, and treatment—can also be counted as meeting all five Title 20 goals. Evidently persons residing in a residential-treatment setting—characterized by Minnesota as a "controlled 24-hour per day live-in setting" (Ibid., p. 9)—can receive services that will maximize their benefit potential for: self-support; self-sufficiency; protection from abuse, neglect, or exploitation; preserving or reuniting families; community/home-based care; and institutional care (Ibid., p. 143). About $18 million out of $24 million allocated to residential treatment—or 75 percent—is classified as meeting the DE goal of "maximum benefit from community/home-based care" (Ibid.). The 1976–77 plan suggests that goal 4 type services for children may make "it possible to *return to the community* as soon as possible"; or for chemically dependent adults, it may "facilitate their *return to the community*" as soon as possible; or for mentally ill or chemically dependent persons living in a halfway house, it may serve as a "transition environment for persons *returning to the community"* (Ibid., pp. 179, 185, 191; italics added). It is evident that residential treatment services can refer to persons living outside of the community, even though goal 4 refers to "community-based care, home-based care."

There is little reason to believe that other state plans are any clearer about the meaning and statistics concerning services and goals. In addition, Minnesota is regarded as a progressive state. As noted in Chapter 5, Minnesota has been a leader in depopulating its state MR institutions and creating alternative, non-traditional, facilities. If the Minnesota data appear to refer to overlapping goals and services, it is likely that other state plans would present comparable problems of interpretation. The blunt fact appears to be that it is extremely difficult to ascertain to what extent service funds are being used to benefit persons living in traditional or alternative institutions, or semiindependent/independent living arrangements.

If we focus only on expenditures by goal classification, then about 8.8 percent of Minnesota's Title 20 expenditures for social services in 1976–77 were directed at the institutionalization goal (State of Minnesota, October 1976, p. 29). If we focus only on services described as providing a "controlled 24-hour per day live-in setting," then about 26 percent of the state's Title 20 service expenditures are devoted to supporting persons residing in traditional and nontraditional institutions. If we combine all services that are "controlled 24-hour per day live-in settings" *and* the portion of other services allocated in favor of goal 5, then the proportion of state funds expended in favor of restrictive living would increase to about 28 percent. This figure may still be overly conservative, for it may exclude a sizable expenditure for health and protection services that include "integral but subordinate medical, room and board and remedial services" occurring in institutions.

If Title 20 funding is assessed according to the service recipients' likely place of residence, then a high proportion of state social service expenditures can be expended for institutional services. However, states can vary in which services to claim for 75 percent reimbursement from federal funds. In Minnesota (for 1976–77), only $39,465,000 of Title 20 money was requested out of $118,648,000 expended—or about one-third of all planned expenditures. Undoubtedly the state wanted to demonstrate that it paid for more services than were allowable under the cap. Of the federal amount requested from Title 20, about 17 percent was for controlled 24-hour living arrangements, compared to the 26 percent obtained by using total state expenditure data. The reason for this total discrepancy is not that the states are picking up the service difference in expenditures; rather, it is due to the heavy reliance on local funding. In Minnesota, local dollars account for the highest proportion of expenditures for total social services—about 52 percent. Funding at the county level is responsible for about 32 percent of funds expended for controlled settings in the total state budget.

As this brief analysis of Title 20 has disclosed, attempting to ascertain the actual institutional distribution of service expenditures is quite complex. State definitions of goals and services are apt to be variable, broad, and imprecise; so too are state allocations of service recipients and dollars. Therefore, any national effort to forge a social-services approach that will enhance ideal DE goals (and that relies on Title 20) will have to recognize this conceptual and fiscal imprecision. Officials could try to decode a sample of state practices in order to understand how to influence actual supportive DE activities on a national scale. To accomplish this, one must understand state-level statutory funding requirements by service type, as well as county variability in defining and delivering services. This approach would work within the existing Title 20 policies. Or in place of another study, one could try a regulatory approach of sharply limiting (or capping) expenditures for goal 5. But unless actual living arrangements of service recipients were determined, focusing merely on stated intentions—or goals— would be an exercise in regulatory futility.

A more direct approach to diverting Title 20 funds away from supporting institutional goals or activities would be to statutorily delete goal 5 and amend the wording about the purposes of Title 20. Deleting goal 5 and amending the wording would be congruent with the earlier recommendation to amend the administration of the total act (see discussion of upgrading, above). An amended Title 20 could read as follows (with added words italicized): "Section 2001. For the purpose of encouraging each State, as far as practicable under conditions in that State, to furnish services *in a manner that is least restrictive to each beneficiary and* directed at the goal of: (1) achieving or maintaining economic self-support. . . ."

The existing goals, except for goal 5, would be included. The amended Title 20 would imply that each beneficiary's service needs would have to be assessed, with the presumption that all federally reimbursed social services be delivered to persons living: at home or with relatives and friends in preference to a foster home; in an independent supervised apartment in preference to a foster home; in a foster home in preference to a free-standing community residence with fewer than 16 beds; in a 15-bed (or fewer) group home in preference to a multiple-unit facility (with distinct units of 15 or fewer beds and near a normal range of community facilities); and in a multiple unit facility (with the aforementioned conditions) in preference to larger facilities (with 4-person bedrooms) or all other facilities. This rank order is, of course, congruent with the proposed definition of "least restrictive" (discussed earlier as an amendment to sec. 1101 [a] [9]).

This direct approach to changing Title 20 could redirect a substantial amount of federal funds away from institutional support and toward programs and services compatible with DE objectives. In Minnesota, for example, this could mean a diversion of a minimum of about 17 percent of federal funds away from controlled 24-hour living. If the states wanted to continue subsidizing these programs, they would have to do so without federal dollars. This diversion of federal funds could influence the states to invest state and local revenues in programs favored by the amended Title 20. This could mean expanding social services on behalf of DE objectives without adding any further funds—federal or state. At a national level this could mean that over $400 million of federal funds could be diverted for DE purposes (based on the Minnesota figure of 17 percent and a $2.5 billion federal cap on Title 20).

These proposed changes would probably be fought by a variety of interests in favor of goal 5; during the drafting stage of Title 20, institutional employee organizations and interested private child welfare leaders pushed for the addition of this goal (Mott 1976). While attempting to overcome this expected opposition to the proposed modification of Title 20, HEW officials could be urged to fulfill their existing statutory obligation. According to Section 2003, HEW officials are required to receive reports from each state "concerning its use of federal social service funds as the Secretary may by regulation provide." To determine the precise amount of federal funds currently supporting institutional programs, states could be required to categorize *all* federal and matching funds by the actual place of residence—or "whereabouts"—of each beneficiary of the "State Plan." These reports could help assess the actual proportion of institutional preferences existing at a state and national level. Proponents of DE would then know whether the proposed amendment would yield $400 million, $500 million, or $600 million of potential new federal dollars for DE activities. These figures might cause local interests, with a stake in noninstitutional programs, to campaign for the deletion of goal 5 and for the amendment redefining the goals of Title 20.

Home Care for Youth in Trouble

Since the turn of the century the country has generally agreed that "normal youth" in trouble, even though poor, should be assisted in a family-type environment. Although the fight against public funding of family assistance, led by private social welfare interests, certainly diminished the level of implementation, the principle of subsidizing home care was widely accepted before World War I, providing youth were not "incorrigible" or "delinquent." This national consensus, first reflected in the passage of mother's pension laws, was later recognized in the initial Social Security Act. Dependent children could be assisted with federal funds only if they resided in the homes of families and relatives; even foster care payments were excluded. In 1962 this national consensus was breached: federal maintenance payments for AFDC-foster care placements were permitted for the first time.

If the definition of foster care had retained the traditional meaning of a "substitute family," then the federal subsidization of private child welfare and other institutions would not have occurred. However, foster care was redefined to include a "foster care institution." By 1967 an institutional placement could be funded as foster care "income maintenance," or as a new federal "social service," or both. Social services were also extended to include former and potential dependents, thereby appreciably expanding the numbers of youth institutionalized with the assistance of federal funds (see Chapter 8). If there had been no congressional cap voted in 1972, then federal social service funding for foster care institutions would have continued to mount—in that states and localities had strong incentives to use new federal funds to replace old state/county funds. When Title 20 was formulated to replace pre-1972 categorical social service programs, the proponents of institutional care were able to insert goal 5 as a legitimate service goal (Mott 1976).

In actual practice, the distinctions between mental health, child welfare, and corrections have become blurred in the current use of Title 4 and Title 20 funding for institutional placements. In addition, the distinctions have become blurred between the goods and services that income-maintenance funds and social service funds can purchase. By failing to deal with this vagueness, institutions have benefited disproportionately. One strategic means for dealing with this blurring could rely on a general legislative mandate to implement a least restrictive policy—as proposed and discussed in the section on "upgrading"; it will be recalled that each individual beneficiary of a Social Security Title would receive benefits in the least restrictive and most humane and normal living arrangement. The general policy mandate would require that *each* title be administered in a least restrictive manner. Regulations could be written to ensure that a Title 4 unit and a Title 20 unit are given to each beneficiary. This could provide a double check to ensure that funds were being used on behalf of national policy. The secretary of HHS, of course, would still be responsible for monitoring compliance.

In addition to this regulatory and monitoring approach, it would be useful to limit federal reimbursement of *all* maintenance and care payments under Title 4 to the level of the maximum monthly home rate, set by each state for traditional or noninstitutional foster care. This would mean that states could not use federal funds to pay institutions at a substantially higher foster rate than now occurs. This limit could be enacted in a statute or regulation superseding the existing "program interpretation" of "federally reimbursable cost items" for foster care. This limit would be congruent with the existing statutory wording that federal "aid to families with dependent children" can pay for "only those items which are included in such term in the case of foster care in the foster family home of an individual" (sec. 408[b] [2]). HEW officials have interpreted allowable items for institutions and homes quite differently (see Chapter 9). For example, in 1977 the following rate disparities, approved for federal matching under Title 4, were noted by the GAO (22 February 1977, p. 14):

Location	Monthly Rates to Institutions	Maximum Monthly Foster Home Rate
Los Angeles County, Calif.	$329–$1,184	$298
Orange County, Calif.	400– 1,251	197
Georgia	133– 311	293
New Jersey	522– 1,594	238
New York	795– 1,107	408

Except for Georgia, each of the surveyed states paid much more for the lowest cost institutional placement than they did for the maximum foster family rate. Under the proposed change, no state could be reimbursed by the federal government for any costs above the maximum foster care rate. This change would force institutional placements to compete on an even footing with foster care homes. If they could not compete on a cost effective basis, institutions would have to demonstrate that functions other than maintenance and care were provided. But if institutions used this type of justification, there would be no statutory basis for reimbursing them under Title 4 for foster care services.

It is quite likely that institutions would seek a greater share of Title 20 funds in order to offset the proposed loss of Title 4 funds. The blurring of the distinctions between maintenance and care versus social service items, approved by HEW officials, could facilitate this increased use of Title 20 funds. This possibility would, of course, be effectively countered by the proposed amendment to Title 20, also reducing support for institutional funding. The dual approach to restricting Social Security funding to support institutional placements for youth in trouble could provide substantial funds on behalf of DE objectives. A reworking of a less significant program—child welfare services (funded under Title 4B)—could add additional funds. This program is also biased toward institutions, in that "funds are primarily used for maintaining children in out-of-home care" (Children's Defense Fund, 1978, p. 107).

The amount of AFDC funds used on behalf of foster care institutional placement remains quite substantial, even in the face of recent efforts to limit the program (for fiscal reasons). In July 1977, about 23 percent of the children in the AFDC Foster Care Program were living in institutions (based on forty-six reporting states); however, 47 percent of all July 1977 federal and state expenditures for this foster care program were allocated for payments to institutions (Ibid., p. 131). In December 1979 (based on forty-four reporting states), the proportion of the AFDC–foster care children living in institutions had dropped to about 14 percent; however, total funds were still allocated at a disproportionate level— about 44 percent of all payments went to institutions (based on forty-one states) (*Social Security Bulletin*, August 1980, p. 45). As of December 1979, the average AFDC payment for a child living in an institution amounted to $1,135 per month; for a child living in a foster family home the average monthly rate amounted to $234 (Ibid.). Meanwhile, all AFDC families received an average of about $280 per family and $93 per recipient (Ibid., p. 43).

In December 1979, child-care institutions received about $14 million and foster families about $18 million (based on forty-one states). If the institutions had received payments on a level with family payments, then the $14 million figure would have been reduced to about $3 million—a savings of about $11 million per month. At a national level this would amount to about $132 million in potential new funds for programs for children receiving home care. (This figure is, of course, a rough approximation because of the nonreporting states and the use of average foster family home payments, rather than the maximum permissible payment.) At a minimum matching rate of 50 percent, approximately $66 million of new federal funds could be used to promote DE objectives. Although this may seem small, it is larger than the $56.5 million usually appropriated annually for the federal share of general child welfare services under Title 4B (American Public Welfare Association, August 1980, p. 6). When added to the proposed new dollars from Title 20 associated with child placements, home care for youth in trouble could be promoted by diverting a substantial amount of federal funds away from institutional programs.

Summary and Conclusions

Whereas Chapter 9 concluded that there are various ideal meanings associated with DE, this chapter revealed that conceptual differences are not merely indications of intellectual disagreement, but rather provide the bases for defining the critical policy issues to be addressed. The conflicts over problem definitions are real ones, and are likely to affect a variety of areas where discretionary decision making could bias decisions and funds in favor of institutional care over DE objectives.

Those interested in "balanced systems" are likely to favor upgrading and maintaining the traditional system. However, even advocates of DE, GAO staff writers, citizens' groups, and legal rights activists support the inclusion of upgrading within a DE mandate. In the competition over funds, it is quite likely that an upgrading of expenditures and programs can reduce the impact of DE efforts. An example from the implementation of the ICF/MR program provides evidence of how institutional buildings and maximization of Medicaid collection, rather than an emphasis on individuals, can profoundly influence a state plan to upgrade care.

The idea that the existing health and welfare programs can impede, as well as promote, DE makes the analysis of strategic issues more complex. Income maintenance, Medicaid, and social services are three types of direct health and welfare programs that have been used by states to promote DE for adults for the past two decades. However, if changes were directed toward modifying health and welfare policies and programs, even further gains could be made toward realizing new DE objectives. This type of strategic approach indicates that a preference for a least restrictive policy is linked to changes in the benefit levels and conditions of SSI grants, redirection of health and welfare policy and funding toward home care for the elderly, and the diversion of federal social service funds away from controlled 24-hour settings.

Loud complaints have been voiced about the dismal living conditions of many former and potential mentally disabled and elderly persons. But unless we are willing to address the basic deficiencies of the income-maintenance programs designed to subsidize persons in their own homes, the conditions will remain. Two flaws have to be remedied: first, grant levels have to be raised to provide disabled and aged persons with a viable opportunity to lead independent, normalized lives; second, if SSI recipients choose to live with families, relatives, or friends they should not be penalized with a one-third reduction in their basic federal grant. If the SSI program were completely federalized, then the states could use the money saved for new and creative housing programs for disabled and elderly persons—including group homes and congregate housing. Complete federalization of SSI—including the changes proposed and accompanied by a legal mandate that the states redirect old SSI dollars to special housing programs—could multiply DE efforts.

Analyzing varied proposals for dealing with the costly overutilization of nursing homes for the elderly revealed that DE goals would be furthered if home care were given adequate, stable funding. A complete DE program for the elderly would include mandated medical and nonmedical screening of the elderly, a deliberate reduction in the use of nursing home days by about 40 percent over a five-year period, and a universal home care program to provide substitute services. Using savings generated by stringent regulation of nursing home admissions, a new Medicare program could provide the funding without stigma to eligible persons.

The proposal to use Medicare, rather than an indigency-based welfare assistance program, is a deliberate choice. It is logically and historically consistent with the Social Security concept of insuring against universal social risks. The likelihood of living beyond 65 years of age has increased dramatically since Social Security was enacted in 1935. Associated with this longevity is the increased risk of living long enough to incur an impairment of physical, personal, and social functioning. Because this is a universal risk affecting all persons beyond the age of 65, and because the old-age and Medicare insurance programs do not adequately address this risk, adding a new Social Security benefit makes a great deal of sense. This risk of becoming impaired while retired could be met by a new addition (Part C) to the existing Medicare program, rather than continuing to rely on an inadequate, complex patchwork of fifty state health and welfare programs.

In contrast to Medicaid, Title 20 social service funds have been used to support a broad array of traditional and nontraditional institutional programs for all ages and social problems. A direct approach to promoting DE objectives would rely on statutory amendments to delete "institutional activities" as one of the five legitimate areas of Title 20, and to add least restrictive language in the introduction to the four remaining goals. A less direct approach would rely on changing reporting requirements to include the residence whereabouts of all Title 20 recipients and funds. This change could occur through an amendment to the regulations, as part of the HEW responsibility to audit expenditures.

A strategy for DE of adults would rely on achieving minimum levels of SSI income and changing the funding and program mechanisms for providing home care. To realize these objectives in an efficient manner, most of the proposals have attempted to stabilize or restrict the opportunities for institutional capital improvements and operating expenses. This deliberate strategy was also used in assessing home care for youth in trouble. Aside from arguments of cost efficiency for any policy proposal, this strategy of opposing institutional upgrading and maintenance is realistic. In a time of nonexpansion of health and welfare programs, the major source of new funds for DE objectives is in the budgets of subsidies for institutional programs. If DE advocates are serious about moving persons away from more restrictive living arrangements and programs, attention will also have to be paid to moving the funds away from these less desirable residences and programs.

Aside from eliminating poverty living conditions among adult recipients, and promoting freedom of choice by eliminating the restriction of living in the household of another, all other funding proposals have been keyed to coincide with proposed savings. The federalization of SSI relied on using state funds for less restrictive housing mortgage financing. Home care for the elderly involved stabilizing the growth rate of nursing home days, or an actual reduction of nursing home use (up to 40 percent). Increased social services for all ages relied on deleting payments for institutional programs, and diverting the funds to DE objectives. Improvement of living standards for retarded persons could rely on diverting Medicaid funds away from a traditional ICF/MR program to community living and programs funded by Medicaid. And home care for youth in trouble could be promoted by restricting payments to institutions at a foster family level. All of these existing institutional sources of funding—whether located in Medicaid, SSI, child welfare, or social service titles—could be redirected to constitute new funds for DE purposes.

Aside from SSI improvements, the new funds could be quite substantial. Although the proposals have been crafted to utilize old money for new purposes, a risk of an "add on" on expenditures could occur. This is particularly likely if institutional supporters are able to weaken any of the proposals for yielding offset funds (and thereby continue the status quo funding in favor of institutional uses). There are HHS officials and legislators who might be unwilling to run the fiscal risks and engage in conflict with institutional interests; therefore, political opposition to actual shifts in funding could be quite formidable.

In the event that the specific substantive proposals are assessed as too risky—fiscally and politically—there remains another proposal that can be argued for on humanitarian grounds alone: amending the Social Security Act to require that all 20 titles are administered by the secretary of HHS and his offices and employees in a least restrictive manner to each beneficiary. This amendment would require, at a minimum, that all existing funds and programs within each title are in compliance with this statutory mandate. The legislation could be passed, initially, without any funding to monitor compliance. If the coalition of persons and groups interested in DE cannot muster the political strength to pass legislation that merely requires purposive attention to the ideals of liberty, humanness, and normal living, then it is unlikely that the substantive proposals discussed in this chapter will be realized in the near future.

11 Summary and Conclusions

This study began by defining two critical terms: institutionalization and its antonym—which we have labeled DE. Examination of the first term led to a conceptual approach that emphasized multiple social functions carried out in nonfamilial residences where more than 4 to 6 persons lived; both traditional and nontraditional, as well as short-term and long-term facilities, were included in the first formulation. From an analytic perspective, DE could be defined narrowly or broadly. Narrowly, DE refers to reduced reliance on traditional institutions; more broadly conceived, it refers to a reduction in the use of traditional institutions *without* offsetting increases in the use of nontraditional facilities. Using both types of definitions where appropriate, this chapter will attempt to answer three broad questions: (1) Is there less institutionalization now than there was twenty, thirty, or fifty years ago? (2) What accounts for the changes in the utilization of traditional institutions? (3) What meaning do these recent trends have for our understanding of the welfare state, American-style?

Institutional Trends in America

Most analyses of DE pay primary attention to traditional institutions and one-day resident counts. As a result, they tend to ignore or underestimate the significance of short-term facilities and new forms of institutionalization. The data presented in this study indicate that when *all* sources are taken into account, the first question posed above is difficult to answer: Is there less institutionalization now than there was twenty, thirty, or fifty years ago? Although there have certainly been various degrees of reductions in the utilization of traditional institutions—state/county mental hospitals, mental retardation facilities, institutions for the dependent/neglected, and juvenile correctional training schools—there is persuasive evidence that offsetting increases have been occurring elsewhere. These increases have occurred in the expanded use of short-term facilities, primarily general hospitals with psychiatric units, and detention and shelter homes for juveniles. They have also occurred in new types of nontraditional institutions: nursing homes for the aged (skilled and intermediate); shelter care homes for the mentally ill and retarded; group homes for delinquents and status offenders; residential treatment centers for "acting out" youth; halfway houses for chemically dependent persons; and community residential facilities for the mentally retarded.

Based on a detailed examination of all sources of institutional living arrangements, question (1) has two answers: "Yes," if only the traditional sites and sources are analyzed; and "No," if nontraditional and short-term facilities are included. Although this paradoxical conclusion may satisfy many, there are critics who might object on the grounds that short-term facilities and newer living arrangements are not really examples of institutions. Whereas they might meet the technical criteria of an institutional definition (discussed in Chapter 1), they are not worth considering as institutions because they are either community-based, do not hold people for more than a few days, or do not offer long-term treatment.

The term "community based" is rarely defined in the DE literature. It is often used as a synonym for a nontraditional residence; anything other than a state training school or a state hospital is not conceptualized as an institution. The term is also used to refer to private—in contrast to public—facilities. After reviewing available literature and after consulting experts, LEAA attempted to define the term by highlighting the characteristics of size, geographical proximity to the resident's family, nonlocked residence, and open access to community resources. Some facilities can be rated highly on the normative ideals of small size, nearness to family, least restrictiveness, and community programming. But anyone familiar with existing facilities knows that their high rating cannot automatically be assumed; nor can their characterization as a "nonnormal" household be denied. They can function, according to consumers, as modern examples of benign, less restrictive, and more normal living arrangements, but they are not independent apartments or households. And, of course, many provide examples of new forms of physical, social, and chemical controls (see Chapter 4).

As for short-term facilities, their omission from customary discussions of institutions is not unusual. Because youth or adults are not *intended* to stay in these facilities for a lengthy term, it can be argued that they do not constitute sites of rehabilitation, treatment, or habilitation. Although short-term facilities may, indeed, operate on behalf of nontreatment goals, it is difficult to overlook the fact that other societal functions, often associated with institutions, are performed by these facilities. They can provide crisis treatment, testing and observational diagnosis, temporary care, and, of course, custody. All detention facilities are locked, as are most (if not all) of the psychiatric units of general hospitals. To continue to ignore their existence and rapid growth is implicitly supportive of a curious conception of an institution—one that omits the societal support for over a half-million annual juvenile admissions to locked detention facilities or over 800,000 admissions to locked psychiatric units of general hospitals (see Chapter 5; and Witkin 1980, p. 12). At any rate, the decennial census of institutions has recognized their existence for over half a century.

By taking into account all of these nontraditional forms of institutionalization, it is possible to deal overtly with the traditional problems of unloving care and supervision within new institutional forms: nursing homes housing over 1.25

million aged persons; or shelter-care homes housing at least a quarter of a million mentally disabled persons. In addition, it is possible to comprehend fully the total institutional system as it actually exists in 1980. The facts appear to support an image of a multifunction system that has gained in breadth, diversity, number, and decentralization of sites. America now has more institutional sites, used by more people during a year, in many more locations, than existed in the recent past. At the same time state mental hospitals have been depopulated and mental retardation facilities reduced in size.

These conclusions mean that America still relies on institutions as acceptable social devices for dealing with social problems for all age groups. It is fairly clear that—controlling for population—there are now more persons 65 years and over admitted to, and living in, a nursing home than occurred in all of the traditional types twenty, thirty, or fifty years ago (see Chapter 2). Similarly, it is clear that there are now many more youths under 18 placed in a psychiatric, detention, private or traditional, correctional or residential treatment facility (controlling for population) than occurred in comparable sites twenty, thirty, or fifty years ago (see Chapter 9). While the evidence is less definitive for persons 19 to 64 years old, it is reasonable to infer that if unduplicated admissions data were available for all types of facilities, rate of institutional use would at least be comparable to that of the past (see Chapters 3 and 5).

Viewing institutions by problem area discloses that, in the specialized mental health field, the total civilian rate of "inpatient care episodes" has not changed between 1955 and 1977; the rate per 100,000 population was 741 in 1955 and exactly the same in 1977 (Witkin 1980, table 3). These figures exclude psychiatric use of nursing homes and such nonmedical facilities as halfway houses, group homes, and shelter-care facilities (see Chapter 3). Although the rates for specialized facilities are the same, it is clear that general hospitals with psychiatric units (whether or not affiliated with federally supported CMHCs) have become the primary focus of care, treatment, and 24-hour supervision (Chapters 3 and 5). In addition, the duration of the stays in all facilities are shorter than they were in earlier years. The public health standard of the 1950s, when a short treatment period was considered to be six months, has been replaced by 72-hour "holds," 14-day "stays," and 30-day "extensions."

The mental retardation (MR) field began reducing its traditional population at a national level about a decade later than the specialized mental health field. Although the number of smaller, more normalized community residential facilities has grown appreciably since the late 1960s, it is clear that gargantuan traditional institutions are still the primary types of nonfamilial residence. The availability of Medicaid funding for all age groups residing in traditional MR institutions has undoubtedly impeded the movement of retarded persons into smaller, more normalized community residences. The total rate of institutionalization appears to have remained stable, dominated by upgraded, large facilities that now are classified as "skilled and intermediate care facilities—MR," instead of traditional state hospitals or schools for the retarded (see Chapters 5 and 10).

Of the three major fields related to youth in trouble, only the child welfare field has undergone an absolute and relative reduction in the utilization of institutions. Traditional facilities for dependent/neglected youth have been affected by sharp reductions, and are likely to disappear as a residential type by the end of the century. Although the emergence of nonmedical residential treatment centers for emotionally disturbed youth has partially offset these reductions, the new balance is in favor of a total reduction of institutionalization in child welfare. The most likely beneficiaries of these long-term trends are "normal" children from poor families, particularly those under 12 years of age (see Chapter 8).

The two other systems dealing with youth in trouble—mental health and juvenile corrections—have experienced sharp rises in institutional use. Juvenile rates of inpatient care/custody/treatment episodes have increased in all types of short- and long-term specialized psychiatric facilities: state/county mental hospitals, private psychiatric facilities, and psychiatric units of general hospitals. In the juvenile corrections field, reductions in the use of long-term training schools have been more than matched by the growth in private facilities; in addition, detention rates have continued to mount (see Chapter 9).

Taken as a whole, the three youth-in-trouble systems indicate that the long-term institutionalization of youth has increased slightly over a fifty-year period, controlling for population. The use of short-term facilities, however, has increased dramatically. A high turnover of more youth passing through short-term facilities is the dominant, unstated, policy of the emergent youth-in-trouble system.

Explaining the Movement Away from Traditional Facilities

The patterns of institutional use described in the section above were not planned at any specific level of government—federal, state, or local. Instead, these patterns evolved as a result of the complex influences interacting within a problem field or system, and factors external to the institutional system. The causes of DE of two traditional systems were examined: private facilities for the dependent/neglected, and state/county mental hospitals. The DE of both traditional systems occurred after there were significant shifts in beliefs about the problem groups and the type of institutions and programs necessary for carrying out the preferred public welfare functions of relief, care, treatment/education, and custody/supervision. Although each system reacted to unique historical influences after the shifts in ideology occurred, both relied on the emergence or expansion of new public funding resources and entrepreneurial leaders to take advantage of these opportunities.

In the field of "child saving," the historical evidence is clear that by the turn of the century, home care and substitute family care were preferred over institutionalization by the influential leaders of private charity organizations. This preference was part of an increased ideological emphasis on promoting family life in all classes, as well as a growing realization that juvenile institutions could be "evil places." Despite these beliefs, the leaders of the Charities Organization Societies and benevolent child-welfare organizations—the dominant leaders of the era—were unwilling to promote or support a publicly subsidized home care policy, primarily because of their arrogant and uncompromising opposition to all forms of outdoor relief. They actively fought the emergence of publicly funded welfare assistance to impoverished mothers, despite the documented knowledge that many parents were using "benevolent institutions" as a form of indoor relief and care for one or more of their children. The placement of their children into these juvenile almshouses appeared voluntary only because their choices were so restricted.

Private child-welfare organizations did not expand the other option to any large extent either, relying primarily on the public sector to finance paid family care in foster homes. However, in most of the nation the increased use of foster care between 1910 and 1933 did not appreciably affect the number or rates of institutionalized youth. Instead, publicly subsidized foster care was added on to the dominant institutional system for the dependent/neglected. One exception to this national trend occurred in Massachusetts, where under cautious, but persistent, entrepreneurial public leadership state and local funds were used to actively substitute institutional care with subsidized foster care; as a result DE occurred without offsetting increases.

DE of institutions for the dependent/neglected did not occur on a national scale until after the passage of the 1935 Social Security Act's Title 4 program— Aid to Dependent Children. Until 1962, no federal funds could be used for institutional or family foster care. By that time state and local governmental leaders had become persuaded that a home care policy of matching federal grants was preferable to subsidizing private child-welfare institutions. The rates of institutionalization in facilities for the dependent/neglected have displayed a sharp reduction in each decennial census since 1933, as well as at intervening surveys by the National Center for Health Statistics. Until the passage of the amendment permitting AFDC payment to private institutions as "foster care" sites, there were no federal funds available to subsidize nontraditional residences. The high cost of these institutional alternatives (i.e., residential treatment centers) probably prevented their utilization rates from exceeding the reductions achieved in the less professional traditional institutions.

DE of the state mental hospitals occurred after beliefs about outdoor public relief were shattered by the Great Depression. In addition, elite leaders within the mental health field, as well as intellectual leaders in a variety of academic disciplines, began to favor the early "parole" of institutional "inmates." By the 1940s, leaders in California (and probably elsewhere) were willing to urge the release of all aged persons to alternative "sanitariums" or to "family care" homes; in addition, they urged freeing from institutions all persons no longer experiencing great distress or constituting a danger to others. Mental patients of reproductive age (particularly women) were no longer feared for their eugenic danger, because environmental theories were also more widely accepted. These ideas continued to grow in the postwar years, but no explicit funding on a large scale was expended by any of the states on behalf of a definitive pro-release policy. Instead, the decade of 1945–55 witnessed a building boom in state hospital construction, mirroring the extensive Veterans' Administration building program of the postwar era. Outpatient funding also developed at a state and local level, but had little or no impact on admissions or release rates.

The invention and dissemination of psychoactive drugs, between 1955 and 1957, triggered a national interest in using these potent (if little understood) chemicals both inside and outside of state/county mental hospitals. California required the hiring and promotion of new state hospital leaders in order to utilize the new technology on behalf of pro-release, rather than institutional maintenance, policies. With the changes in federal regulations and statutes permitting federal subsidization of all existing and potential mental patients, states with a pro-release leadership were able to accelerate DE activities. States whose leaders exhibited entrepreneurial skills, and who were supported by executives and legislators willing to risk increased spending in order to gain long-term fiscal benefits via deferred construction and maintenance of facilities, displayed marked population reductions by 1969. Laggard states waited until Supplementary Security Income (SSI) was passed in 1972.

Unlike the DE of institutions for the dependent/neglected (for the first thirty years), federal funds were available for subsidizing alternative living arrangements—institutional and noninstitutional. Old Age Assistance (OAA), Medical Assistance for the Aged (after 1960), Medicaid (after 1965), and Medicare (after 1965) subsidized the placement of potential and former geriatric patients in families or in skilled and intermediate nursing care homes. Younger patients were supported with Aid to Permanently and Totally Disabled (APTD) funds after 1962. They were released in increasing numbers to the less costly shelter-care homes, single-room occupancy hotels, and family care homes.

Because many of these depopulating activities were carried out in an expedient fashion, particularly in the first decade of acceleration, mental health leaders were accused of "dumping" patients in order to gain federal dollars. Although many of these charges could be substantiated, it is a fact that California (and probably every other state) did *not* realize immediate actual fiscal benefits. Instead actual costs increased due to the expense of matching funds necessary to support the new nontraditional alternatives, expanding public assistance payments, and growing outpatient services. Not until the advent of SSI (after 1972) were states able to rely on nonmatching federal grants to subsidize patient releases. Therefore, the states' long- and short-term fiscal benefits should not be confounded; nor should the national timing of mental health DE be confused with its acceleration or the extensive state variations in responding to the expansion of the welfare state in the 1960s.

Social Security Legislation and the Deinstitutionalization
of Traditional Public Welfare

Prior to the passage of the Social Security Act in 1935, American public welfare was institution-centered to a marked degree. In a broad sense, institutional relief and care became virtually synonymous with public welfare from the post-Civil War period to the Great Depression. At the local level public welfare funds were expended primarily on almshouses, workhouses, and municipal lodges; there were also episodic and uncertain public dollars paid for foster care and meager forms of mothers' and old age pensions. The elite bias against outdoor relief was so strong that by 1900 more than half of the cities with populations over 200,000 ceased to provide any form of public outdoor relief (Warner 1908, p. 236). Instead, the public authorities openly deferred to the Charity Organization Societies and other "benevolent" organizations. Even at the private level, it is evident that a great many more philanthropic funds were expended on behalf of benevolent institutions for dependent/neglected youth, homeless and friendless adults, and wayward women, than were spent on home-based charity or foster care.

At the state level, Massachusetts and a few other states were virtually alone in providing child foster care or mental health family care from public funds. Even as late as 1937, the census reported that the entire country had 893 "paroled" mental hospital patients living in a "family care" home as a state-subsidized "boarder" (U.S. Bureau of the Census, *Patients in Hospitals for Mental Disease: 1937*, table 5); this figure constituted only 0.2 percent of all persons on the state hospital "books." Seven years later the country reported 2,164 patients as family care parolees—or 0.4 percent of those on the "books" (Ibid., 1944, table 4). Comparable figures can be cited for institutions for the retarded. Because inmates of public institutions and hospitals for mental diseases were statutorily ineligible to receive any federally subsidized public assistance funds, state-supported family care constituted the most generous pre-1950s state home care policy toward the released mentally ill or retarded. Clearly, the major resources of the state were devoted to constructing and maintaining traditional institutions.

It is difficult to obtain precise fiscal measures of the relative dominance of institutions in the field of public welfare before passage of the 1935 Social Security Act. The best available national data for assessing expenditures from all government levels—federal, state, and local—for an earlier period appear to be for 1929. Even though this year marked the onset of the Great Depression, the data reveal that about $60 million was spent on all forms of public assistance and $75 million for institutional care; the latter figure does *not* include any expenditures for hospital care, for it was impossible to disaggregate federal funds (civilian and military) for this form of public welfare (U.S. Social Security Administration, September 1980, *Social Security Bulletin: Annual Statistical Supplement, 1977–79*, table 3). In 1929 the federal government contributed very few (if any) funds for public assistance and institutional forms of public welfare; therefore, the distribution of the $135 million refers primarily to state and local expenditures. In contrast to the institutional dominance of public welfare spending by state and local governments in 1929, the distribution of funds for institutional public welfare amounted to $125 million in 1950, out of a local/state outlay of $1.4 billion (*Social Security Bulletin*, May 1980, p. 7). The emergence of federal responsibility for public welfare functions finally ended almost a century of institutional dominance in capturing local and state tax funds.

Besides breaking the fiscal dominance of traditional institutions at the state and local level, federal matching of responsibility for social and economic problems created new or modified forms of noninstitutional welfare programs. These federal welfare programs created new societal mechanisms for assuming many of the old public welfare functions carried out by institutions. Instead of indoor relief in almshouses, workhouses, and municipal lodges, modern public welfare provided old-age services and disability insurance payments (OASDI), as well as income-maintenance assistance grants for categories of persons determined to be in economic need (Old Age Assistance, Aid to Dependent Children, Aid to Permanently and Totally Disabled). Instead of traditional institutional custody, public welfare increasingly subsidized alternative forms of medical, nursing, and social service supervision. Instead of institutional treatment, the public sector first provided Medical Assistance for the Aged, followed by Medicare for the elderly and Medicaid for the medically indigent. Instead of institutional protection, public funds subsidized protective services for the elderly and children living in their own homes. One important function carried out in a traditional institution—physical, personal, and social care—has become eligible for federal subsidization in skilled and intermediate nursing care homes, and to a limited extent in shelter-care homes. Although some noninstitutional home health, personal, and social care services have begun to be provided, the care function has not been as fully replaced as have other functions (Morris 1977).

The Emergence of Institutional Funding by the Welfare State

For over twenty-five years after the passage of the Social Security Act, all of the public welfare titles were explicitly antiinstitutional. Beginning in the 1960s this policy preference was modified so that the welfare state could promote, as well as impede, various forms of institutional care. In 1960 the explicit preference for home care led to the passage of Medical Assistance to the Aged; skilled nursing home care was classified as an eligible type of medical treatment, even if it occurred in a nonhospital facility. Passage of Medicaid and Medicare in 1965 enhanced the legitimation of skilled nursing home care as a type of public welfare; by 1967 intermediate care homes were included under Medicaid. For aged persons, the welfare state no longer insisted on providing assistance only in the home or, when necessary, in hospitals. Since that time a large portion of Medicaid expenditures for the aged has been on behalf of a new form of institutional care (see Chapter 10).

Until 1961 ADC (later AFDC) payments could only be made to dependent children residing in a home with family or relatives. In that year foster care payments were permitted, and a year later institutional foster care was added to the legislation. Both types of foster care were optional until 1967, when they became a mandatory part of any state plan. By the late 1970s it was evident that institutions received a disproportionate amount of foster care funding (see Chapter 10).

In 1972 the welfare state, for the first time, began to subsidize traditional institutions, particularly state and private psychiatric facilities and those for the retarded. Persons over 65 could have their stay in a mental hospital reimbursed by Medicaid, providing the building met the standards of the Joint Commission on the Accreditation of Hospitals (JCAH); in 1974 persons under 18 also became eligible. At about the same time all state facilities for the retarded became eligible for Medicaid funding as skilled nursing or intermediate care facilities (SNF-MR or ICF-MR), providing they were upgraded to meet JCAH, Life Safety Code, and federal standards. Presumably, upgrading is intended to improve the medical care, treatment, and habilitation capabilities of traditional institutions, so that they can once again attempt to become more like hospitals. At present, available data indicate that public and private traditional MR institutions and private mental hospitals have been the primary beneficiaries of these funding changes. In addition, it is clear that the Medicaid MR program distributes an inordinate share of federal funds to traditional ICF-MR facilities, rather than to ICF-MR residences with fewer than sixteen beds, located in normal neighborhoods (see Chapter 10).

Regardless of the initial motivation by legislators, these program and funding changes have created fiscal incentives for the states to deal with social problems by using new or modified institutions as the instruments for carrying out public welfare functions. The welfare state now both promotes and impedes DE. Paradoxically, federal funds now support home care and institutional care, even though the welfare state initially created programs to assist only needy persons in their own homes. Unless this paradox is forthrightly addressed at a national level, the ideals of DE will continue to be compromised by a creeping bias toward more restrictive upgraded and nontraditional institutions.

Subsidization of Proprietary Provisions of Public Welfare Functions

The growth of proprietary nursing home and shelter-care facilities, subsidized heavily by federal and state funds in exchange for providing public welfare functions, appears to be a recent American phenomenon. This growth is directly linked to the emergence and expansion of the welfare state. The increase in federal assumption of responsibility for the social and economic welfare of its citizens was paradoxically accompanied by a willingness to transfer part of this responsibility to private parties for a profit. This privatization of public welfare functions is integrally related to DE activities and, therefore, important to comprehend. The birth of a subsidized nursing home industry is particularly significant, in that the U.S. Congress has continually expressed displeasure at the performance of proprietary operators.

In 1933, when the federal government began its first experiment in providing public outdoor assistance through the Federal Emergency Relief Administration, program head Harry Hopkins directed that federal funds should be spent by public agencies (Leiby 1978, p. 225). In many communities local officials had arranged for private charitable organizations to assume the responsibility for determining eligibility and the size of the public relief grant. Hopkins, however, thought that relief should be a matter of citizenship right, "not dependent on anybody's voluntary generosity"; and the people who administered the grant should be responsible public employees (Ibid.). This policy later became incorporated into the Social Security Act, by which state agencies were made legally responsible for preparing and administering a state welfare plan. What now seems like a ritualistic requirement was actually a distinctive public policy.

Although public welfare orgranizations at state and county levels did assume these new responsibilities, they continued the established practices of using public funds to purchase foster care via private agencies and subsidizing many private child welfare institutions, as well as funding a small amount of family care for adults. These traditional "purchase of care" arrangements were not reimbursable by the federal government from 1935 to 1962. Purchase of care of this type occurred with nonprofit organizations, except for family care homes. Family care homes with boarders may have made a profit, but they were considered akin to a group foster home—or, at most, a "mom and pop" commercial venture. After 1935, this tradition of purchase of care from private nonprofit organizations was expanded to include proprietary organizations.

In 1935 the Social Security Act provided for Old Age Assistance (OAA) to persons living in their own homes, and specifically barred payments to an individual "who is an inmate of a public institution or any individual who is a patient in an institution for tuberculosis or mental diseases" (Title 1, sec. 6 [a] [1]). It was understood that this prohibition was particularly aimed at public poorhouses (U.S. Senate Committee on Aging, Supporting Paper no. 7, March 1976, p. xii). Barred from using federal funds for discredited almshouses as a residence for elderly persons requiring physical, personal, and social care, families and social workers attempted to use OAA payments for boarding homes.

In the fourth *Annual Report of the Social Security Board* (1939), this new development was noted by federal officials. About 5.3 percent of OAA recipients in 1937–38 were classified as residing in a "household group but not with relatives"; however, "probably many . . . were boarders, since households with less than 10 lodgers were not classified as institutions" (U.S. Federal Security Agency, 1940, p. 93). The board was deeply concerned about reports of "serious fire hazards and other deplorable conditions" in other boarding homes (Ibid., p. 94). This link between OAA and boarding homes was documented in a 1944 federal report, *Sheltered Care and Home Services for Public Assistance Recipients*. The study of six localities revealed the following information about 208 "commercial homes":

> About half of these homes for which the date of establishment was known had been in existence less than 2 years. Three-fourths had been established since passage of the Social Security Act.
>
> One agency, responsible for licensing homes in the state caring for the aged, reported that there were 501 licensed homes in 131 cities and towns in 1938 and 786 in 164 cities and towns in 1941, and that in March 1942 there were approximately 800 licensed homes. The annual report of the agency declared: "The old-age assistance law has been responsible for the rapid mushrooming of these homes. Fully 50 percent of the inmates are recipients of old age assistance." [U.S. Federal Security Agency, Public Assistance Report no. 5, 1944, p. 14]

Of the 207 commercial homes studied in the 1944 report, 53 provided medical care and 127 provided medical and nursing care in combination. The services of a registered or a graduate nurse were reported for 86 homes, and those of a practical nurse for 164 homes. An unknown number also provided "the protective care that is present to some degree in congregate living arrangements" (Ibid., p. 15).

It is clear now that the "seeds of the nursing home industry" began in these early years of the Social Security Act (Vladeck 1980, p. 37). Dissatisfied with the quality of these early proprietary nursing homes, Congress in 1950 changed the law to permit public assistance payments to public medical facilities; it was hoped that the public sector would be encouraged to develop programs and compete with the commercial sector. In continued preference for noncommercial nursing home care, the Hill-Burton Hospital Construction Act was amended in 1954 to allow public and nonprofit organizations to construct nursing homes for the elderly. This action again symbolized legislative support for public nonprofit facilities; but this action also transformed nursing homes from a welfare-oriented care facility into a medical facility. As Vladeck noted, "nursing homes would never again be solely an extension of the welfare system; they now belonged to health policy as well" (Ibid., p. 43).

Private interests were quick to expand and take advantage of this legitimation of nursing homes. In 1956 the American Nursing Home Association (ANHA) was finally successful in obtaining legislative authorization for loans from the Small Business Administration. In 1959 federal loan insurance, under housing programs of the Federal Housing Administration (FHA), was made available to proprietary nursing homes. The FHA soon guaranteed almost a billion dollars in mortgage loans; this action probably legitimated additional loans from savings banks and mortgage-granting facilities.

This availability of low-cost capital construction funds meshed nicely with the 1960 passage of Medical Assistance for the Aged (MAA). MAA, for the first time, defined medical need independently of OAA eligibility. It also included "skilled nursing home services," without defining these new medical services. Between 1960 and the 1965 passage of Medicare and Medicaid, MAA vendor payments for nursing homes increased ten times, and contributed one-third of the total program expenditures. By 1965 public funds provided by a public welfare program (MAA) were subsidizing a significant share of the costs of the nursing home industry. With the passage of Medicare and Medicaid, "the welfare-based nursing home system was incorporated, willy nilly, into new programs designed to finance health services" (Ibid., p. 48).

Whereas profit motives of the nursing home association (ANHA), coupled with support of strategically located legislators, helped achieve the public subsidization of a profit-making welfare function, there are additional reasons for its occurrence and acceptance. In the late 1950s and early 1960s, entrepreneurial public officials, interested in depopulating state mental hospitals, created an extra source of demand for beds for released geriatric patients. Nursing homes figured prominently in the plans of mental hospital after-care workers. Potential mental hospital admissions of elderly persons were also redirected to nursing homes, creating another source of demand. It is clear, too, that many families, general hospitals, and welfare agencies were receptive to the idea of taking care of geriatric problems via this new, specialized, community treatment resource.

There appears to have been little opposition by families or workers in public agencies to the idea of making a profit for performing welfare functions. The notion that few, if any, goods or services may not provide legitimate profit-making opportunities must be considered another influential variable associated with the privatization of health and welfare programs.

Many of these critical variables can be observed in the "birth of a for-profit Boarding Home Industry" (U.S. Senate Special Committee on Aging, Supporting Paper no. 7, March 1976). This industry also emerged in an unplanned fashion. In 1972 the passage of the new SSI legislation prohibited payments to "inmates in public institutions," and required that SSI funds be reduced if SSI recipients "lived in the household of another." SSI funds, however, could be received in full by persons residing in boarding homes with unrelated individuals. A belated amendment, in 1976, permitted public boarding homes housing sixteen or fewer persons to receive SSI payments. This modest amendment does not appear to have changed the relative balance between commercial and nonproprietary, nonmedical, shelter-care homes.

Although many persons accepted these new examples of the spirit of capitalism, there have also been some who doubt the positive value of this unusual development. Critics are often confronted with the truism that "private industry can do it better," whether the "it" be a nursing home service, delivery of a postal package, or garbage collection. Although a comparison is rarely put to a strict empirical test, there is little doubt in the superiority of private enterprise. Despite this unchallenged belief, Vladeck recently characterized American nursing homes as new forms of *Unloving Care* (1980). Nor has this belief dissuaded the U.S.

Senate Special Committee on Aging from labeling a lengthy series of reports, summarizing a decade of investigation, as follows: *Nursing Home Care in the United States: Failure in Public Policy* (U.S. Senate Subcommittee on Long-Term Care, 1974).

Although the Senate Special Committee on Aging believed there was a failure, it was not just due to poor planning or faulty implementation. The record reveals that the nation has never developed a purposeful federal policy for the aged, the chronically mentally ill, or any other problem group; nor was there a formal policy for DE and the development of alternative living arrangements. Nursing homes and shelter-care homes, like DE, emerged in an ad hoc fashion as the result of a variety of influences. It is the accumulation of ad hoc decisions that can now be characterized as a "failure in public policy." Understanding the emergent accumulation of choices alerts us to the fact that many persons, organizations, and interests participated in the creation of proprietary welfare agencies. Many of these same parties can be expected to oppose any proposals favoring home care—unless, of course, home care is also delivered by proprietary organizations.

The Expansion of Citizenship Rights

There is persuasive evidence that many nontraditional institutional alternatives do, in fact, provide "unloving care." Of course, similar charges have been made about many traditional institutions. When residents of shelter-care facilities are asked to compare the traditional and nontraditional, however, they do not tend to rate them as equally bad. Instead, over 85 percent of those who have experienced both types of institutions prefer the nontraditional to the traditional. "Life is better than the hospital as one is free to come and go as one pleases," commented one ex-patient (see Chapter 4). Granting to former patients the freedom to come and go as one pleases constitutes one of the most significant products of emergent DE policy.

To some professional critics of DE, particularly in the mental health field, the movement from a hygienic, professionally managed state or county hospital to an untidy, nonprofessionally administered shelter-care home may appear to be a poor consumer bargain. However, from a consumer perspective, both forms of care may appear equally "unloving." In addition, psychoactive drugs, the major form of institutional psychiatric treatment, may be similarly regarded, regardless of where the supervision of the ingestion takes place. For those residing in nonmedical facilities, the right to freely come and go may even outweigh any perceived differences associated with superior treatment and care services offered by a lengthy hospital stay.

Although the movement out of traditional facilities is associated with expanded citizenship rights, DE is also, paradoxically, associated with new forms of social control. Newer institutions for former mentally disabled persons often enforce curfews, drug supervision, program scheduling, and other forms of personal, social, and chemical control. However, the nonmedical facilities still appear to be perceived as less onerous than the more closed form of care, treatment, and control associated with traditional facilities. Granting increased citizenship rights has certainly not been absolute, nor does it uniformly occur in all nontraditional settings (for example locked nursing homes). Yet the gain in relative freedom has been significant enough to characterize DE for adults as a policy associated with a general diminution in the type, degree, and duration of social control. These gains occurred primarily after 1960, but it is evident from the historical record that expanded rights could not have occurred without earlier changes in ideologies and practices supportive of a proinstitutional policy.

In the 1840s and 1850s, when "moral treatment" of the insane and education for educable retarded youth were initiated, residential programs were designed to house occupants for a relatively short period of time. It was believed that the benign treatment of insane persons, and training retarded youth so they could function in the community, would occur within a period of six months to a year. For Samuel Gridley Howe, a pioneer in the instruction of deaf, blind, and retarded youth, the new institutions for youth were designed to serve as a "link in the chain of common schools"—not as places of isolation and segregation from normal community life (Wolfensberger 1976, p. 49). By the time of the 1880 census these benign beliefs and ideals were replaced with harsher perceptions and policy goals. Institutions were now perceived as segregated facilities for the "defective, dependent and dangerous classes." Instead of educative hospitals and schools, institutions became sites for "incurables." These perceptions, and related policy goals, survived until after America's Progressive period and the prosperity of the 1920s.

As the nineteenth century drew to a close, insanity and mental retardation were increasingly perceived as visible signs of physical, moral, and social danger. Institutional leaders accepted new theories of hereditary causation that threatened the social order with the future "evil" of reproducing "defectives" and debasing the "social stock" of the nation. From 1874 until 1926 major studies of family genealogies, empirically demonstrating the hereditary lines of degeneration of families like the Jukes and Kalliaks, were sponsored by an array of respectable persons or organizations: the Prison Association of New York; Indianapolis Charity Organization Society; Vineland Training School of New Jersey; Ohio Board of Administration; John D. Rockefeller, Jr.; and the Carnegie Institution (Hahn 1980). These ideas were provided further legitimation in pre-1930 statutes prohibiting the marriage of insane and retarded persons and permitting the sterilization of "defective" persons (Wolfensberger 1976; Leiby 1978; Rosanoff 1927). Marriage laws were difficult to enforce, and sterilization statutes were often deemed morally offensive; but segregation was considered a viable policy (Rosanoff 1927).

During this fifty-year period, there was a continued demand to multiply the number of institutions to house an increasing proportion of the "defective classes." The 1880 census actually attempted to conduct a national count of all "outdoor" members of these classes, in order to help determine the potential number requiring institutionalization. There was an "urgency of the demand for institutions" (U.S. Bureau of the Census, 1882, p. 1,664). The "three great classes" constituted "drains upon the vitality of the community" and represented "evils which are like a canker at the heart of all our prospects" (Ibid., p. 1,665). Instead of persons to be helped, treated, and educated, inmates were perceived as "burdens to be borne" for an indefinite period. These views, expressed in an official census document, were in sharp contrast to the earlier statements by Howe, who referred to all persons in public institutions as "brothers and sisters" and "members of the human family."

In the early twentieth century reformers supported "parole of inmates" from institutions, on a trial basis. But parole was primarily a means to relieve over-crowding, given the persistent urgency to institutionalize a larger proportion of the insane and feeble-minded. The 1910 census reporter wrote of "the increasing conviction that the segregation and institutional care of the feeble-minded is nec-essary, even more as a protection to the public than of benevolence for the in-mates" (U.S. Bureau of the Census, 1910, p. 184). The reporter also wrote that "beyond question the extension of the practice of placing the insane under in-stitutional care has had a very great influence upon the statistics" (Ibid., p. 14).

The marked difference between viewing institutionalized persons as members of the "human family" worth returning to their communities, or as an "evil and burden to be borne" for an indefinite period was reinforced at the turn of the century by an additional ideological concern: the "new immigrants" problem. Besides being regarded as a competitive danger to the economic interests of "na-tive labor" (i.e., older immigrants, arriving prior to 1880), the new immigrants were also depicted as contributing a disproportionate number of defectives to the nation; their ethnic and religious heritage indicated that they were of "inferior stock." Madison Grant, a distinguished anthropologist of the American Museum of Natural History, wrote a widely cited and popular book, *The Passing of the Great Race* (1916). A dozen years later a new edition appeared and sold more widely than the first edition (Handlin 1950, pp. 77, 141). Grant argued in both editions that the new immigrants were not "members of the Nordic race as were the earlier ones." Rather,

> the new immigration contained a large and increasing number of the weak, the bro-ken, and the mentally crippled of all races drawn from the lowest stratum of the Mediterranean basin and the Balkans, together with hordes of the wretched, sub-merged populations of the Polish ghettos. Our jails, insane asylum, and almshouses are filled with this human flotsam and the whole tone of American life, social, moral, and political, has been lowered and vulgarized by them." [Ibid., p. 77]

In the 1920s beliefs about the biological and hereditary inferiority of certain nationalities and races, as well as the defective classes, received further legitimation. Congress passed the nation's first quota statute, restricting immigration by origin of birth. In 1924 the law was amended to ensure that the "Nordic race" was given greater preference; works by Grant and others legitimated the congressional action.

The eugenic danger of the defective classes was also represented in the sixth edition of a reputable psychiatric textbook. Writing in 1927, Rosanoff, although a member of a "new immigrant" group, supported the argument that the "best prevention for insanity, feeble-mindedness and maladjustment" would consist of a eugenics segregation policy. Parole could be granted to inmates, but only to check the eugenic capability of adjusting to the community, or because of age and harmless incapacity (see Chapter 6).

This repressive ideology was not entirely unchallenged during the Progressive and postwar eras. But it is now evident that the 1920s harbored the continued acceptance and dominance of restrictive policies. Sometime during the 1930s these views became ideologically discredited; newer, less hostile emphases began to prevail. The devastating experiences of the Depression may have facilitated the acceptance of ideas emphasizing social, economic, and environmental influences as causes of the nation's social problems. By the end of the 1930s, Rosanoff's seventh edition would no longer contain arguments to segregate a minimum of 1 percent of the nation's population. Instead, as head of the California institutional system, Rosanoff would argue that inmates were to be considered as persons overcoming distressing experiences, and once they could no longer benefit from the hospital, they should be quickly released. Instead of being on "parole," they should receive "extramural or after care." If unable to work, many even had a right to family care, at state expense.

Until the late 1960s and early 1970s witnessed changes in state commitment laws and judicial standards of least restrictiveness and human decency, the mentally disabled were not included in a formal declaration of minimum citizenship rights. However, in retrospect, it is now evident that informal rights were increasingly granted, as a result of the discretionary actions taken by leaders with new beliefs about the personhood of inmates, the functions of state institutions, and the paradigms of treatment. This ideological shift occurred prior to World War II, but was sidetracked by the war and the postwar building boom. The aged and chronically ill, considered of danger to no one, were singled out as candidates for early release. However, until the early 1960s, alternative public resources were not provided to support released persons outside the hospitals and to continue the maintenance of traditional facilities.

It is evident, too, that granting more citizenship rights to more persons required political support within the psychiatric and retardation establishment of a new generation of leaders. These new leaders were interested in using the recent drug technology and in expanding welfare programs to "break down the walls" and accelerate the depopulation of traditional institutions. However, they could not have proceeded so rapidly in a hostile environment. It is now clear that the

receiving communities did not share the fears of earlier generations about released mental and retarded patients; there existed, in fact, a greater degree of
community tolerance.

There are well-known difficulties in procuring and developing, in local neighborhoods, small group residences for the mentally and physically disabled. But it
helps to place these objections into perspective. Earlier generations of populists,
progressives, and prohibitionists would not have been as ready to concede that
local inmates of civil institutions deserved normal citizenship rights, let alone the
status of new community neighbors. Although today's opposition groups might
argue that those released from institutions do not belong on "our block," it is rare
to encounter the position that former patients—even if strangers—do not have a
natural right to live their lives outside of a state institution. State legislators have
even begun to codify this right by amending state zoning laws and legally defining community residential facilities of limited size as a "permitted use in all residential zones" (Lauber and Bangs 1974). The "moral majority" of an earlier
generation would hardly have countenanced such a eugenically foolish idea.

Assessing the Paradoxes of Deinstitutionalization

A probing study of DE reveals a number of surprising paradoxes. Whereas traditional institutions have been depopulated or reduced in size, new institutional
forms have also emerged during the last quarter century. Although the welfare
state has helped DE by subsidizing ex-patients outside of institutions, it has also
been a major patron of the nursing home industry and provided traditional MR
institutions with a renewed chance of survival for many years. Public welfare has
increased the number of institutional-type social functions supported by federal
and state dollars, but it has also introduced more opportunities to profit from this
welfare expansion. The mentally disabled have been granted greater freedom of
treatment, care, and supervision outside of traditional institutions, but they have
also been subject to new forms of physical, personal, and social control. And
more persons are experiencing a stay—albeit short—in an institutional facility
in 1980, than occurred twenty, thirty, or fifty years ago.

These are not the only paradoxes that emerge from the analysis. Persons over
65 and under 18 are increasingly singled out as the two age groups that are "underserved." Yet, the more they are "served" by professional agencies, the greater the
likelihood that their rates of institutionalization will increase. These two age
groups, in fact, display the sharpest increases in institutionalization over a fifty-
year period. It appears, too, that the greater the increase in "service," the greater
the likelihood of institutional bias in funding. Service promoters might argue that
more adults are living past 65 years of age, thereby increasing the chance that
they will require physical, social, and personal care at some time in their lives.
This is undoubtedly true, but other societies appear to deal with these problems
by creating a greater array of home care services (see Chapter 10).

As for youth, it could be argued that more "acting out" youth are emotionally disturbed today than fifty years ago, or that more youth today require a detention lockup prior to receiving a judicial hearing than was true in the 1920s. However, neither argument is valid. There is no evidence that youth admitted to psychiatric units of general hospitals, public and private mental hospitals, or residential treatment centers are any "sicker" than those of a previous generation or that the "treatment" is effective. Nor is there evidence that youth experiencing detention, with or without an adjudication of delinquency, are more likely to desist from future troublesome behaviors. Instead mental health professionals and court officials (including judges) behave as if increasing the use of institutional services is the preferred policy. One group uses a therapeutic rationale, while the other relies on a theory of deterrence; the policy result appears similar.

Given all of these paradoxes, how are we to assess the impacts of DE policies and activities? Critics, of course, emphasize the negative results, while proponents of DE understandably accentuate the positive outcomes. At present it is impossible to categorize these results neatly according to effectiveness or cost criteria. Instead, one must rely primarily on judgments based on nuances of interpretations of data; these judgments, however, are informed by assumptions and value preferences. Relying solely on technical criteria of the effectiveness of DE presents difficulties because the policies were not really chosen on these grounds. In addition, clear-cut technologies do not exist for curing mental illness, habilitating the retarded, restoring senile persons to normal functioning, or transforming "acting out" youth into conformers (Mechanic 1980; Balla 1976; Lerman 1975).

Cost-effectiveness analysis, another popular criterion for assessing alternatives, also presents difficulties. This mode of analysis assumes that all program efforts and outcomes can be quantified, but how does one allocate cost values to unnecessary restrictions on liberty? Aside from this complex problem, studies providing a comparison of the relative costs of traditional and nontraditional programs have yielded mixed results. A uniform accounting scheme does not yet exist for determining whose costs should be computed, what items are to be included, the time period to use, the present discount rates that are applicable, or other technical matters. After a recent sophisticated effort, Weisbrod noted: "What is controversial is not whether benefits and costs should be compared, but *what* to count as benefits and costs, and *how* to compare them" (Weisbrod et al. 1980, p. 1). After a serious attempt to estimate the economic benefits and costs of a random experiment involving a professionally staffed community-support versus state-hospital program, Weisbrod (an economist), Test (a social work educator), and Stein (a psychiatrist) commented about their major findings as follows:

> (1) Total costs of treating mental patients are very high—more than $7,200 per patient per year, whether a hospital-based (C type) program or a community-based (E type) program is used.

(2) A very sizable proportion of costs (between 40 and 50 percent) are in forms other than direct treatment costs for either treatment.

(3) While the experimental, community-based treatment program involved *larger* direct treatment costs per patient than did the hospital-based program, the community-based program involves *smaller* costs in every other form—indirect treatment, law enforcement, maintenance, and family burdens. Considering all forms of costs in total, the hospital-based program is about 10 percent cheaper per patient.

(4) On the benefit side, the community-based program is associated with a doubling of work productivity as gauged by the differential in total earnings of the patients in the two programs.

(5) Considering all the forms of benefits and costs we have been able to derive in monetary terms, the experimental program provides both additional benefits and additional costs as compared to the conventional treatment approach, but the added benefits, $1,196 per patient per year, are nearly $400 more per patient per year than the added costs, $797." [Weisbrod et al. 1980]

This study reveals that if only *direct* costs are counted, an ideal community-based training and social support program can be more expensive than a state hospital program over a one-year period (about $3,138 to $4,798); if *indirect* costs are included—the use of general hospitals, sheltered workshops, and community health, employment, and social service agencies—the comparison still favors the hospital, although indirect costs are less expensive for the E type program; if *income maintenance* payments and in kind costs are included, the comparison still favors the hospital, although these costs are less for the E type program. The economic evaluation is reversed when benefits accruing from a greater amount of earnings from competitive employment and sheltered workshops are included; the benefit differential yields the following results per person (Weisbrod et al. 1980, table 1):

	C Type/ Hospital Group	E Type/ Community Group
Value of all costs	−$7,296	−$8,093
Value of all benefits	1,168	2,364
Net costs	−$6,128	−$5,729

From a *government budget* perspective, the state hospital program is economically preferable to an ideal community-support program, in that the difference in costs stems mainly from this source. However, from a *societal* perspective, the benefits accruing to the individual, for valued work, are high enough to reverse the cost assessment—about $400 less per person for the E type group. Added to these benefits are others that were not amenable to fiscal quantification: fewer hospitalizations for nonpsychiatric illness; lower rates of clinical symptomatology; higher levels of expressed "satisfaction with life"; and less time unemployed. These benefits, however, only lasted during the one year when intensive services were provided to the experimental group.

Because this is one of the most thorough social and economic evaluations in the mental health literature, one might attempt to use this study for policy guidance. Yet, this is extremely difficult for a variety of reasons: (1) The site where comparisons were made is in a county surrounding a university community (Madison) in a "progressive" state (Wisconsin). (2) The hospital cost per diem was estimated to be $99; the average length of use, per patient during 12 months, was about 32 days. In 1976–77, at the time of the experiment, the average stay in all Wisconsin hospitals was about 56 days—much longer than that of the control group (NIMH, *Statistical Note*, no. 153, table 6). If a statewide rather than a local sample had been used, the state hospital direct costs would have been much higher. (3) Compared to a national sample, time spent in the experimental control hospitals is even longer than in the Wisconsin state figures; in 1976–77 nationwide, the length of stay per resident under care during a year was about 108 days. At this rate, the direct cost would have amounted to about $5,400; this is much higher than the control hospital cost ($3,138) or the direct experimental program cost ($4,798) (Ibid., tables 6 and 7).

It is evident that differences in annual average length of institutional stay and per diem costs can appreciably alter the fiscal outcome. Thus, it is extremely difficult to project the results from an atypical county hospital in Madison, Wisconsin, onto other parts of the state, other states, or the nation as a whole. Indirect and income-maintenance values might also be expected to vary, although perhaps not as sharply as the direct cost data.

The benefits could also be expected to vary. It is possible that other community-support programs might not make as strong an effort to influence pro-employment activities. Even if other programs simulated the Wisconsin experiment, employment opportunities vary by community. Paid work, however, is a value not under the control of the treatment program professionals. If all other values were equal, and just employment opportunities varied, those programs relying on the fiscal benefits of paid work to offset higher community program costs would, of course, be at a disadvantage.

Given these difficulties, as well as the lack of consensus about *what* should be counted and *how* to compare costs and benefits, analysts are forced to rely on judgment to assess policy choices. As noted earlier, this judgment depends heavily on normative ideals. Although analysts, like legislators and administrators, share many ideals, variability often occurs in the ranking of preferences. HEW officials favor "balanced systems," cost effectiveness, and the "ultimate ideal" of least restrictiveness. The GAO favors a least restrictive, normalization doctrine, but also includes a proposal to upgrade traditional facilities. In contrast, I deliberately minimize upgrading and balanced systems, so that the least restrictive doctrine can capture a greater share of the resources disproportionately allocated to the traditional system.

Regarding the least restrictive doctrine, progress has been made in expanding citizenship rights for the mentally disabled, and increasing their access to public welfare resources outside of a traditional institution. However, a fair assessment of the past two decades reveals that these benefits have accrued mainly to persons between 21 and 64 years of age. I believe that it is possible both to promote these benefits even further, and to diminish the added social costs that have accompanied DE of the young and the aged.

Prospects for the Future

Chapter 10 provided suggestions for diminishing the impact of the fundamental law—contained in the Social Security Titles—that impedes rather than promotes a least restrictive policy. These proposals are based on the assumption that the provision of food, shelter, clothing, medical care, and other basic amenities is a necessary requisite for living the most normal life possible outside of an institutional setting. In addition, many of those persons who would have been candidates for traditional institutions often require physical, personal, and social care, support, or assistance, in living. Although the Social Security Act provides for basic provisions, it does not yet provide for a full program of home care. However, it probably offers the most viable basis for expanding this traditional welfare function.

The proposed amendments to the Social Security Title are based on the view that accessible fiscal resources are being used to upgrade MR institutions, support unnecessary nursing home placements, subsidize maintenance payments for institutional foster care, and legitimate social services in traditional institutions. These resources could be diverted toward alternative, less restrictive forms of living, care, and social support programs. In addition, if SSI were federalized at a higher payment level, mentally disabled adults could be offered a realistic choice of whether to live alone, with relatives, or in a shelter home. In 1979, this latter proposal meant that eligible individuals would receive income sufficient to raise them above the poverty level of $3,490 per year for persons 65 or older, and $3,780 for persons under 65 (*Social Security Bulletin, Annual Statistical Supplement, 1977–79*, table 9). On 1 July 1979, the maximum federal payment was $208.20, or about $2,500 per year (Ibid., p. 40). Because the average optional supplements provided by the states are far below the poverty threshold gaps of $1,000 to $1,200, it is evident that many disabled and aged SSI recipients will continue to live at substandard levels (see Chapter 10).

With the exception of the SSI proposal, the proposed changes are keyed to reducing federal payments for institution-oriented programs and diverting funds to alternative home-based programs. The proposed benefits are expected to be social rather than fiscal, but the non-SSI changes are expected to occur within a program for achieving fiscal savings. Although enactment of these proposals could result in unexpected outcomes, the alternative—accepting the status quo —runs the risk of continually multiplying costs, fiscal and social.

Bibliography

Abbott, E. 1933. *Some American Pioneers in Social Welfare*. Chicago: University of Chicago Press. Reprint. Chicago: Midway, 1974.

American Federation of State, County, and Municipal Employees. 1975. *Deinstitutionalization: Out of Their Beds and into the Streets*, prepared by Henry Santiestaven. Washington, D.C.: The Federation.

American Psychiatric Association. 1949–1954. *Mental Hospital Institute Proceedings*. Washington, D.C.: American Psychiatric Association.

———. 1955. *Pharmacologic Products Recently Introduced in the Treatment of Psychiatric Disorders*. Washington, D.C.: American Psychiatric Association.

———. 1956. *Psychiatric Research Report 4: An Evaluation of the Newer Psychopharmacologic Agents and Their Role in Current Psychiatric Practice*. Washington, D.C.: American Psychiatric Association.

———. 1958–1968. *Biographical Directory of Fellows and Members of the American Psychiatric Association*. 1958 and 1968 eds. New York: Bowker and Co.

———. 1964. *Standards for Hospitals and Clinics*. 1958 rev. ed. Washington, D.C.: American Psychiatric Association.

American Public Welfare Association. 1978–1980. *Washington Report*. Washington, D.C.: American Public Welfare Association.

Anderson, N. N.; Patten, S. K.; Greenberg, J. N.; and Fine, R. E. 1977. *A Comparison of In-Home and Nursing Home Care for Older Persons*. Minneapolis: School of Public Affairs, University of Minnesota.

Arnhoff, F. N. 1975. Social Consequences of Policy toward Mental Illness. *Science* 188: 1277–81.

Association for Research in Nervous and Mental Disease. 1959. *The Effects of Pharmacologic Agents on the Nervous System*. Vol. 37. Baltimore: Williams and Wilkins Co.

Aviram, U. 1972. "Mental Health Reform and the After Care State Service." Ph.D. dissertation, pts. 1 and 2. University of California at Berkeley.

Aviram, U., and Segal, S. P. 1973. Exclusion of the Mentally Ill: Reflections on an Old Problem in a New Context. *Archives of General Psychiatry* 29: 122–31.

Aviram, U.; Syme, L. S.; and Cohen, J. B. 1976. The Effects of Policies and Programs on Reduction of Mental Hospitalization. *Social Science and Medicine* 10: 571–77.

Bachrach, L. 1976. *Deinstitutionalization: An Analytical Review and Sociological Perspective*. In National Institute of Mental Health, *Conference on Committee Reports, and Analytical Reviews of Literature*, Series D, no. 4. Washington, D.C.: U.S. Government Printing Office.

Bakal, Y. 1973. *Strategies for Restructuring the State Department of Youth Services*. (SRS) 73–26034. U.S. Department of Health, Education, and Welfare, Office of Youth Development. Washington, D.C.: U.S. Government Printing Office.

225

————. 1973. *Closing Correctional Institutions: New Strategies for Youth Services.* Lexington, Mass.: Lexington Books.

Balla, D. A. 1976. Relationship of Institution Size to Quality of Care: A Review of the Literature. *American Journal of Mental Deficiency* 81: 117–24.

Bardach, E. 1972. *The Skill Factor in Politics: Repealing the Mental Commitment Laws in California.* Berkeley: University of California Press.

Bassuk, E., and Gerson, S. 1978. Deinstitutionalization and Mental Health Services. *Scientific American* 338: 46–53.

Bennett, D. 1979. Deinstitutionalization in Two Cultures. *Health and Society* 57: 516–32.

Bernstein, B.; Snider, D.; and Meezan, W. 1975. *Foster Care Needs and Alternatives to Placement.* New York: Center for City Affairs, New School for Social Research. Reprint. U.S. Senate Committee on Labor and Public Welfare, pt. 1:153–282, 1975.

Blain, D. 1956. Changing Patterns of Mental Hospital Patients. *Mental Hospitals* (Supplement) 10:1–8.

Bock, W. February 1977. *An Analysis of Minnesota's Effort to Reintegrate Its Mentally Retarded Citizens into the Community.* State of Minnesota Mental Retardation Program Division. St. Paul, Minn.: Department of Public Welfare. Mimeographed.

Brace, C. L. 1872. *The Dangerous Classes of New York and Twenty Years' Work among Them.* Reprint, pp. 223–45. Washington, D.C.: National Association of Social Workers, 1973.

Bremner, R. H.; Barnard, J.; Haraven, T. K.; and Mennel, R. M. 1971. *Children and Youth in America: A Documentary History.* 2 vols. Cambridge, Mass.: Harvard University Press.

Cahn, F., and Bary, V. 1936. *Welfare Activities of Federal, State, and Local Governments in California, 1850–1934.* Berkeley: University of California Press.

California Medical Association. 1962. Editorial. *California Medicine* 96:204–5.

Callahan, J.; Diamond, L.; Giele, J.; and Morris, R. 1980. Responsibility of Families for their Severely Disabled Elders. *Health Care Financing Review* 1, no. 3:29–49.

Callison, James C. 1974. Early Experience under the Supplemental Security Income Program. *Social Security Bulletin* 37:3–12.

Cameron, D. E. 1950. Day Hospital Care in Canada. American Psychiatric Association. 1949–1954. *Mental Hospital Institute Proceedings.* Washington, D.C.: American Psychiatric Association.

Chase, J. 1973. Where Have All the Patients Gone? *Human Behavior* 2, no. 10:14–21.

Child Welfare League of America. 1974. *Newsletter* 4, no. 2:1–8.

Children's Defense Fund. April 1977. *Children without Homes: An Examination of Public Responsibility to Children in Out of Home Care. An Overview.* Prepared by J. Knitzer and M. Allen. Washington, D.C.: Children's Defense Fund. Mimeographed.

————. 1978. *Children without Homes.* Washington, D.C.: Children's Defense Fund.

City of New York. 1978. *The Children Are Waiting: The Failure To Achieve Permanent Homes for Foster Children in New York City.* New York: New York City Comptrollers Office.

Coates, R.; Miller, A.; and Ohlin, L. July 1975. *Quarterly Report of the DYS Project.* Cambridge, Mass.: Harvard Law School, Center for Criminal Justice. Mimeographed.

————. July 1976. *Social Climate, Extent of Community Linkages, and Quality of Community Linkages: The Institutionalization-Normalization Continuum.* Cambridge, Mass.: Harvard Law School, Center for Criminal Justice. Mimeographed.

Cohen, F. 1980. *The Law of Deprivation of Liberty: A Study in Social Control, Cases and Materials.* St. Paul, Minn.: West Publishing Co.

Cole, J. O.; Gardos, G.; and Nelson, M. 1978. "Alternatives to Chronic Hospitalization." In *Alternatives to Mental Hospital Treatment,* edited by L. I. Stein and M. A. Test. New York: Plenum Press.

Connery, R. H.; Backstrom, C. H.; Deewer, D. R.; Friedman, J. R.; Krull, M.; Marden, R. H.; McCleskey, C.; Meekison, P.; and Morgan, J. A. 1968. *The Politics of Mental Health.* New York: Columbia University Press.

Council of State Governments. 1950. *The Mental Health Programs of the Forty-Eight States: A Report to the Governor's Conference.* Chicago: Council of State Governments.

Crutcher, H. B. 1944. *Foster Home Care For Mental Patients.* New York: Commonwealth Fund.

Cupaiuolo, A. A. 1977. Community Residences and Zoning Ordinances. *Hospital and Community Psychiatry* 28:206–10.

Derthick, M. 1975. *Uncontrollable Spending for Social Service Grants.* Washington, D.C.: The Brookings Institution.

Edwards, R. M. 1964. Functions of the State Mental Hospital As a Social Institution. *Mental Hygiene* 48:666–71.

Enki Research Institute. 1972. *A Study of California's New Mental Health Law.* Chatsworth, Calif.: Enki. Mimeographed.

Ferleger, D. 1976. *Kramens* v. *Bartley: The Right to be Free. Hospital and Community Psychiatry* 27, no. 10:708–12.

————. 1978. The Future of Institutions for Retarded Citizens: The Promise of the Pennhurst Case. In *Mental Retardation and the Law,* pp. 28–42. President's Committee on Mental Retardation.

Fox, R. W. 1978. *So Far Disordered in Mind: Insanity in California, 1870–1930.* Berkeley: University of California Press.

Freeland, M.; Calat, C.; and Schewdler, C. 1980. Projections of National Health Expenditures. *Health Care Financing Review* 1, no. 3:1–29.

Gary, W., et al. v. *State of Louisiana.* July 1976. Reprint of U.S. Senate Committee on Labor and Public Welfare, 1975, pt. 2:310–421.

Gottfredson, M. R.; Hindelang, M. J.; and Parisi, N. 1978. *Sourcebook of Criminal Justice Statistics—1977.* U.S. Law Enforcement Assistance Administration, National Criminal Justice Information and Statistics Service. Washington, D.C.: U.S. Government Printing Office.

Grob, G. N. 1966. *The State and the Mentally Ill: A History of the Worcester State Hospital in Massachusetts, 1830–1920.* Chapel Hill: University of North Carolina Press.

————. 1973. *Mental Institutions in America: Social Policy to 1875.* New York: Free Press.

Hahn, N. F. 1980. Too Dumb To Know Better: Cacogenic Family Studies and the Criminology of Women. *Criminology* 18:3–26.

Halderman v. *Pennhurst State School and Hospital.* December 1977. 446 Federal Supplement 1295 (Eastern District, Pennsylvania, 1977).

————. December 1979. 612 Federal 2nd District 84 (Third Court of Appeals 1979).

————. July 1978. Discussion of case by Attorney for Plaintiffs. See Ferleger, D., July, 1978.

Handlin, O. 1950. *Race and Nationality in American Life*. Boston: Little Brown & Co.

Hargrove, E. C. July 1975. *The Missing Link: The Study of the Implementation of Social Policy*. Washington, D.C.: Urban Institute. Mimeographed.

Harvard Law School, Center for Criminal Justice. July 1975. *Quarterly Report of the DYS Project*. Mimeographed.

Hawkins, S. 1980. SSI: Trends in State Supplementation, 1974–78. *Social Security Bulletin* 43, no. 7:19–28.

Health and Society Issue. 1979. Deinstitutionalization: The Evolution and Evaluation of Health Care Policy in the United States and Great Britain. *Health and Society* 57, no. 4.

Health Care Financing Administration. May 1977. Additions to pt. t of Medical Assistance Manual at 5-81-00. Washington, D.C.: Health Care Financing Administration, U.S. Department of Health, Education, and Welfare. Action transmittal memo to State Agencies Administering Medical Assistance Program. Mimeographed.

Hennepin County MH/MR/CD Department. July 1976. *Proposed Service Plan for Mentally Retarded People in Hennepin County*. Minneapolis, Minn. Mimeographed.

————. June 1977, 1978. *County Budget Overview: Mental Retardation*, prepared by Robin Reich. Minneapolis, Minn.

Hindelang, M. J.; Gottfredson, M. R.; Dunn, C. S.; and Parisi, N. 1975–77. *Sourcebook of Criminal Justice—1974 and 1976*. Washington, D.C.: U.S. Department of Justice, Law Enforcement Assistance Administration.

————. 1977. *Sourcebook of Criminal Statistics—1976*. Washington, D.C.: U.S. Department of Justice, Law Enforcement Assistance Administration.

Hofstadter, R. 1955. *Social Darwinism in American Thought*. Rev. ed. 1969. New York: George Braziller.

Kadushin, A. 1974. *Child Welfare Services*. 2d. ed. New York: Macmillan.

Kahn, K. A.; Hines, W.; Woodson, A. S.; and Burkhan-Armstrong, G. 1977. A Multidisciplinary Approach to Assessing the Quality of Care in Long-Term Care Facilities. *Gerontologist* 17, no. 1:61–65.

Kochhar, S. 1977. SSI Recipients in Domiciliary Care Facilities: Federally Administered Optional Supplementation, March 1976. *Social Security Bulletin*. HEW Pub. no. (SSA) 78-117000:17–28. Washington, D.C.: U.S. Department of HEW, Social Security Administration.

Kramer, M. 1977. *Psychiatric Services and the Changing Institutional Scene, 1950–1985*. In National Institute of Mental Health, *Analytical and Special Study Reports*, Series B, no. 12. Washington, D.C.: U.S. Government Printing Office.

Lamb, H. R. 1975. The New Asylums in the Community. *Archives of General Psychiatry* 36: 129–34.

Lauber, D., and Bangs, F. S., Jr. 1974. *Zoning for Family and Group Care Facilities* ASPO Report no. 300. Washington, D.C.: American Society of Planning Officials.

Leiby, J. 1967. *Charities and Corrections in New Jersey*. New Brunswick, N.J.: Rutgers University Press.

————. 1978. *A History of Social Welfare and Social Work in the United States*. New York: Columbia University Press.

Lerman, P. 1975. *Community Treatment and Social Control*. Chicago: University of Chicago Press.

————. 1977. Discussion of Differential Selection of Juveniles for Detention. *Journal of Research in Crime and Delinquency* 14, no. 2:166–73.

————. 1977. Delinquency and Social Policy: An Historical Perspective. *Crime and Delinquency* 23, no. 4:383–94.

————. 1980. Trends and Issues in Deinstitutionalization of Youths in Trouble. *Crime and Delinquency* 24, no. 4:281–98.

Lerman, P.; Dickson, D.; Lerman, C.; and Lagay, B. July 1974. *The New Jersey Training School for Girls: A Study of Alternatives.* Final Report of State Contract Between Dr. Paul Lerman and the State of New Jersey. Mimeographed.

Levin, M., and Sarri, R. 1974. *Juvenile Delinquency: A Study of Juvenile Codes in the U.S.* In National Assessment of Juvenile Corrections, *Juvenile Delinquency: A Study of Juvenile Codes in the U.S.* Ann Arbor: University of Michigan.

Levine, D. S., and Levine, D. R. 1975. *The Cost of Mental Illness—1971.* In National Institute of Mental Health, *Analytical and Special Study Reports,* Series B, no. 7. Washington, D.C.: U.S. Government Printing Office.

Lewis, C. E.; Fein, R.; Mechanic, D. 1976. *A Right to Health: The Problem of Access to Primary Health Care.* New York: John Wiley and Sons.

Little, V. C. 1978. Open Care for the Aged: A Swedish Model. *Social Work* 23, no. 4:282–88.

Liu, K., and Mossey, J. 1980. The Role of Payment Source in Differentiating Nursing Home Residents, Services, and Payments. *Health Care Financing Review* 2, no. 1:51–63.

Lubove, R. 1968. *The Struggle for Social Security.* Cambridge, Mass.: Harvard University Press.

McCormick, M.; Balla, D.; and Zigler, E. 1975. Resident Care Practices in Institutions for Retarded Persons: A Cross-Institutional, Cross-Cultural Study. *American Journal of Mental Deficiency* 80, no. 1:1–17.

Maluccio, A. N., and Marlow, M. D. 1972. Residential Treatment of Emotionally Disturbed Children: A Review of the Literature. *Social Service Review* 46, no. 2: 230–51.

Mead, L. M. April 1977. *Institutional Analysis: An Approach to Implementation Problems in Medicaid.* Washington, D.C.: The Urban Institute. Mimeographed.

Mechanic, D. 1969. *Mental Health and Social Policy.* Rev. ed., 1980. Englewood Cliffs, N.J.: Prentice-Hall.

Mental Health Association. 1978. *Back Wards to Back Streets: A Study of People in Transition from Psychiatric Hospital to Community.* East Orange, N.J.: Mental Health Association of Essex County. Mimeographed.

Mercer, J. R. 1973. *Labeling the Mentally Retarded.* Berkeley: University of California Press.

Milazzo-Sayre, L. 1978. State Trends in Resident Patients—State and County Mental Hospital Inpatient Services, 1971–75. In National Institute of Mental Health, 1967– 80. *Statistical Note, no. 150.* Washington, D.C.: U.S. Government Printing Office.

Miller, D., and Miller, D. October 1976. *Runaway, Illegal Aliens in their Own Land: Implications for Service.* San Francisco: Scientific Analysis Corp. Mimeographed.

Miller, R. B., and Kenney, E. 1966. Adolescent Delinquency and the Myth of Hospital Treatment. *Crime and Delinquency* 12, no. 1:38–48. Reprinted in *Delinquency and Social Policy,* edited by P. Lerman. New York: Praeger, 1970.

Moos, R. H. 1975. *Evaluating Correctional and Community Settings*. New York: John Wiley and Sons.

Moroney, R. M. 1976. *The Family and the State—Considerations for Social Policy*. London: Longman Group.

Morris, R. 1977. Caring for vs. Caring about People. *Social Work* 22:353–60.

Mott, P. E. February 1976. *Meeting Human Needs: The Social and Political History of Title XX*. Columbus, Ohio: National Conference on Social Welfare. Mimeographed.

Mulhearn, J. May 1974. Closing State Hospitals: Accreditation as a Factor. In *Where Is My Home?* Proceedings of a Conference on the Closing of State Mental Hospitals. Menlo Park, Calif.: Stanford Research Institute. Mimeographed.

Murphy, J. G., and Datel, W. 1976. A Cost-Benefit Analysis of Community vs. Institution Living. *Hospital and Community Psychiatry* 27, no. 3:165–70.

National Assessment of Juvenile Corrections. 1974. *Juvenile Delinquency: A Study of Juvenile Codes in the U.S.* Ann Arbor: University of Michigan.

———. 1974. *Under Lock and Key: Juveniles in Jails and Detention*. Ann Arbor: University of Michigan.

———. 1975. *Juvenile Corrections in the States: Residential Programs and Deinstitutionalization*. Ann Arbor: University of Michigan.

National Association for Retarded Citizens. 1977. Statement on Welfare Reform. In President's Commission on Mental Health 4:2055–65.

National Center for Health Statistics. February 1965. Development and Maintenance of a National Inventory of Hospitals and Institutions. Washington, D.C.: U.S. Department of HEW, Public Health Service. Mimeographed.

———. 1965–80. Data on Health Resources Utilization. Series 13. Washington, D.C.: U.S. Department of Health, Education, and Welfare, Public Health Service.

———. 1972–80. Data on Health Resources: Manpower and Facilities. Series 14. Washington, D.C.: Department of Health, Education, and Welfare, Public Health Service.

National Council on Aging. 1976. Public Policy Agenda, 1976–77. *Perspectives on Aging* 5:40–42.

National Fire Protection Association. 1975. Code for Safety to Life from Fire in Buildings and Structures (NFPA 101-1973). In *National Fire Codes* 9 (1975). Boston: National Fire Protection Association.

National Institute of Mental Health. 1967–80. *Mental Health Statistical Notes*, nos. 1–153. Washington, D.C.: U.S. Government Printing Office.

———. 1969–78. *Mental Health Facility Reports*, Series A. Washington, D.C.: U.S. Government Printing Office.

———. 1968–78. *Analytical and Special Study Reports*, Series B. Washington, D.C.: U.S. Government Printing Office.

———. 1969–78. *Methodology Reports*, Series C. Washington, D.C.: U.S. Government Printing Office.

———. 1970–75. *Conference on Committee Reports, and Analytical Reviews of Literature*, Series D. Washington, D.C.: U.S. Government Printing Office.

———. May 1976. *List of Publications*, prepared by staff of Division on Biometry and Epidemiology. Washington, D.C.: U.S. Government Printing Office.

National Institute of Mental Health, Survey and Reports Branch. No date. *1973 Profile for Federally Funded Community Mental Health Centers*. Washington, D.C.: NIMH, Division of Biometry. Mimeographed.

Noyes, A. P. 1953. *Modern Clinical Psychiatry*. 4th ed. Philadelphia: W. B. Saunders.

Noyes, A. P., and Kolb, L. C. 1958. *Modern Clinical Psychiatry.* 5th ed. Philadelphia: W. B. Saunders.

O'Connor, G. 1976. *Home Is a Good Place.* AMD Monograph no. 2. Washington, D.C.: American Association on Mental Deficiency.

O'Connor, G., and Sitkei, E. G. 1975. Study of a New Frontier in Community Services: Residential Facilities for the Developmentally Disabled. *Mental Retardation* 13, no. 4:35–39.

Ohlin, L.; Coates, R.; and Miller, A. 1974. Radical Correctional Reform: A Case Study of the Massachusetts Youth Correctional System. *Harvard Educational Review* 44, no. 1:74–111.

Ohlin, L.; Miller, A.; and Coates, R. 1977. *Juvenile Correctional Reform in Massachusetts: A Preliminary Report of the Center for Criminal Justice of the Harvard Law School.* U.S. Law Enforcement Assistance Administration, Office of Juvenile Justice and Delinquency Prevention. Washington, D.C.: U.S. Government Printing Office.

Ozawa, M. N. 1974. SSI: Progress or Retreat. *Public Welfare* 32, no. 2:33–40.

———. 1978. Issues in Welfare Reform. *Social Service Review* 52, no. 1:37–56.

Pappenfort, D. M.; Kilpatrick, D. M.; and Dinwoodie, A. 1970. *Population of Children's Residential Institutions in the United States.* Social Service Monographs, Series no. 4, vols. 1–7. Chicago: Center for Urban Studies, University of Chicago.

Pasamanick, B.; Scarpitti, F.; and Dinitz, S. 1967. *Schizophrenics in the Community.* New York: Appleton-Century-Crofts.

Paul, J.; Stedman, D.; and Newfield, G., eds. 1977. *Deinstitutionalization: Program and Policy Development.* Syracuse, N.Y.: Syracuse University Press.

Pennhurst State School v. *Halderman.* April 1981. 67L. Ed 2d 694, 101 Sup. Court.

Pers, J. S. 1974. *Somebody Else's Children: A Report on the Foster Care System in California.* Prepared for University of California School of Law (Berkeley) Childhood and Government Project. Reprinted in U.S. Senate Committee on Labor and Public Welfare, pt. 1:441–605. Washington, D.C.: U.S. Government Printing Office.

Piasecki, J. R.; Pittinger, J. E.; and Rutman, I. D. 1978. *Determining the Costs of Community Residential Services for the Psychosocially Disabled.* In National Institute of Mental Health, *Analytical and Special Study Reports,* Series B, no. 13. Washington, D.C.: U.S. Government Printing Office.

Piven, F. F., and Cloward, R. A. 1971. *Regulating the Poor: The Functions of Public Welfare.* New York: Random House.

President's Commission on Mental Health. September 1977. *Preliminary Report to the President, 1977.* Mimeographed.

———. 1978. *Report and Recommendations to the President,* vol. 1. Washington, D.C.: U.S. Government Printing Office.

———. 1978. *Task Panel Reports,* vols. 2–4. Washington, D.C.: U.S. Government Printing Office.

President's Committee on Mental Retardation. 1968. *Changing Patterns in Residential Services for the Mentally Retarded.* Washington, D.C.: U.S. Government Printing Office.

———. 1976. *Changing Patterns in Residential Services for the Mentally Retarded.* Rev. ed. Washington, D.C.: U.S. Government Printing Office.

———. 1976–1978. *Mental Retardation and the Law: A Report on Status of Current Court Cases.* DHEW Publication nos. (OHD) 76-21012; (OHD) 77-21012; (OHD) 78-21012. Washington, D.C.: U.S. Government Printing Office.

————. 1976. *Mental Retardation: The Known and the Unknown*. Washington, D.C.: U.S. Government Printing Office.

————. 1976. *Mental Retardation—Trends in State Services*. Washington, D.C.: U.S. Government Printing Office.

Reich, R. July 1976. *Proposed Service Plan for Mentally Retarded People in Hennepin County*. Hennepin County MH/MR/CD Department. Minneapolis, Minn. Mimeographed.

————. June 1977. *1978 County Budget Overview*. Hennepin County MH/MR/CD Department. Minneapolis: Minn. Mimeographed.

Robertson, A. G. 1974. The California Plan. In *Where Is My Home?* Proceedings on a Conference of the Closing of State Mental Hospitals. Menlo Park, Calif.: Stanford Research Institute. Mimeographed.

Robins, L. N. 1966. *Deviant Children Grown Up*. Baltimore: Williams and Wilkins.

Rosanoff, A. J. 1927. *Manual of Psychiatry*. 6th ed. New York: John Wiley and Sons.

————. 1938. *Manual of Psychiatry and Mental Hygiene*. 7th ed. New York: John Wiley and Sons.

————. 1939. California State Hospitals: The Problem of Overcrowding. *California and Western Medicine* 50:109–11.

Rosenthal, M. June 1977. *Report on Residential Care of the Department of Youth Services in Massachusetts*. Trenton, N.J.: Child Advocacy Program of the N.J. Public Defender's Office. Mimeographed.

Rothman, D. J. 1971. *The Discovery of the Asylum: Social Order and Disorder in the New Republic*. Boston: Little, Brown & Co.

————. 1980. *Conscience and Convenience: The Asylum and Its Alternatives in Progressive America*. Boston: Little, Brown & Co.

Rutherford, A. 1974. *The Dissolution of the Training Schools in Massachusetts*. Crime and Justice Paper no. 1. Columbus, Ohio: Academy for Contemporary Problems.

Rutherford, A., and Bengur, O. 1976. *Community-Based Alternatives to Juvenile Incarceration*. National Institute of Law Enforcement and Criminal Justice National Evaluation Program, Series A, No. 7. Washington, D.C.: U.S. Government Printing Office.

Sabatier, P., and Mazmanian, D. 1980. The Implementation of Public Policy: A Framework of Analysis. *Policy Studies Journal* 8:538–60.

Saleeby, G. 1975. *Hidden Closets: A Study of Detention Practices in California*. Sacramento: California Youth Authority.

Sarri, R. C. 1974. *Under Lock and Key*. In National Assessment of Juvenile Corrections, *Juvenile Delinquency: A Study of Juvenile Codes in the U.S.* Ann Arbor: University of Michigan.

Scheerenberger, R. C. 1974. A Model for Deinstitutionalization. *Mental Retardation* 12, no. 6:3–5.

————. 1976. A Study of Public Residential Facilities. *Mental Retardation* 14, no. 1:32–35.

————. 1976. *Deinstitutionalization and Institutional Reform*. Springfield, Ill.: Charles C. Thomas.

Schlossman, S. L. 1977. *Love and the American Delinquent: The Theory and Practice of "Progressive" Juvenile Justice, 1825–1920*. Chicago: University of Chicago Press.

Scull, A. T. 1977. *Decarceration: Community Treatment and the Deviant—A Radical View*. Englewood Cliffs, N.J.: Prentice-Hall.

Segal, S. P., and Aviram, U. 1978. *The Mentally Ill in Community-Based Sheltered Care: A Study of Community Care and Social Integration.* New York: John Wiley and Sons.

Stanford Research Institute. 1974. *Where Is My Home?* Proceedings of a Conference on the Closing of State Mental Hospitals. Menlo Park, Calif.: Stanford Research Institute. Mimeographed.

State of California Department of Health. 1975. *Laws and Regulations Relating to Licensing of Community Care Facilities.* Sacramento: California Department of Health.

————. April 1977. *Plan of the Community Development Task Force for Services to the Mentally Ill.* Sacramento: California Department of Health Treatment Services Division. Mimeographed.

————. July 1977. Memo. County Mental Health Plan Instructions, 1978–79. Sacramento: California Department of Health. Mimeographed.

State of California Department of Mental Health. January 1976. *State Hospitals Utilization Project Report.* Sacramento: California Department of Health. Mimeographed.

State of Massachusetts Department of Youth Services. July 1976. *Task Force on Secure Facilities: Preliminary Report to Commissioner John A. Calhoun.* Boston: Department of Youth Services. Mimeographed.

————. 1976. *The Department of Youth Services, 1976: Progress Report.* Boston: Department of Youth Services. Mimeographed.

————. 1977. Budget Data for 1977 and 1978. Boston: Department of Youth Services. Mimeographed.

State of Michigan. April 1976. *Final Report of the Joint Legislative Committee to Study Community Placement in Michigan.* Lansing, Mich.: House of Representatives, Committee on Appropriations.

State of Minnesota, Cambridge State Hospital. May 1975. *June 1925 to June 1975. 50 Years for CSH.* Cambridge, Minn.: Cambridge State Hospital. Mimeographed.

State of Minnesota Chemical Dependency Division. June 1975. *A Policy Change toward Public Drunkenness: Minnesota's Experience with Detoxification Programs.* St. Paul, Minn.: Department of Public Welfare.

State of Minnesota Department of Corrections. January 1977. *Impact of the Community Corrections Act on Sentencing Patterns,* prepared by K. Larimore. St. Paul, Minn.: Department of Corrections.

————. June 1977. *The Effect of the Availability of Community Residential Alternatives to State Incarceration on Sentencing Practices: The Social Control Issue,* prepared by K. Knapp. St. Paul, Minn.: Department of Corrections.

State of Minnesota Department of Public Welfare. October 1975. *Title XX Minnesota Comprehensive Annual Services Program Plan, Oct. 1, 1975–Sept. 30, 1976.* St. Paul, Minn.: Department of Public Welfare.

————. October 1976. *Final Plan: Title XX, Oct. 1, 1976–Sept. 30, 1977.* St. Paul, Minn.: Department of Public Welfare.

————. October 1977. *Proposed Plan: Title XX, Oct. 1, 1977–Sept. 30, 1978.* St. Paul, Minn.: Department of Public Welfare.

————. November 1977. *DPW Rule 34: Standard For the Operation of Residential Facilities and Services for Persons who are Mentally Retarded.* St. Paul, Minn.: Department of Public Welfare. Mimeographed.

————. June 1977. Memo. Role of the State Institutions in the Continuum of Care, prepared by J. Doyle Kirby. St. Paul, Minn.: Department of Public Welfare.

State of Minnesota Mental Retardation Program Division. February 1977. *An Analysis of Minnesota's Effort to Reintegrate Its Mentally Retarded Citizens into the Community.* St. Paul, Minn.: Department of Public Welfare. Mimeographed.

———. February 1977. *Report to the Minnesota Legislature concerning Trends in Mental Retardation Services.* St. Paul, Minn.: Department of Public Welfare. Mimeographed.

———. July 1977. Memo. Role and Function of State Institutions, prepared by A. Wrobel, director. St. Paul, Minn.: Department of Public Welfare.

State of New Jersey Division of Mental Retardation. June 1978. *Plan to Address the Impact of the Conversion of New Jersey State Schools for the Retarded to ICF/MR Facilities on the Displaced Population.* Trenton, N.J.: Mental Retardation Planning Project. Mimeographed.

State of New Jersey State Commission of Investigation. April 1977. *Property Cost Reimbursement System for Nursing Home Participation in the New Jersey Medicaid Program.* Trenton, N.J.: New Jersey State Commission of Investigation.

———. November 1978. *Abuses and Irregularities in New Jersey's Boarding Home Industry.* Trenton, N.J.: State Commission of Investigation.

State of New York. March 1976. *Mental Health in New York.* Report to Speaker from Assembly Joint Committee to Study Department of Mental Hygiene. Albany, N.Y.: Assembly Committee on Mental Health and Ways and Means Committee.

State of New York Department of Social Services. 1975. *Report on Provision of Child Welfare Services in New York State, 1974–1975.* Albany, N.Y.: New York State Department of Social Services. Reprinted in U.S. Senate Committee on Labor and Public Welfare, pt. 1 : 665–714.

———. 1976. *Foster Care Needs and Alternatives to Placement: A Plan for Action.* Albany, N.Y.: New York State Department of Social Services. Reprinted in U.S. Senate Committee on Labor and Public Welfare, pt. 1 : 715–732.

State of New York Moreland Act Commission. January 1976. *Reimbursement of Nursing Home Property Costs: Pruning the Money Tree.* Albany, N.Y.: Report of the New York State Moreland Act Commission on Nursing Homes and Related Facilities.

State of Pennsylvania Division of Community Living Arrangements of Office of Mental Retardation. 1976. *Community Living Arrangements Plan (Five-year Projection) Fiscal Years 1976–77 through 1980–81.* Harrisburg, Pa.: Department of Public Welfare. Mimeographed.

———. 1973–77. *Population and Dispersal Report* (through June 1974 and 1975). Harrisburg, Pa.: Department of Public Welfare. Mimeographed.

State of Pennsylvania Legislative Budget and Finance Committee. February 1975. *A Program Evaluation Report on the Small Unit Residential Treatment Program for the Mentally Retarded.* Harrisburg, Pa.: State Senate and House of Representatives. Mimeographed.

———. August 1976. *Follow-up Report of Evaluation Report on the Department of Public Welfare Community Living Arrangements Program for the Mentally Retarded.* Harrisburg, Pa.: State Senate and House of Representatives. Mimeographed.

Stein, L. I., and Test, M. A. 1978. *Alternatives to Mental Hospital Treatment.* New York: Plenum Press.

Steiner, G. Y., with assistance of Milius, P. H. 1976. *The Children's Cause.* Washington, D.C.: The Brookings Institution.

Thalheimer, D. 1975. *Cost Analysis of Correctional Standards: Halfway Houses*, 2 vols. Prepared for U.S. Law Enforcement Assistance Administration under a Contract to the American Bar Association, Correctional Economics Center. Washington, D.C.: U.S. Government Printing Office.

Thomas, G. 1975. *Is Statewide Deinstitutionalization of Children's Services A Forward or Backward Social Movement?* Urbana, Ill.: University of Illinois School of Social Work.

Tizzard, J.; Sinclair, J.; and Clark, R. J. 1975. *Varieties of Residential Experience*. London: Routledge & Kegan Paul.

U.S. Bureau of the Census. 1883. *Report on the Defective, Dependent, and Delinquent Classes of the Population of the U.S. 1880*. Washington, D.C.: U.S. Government Printing Office.

————. 1905. *Benevolent Institutions, 1904*. Washington, D.C.: U.S. Government Printing Office.

————. 1906. *Insane and Feeble-Minded in Hospitals and Institutions*, 1904. Washington, D.C.: U.S. Government Printing Office.

————. 1906. *Paupers in Almshouses, 1904*. Washington, D.C.: U.S. Government Printing Office.

————. 1907. *Prisoners and Juvenile Delinquents in Institutions, 1904*. Washington, D.C.: U.S. Government Printing Office.

————. 1913. *Benevolent Institutions, 1910*. Washington, D.C.: U.S. Government Printing Office.

————. 1910. *Insane and Feeble-Minded in Institutions, 1910*. Washington, D.C.: U.S. Government Printing Office.

————. 1915. *Paupers in Almshouses, 1910*. Washington, D.C.: U.S. Government Printing Office.

————. 1918. *Prisoners and Juvenile Delinquents in the United States, 1910*. Washington, D.C.: U.S. Government Printing Office.

————. 1926. *Feeble-Minded and Epileptics in Institutions, 1923*. Washington, D.C.: U.S. Government Printing Office.

————. 1926. *Patients in Hospitals for Mental Disease, 1923*. Washiington, D.C.: U.S. Government Printing Office.

————. 1926. *Prisoners, 1923*. Washington, D.C.: U.S. Government Printing Office.

————. 1927. *Children under Institutional Care, 1923*. Washington, D.C.: U.S. Government Printing Office.

————. No Date. *Prisoners in State and Federal Prisons and Reformatories, 1926–1929*. Washington, D.C.: U.S. Government Printing Office.

————. 1930–39. *Patients in Hospitals for Mental Disease, 1926–1937*. Washington, D.C.: U.S. Government Printing Office.

————. 1930–39. *Mental Defectives and Epileptics in Institutions, 1926–37*. Washington, D.C.: U.S. Government Printing Office.

————. 1935. *Children under Institutional Care and in Foster Homes, 1933*. Washington, D.C.: U.S. Government Printing Office.

————. 1935. *County and City Jails, 1933*. Washington, D.C.: U.S. Government Printing Office.

————. 1936. *Juvenile Delinquents in Public Institutions, 1933*.

————. 1943. *Special Report on Institutional Population: 14 Years Old and Over, 1940*.

————. 1953. *Institutional Populations, 1950*. Vol. 4, Special Reports, Part 2, Chapter C.

————. 1960. *Historical Statistics of the United States: Colonial Times to 1957*. Washington, D.C.: U.S. Government Printing Office.

————. 1963. *Inmates of Institutions, 1960*. Final Report PC(2)–8A.

————. 1973. *Persons in Institutions and Other Group Quarters*, 1970. Final Report PC(2)–4E.

————. June 1978. *1976 Survey of Institutionalized Persons: A Study of Persons Receiving Long-Term Care*. Current Population Reports Special Studies Series P-23, no. 69. Washington, D.C.: U.S. Government Printing Office.

U.S. Children's Bureau. 1966. *Foster Care of Children: Major National Trends and Prospects*. U.S. Department of Health, Education, and Welfare. Also reprinted in U.S. Senate Committee on Labor and Public Welfare, pt. 1 : 324–34.

U.S. Congressional Budget Office. February 1977. *Long-Term Care for the Elderly and Disabled*. Washington, D.C.: U.S. Government Printing Office.

U.S. Department of Health, Education, and Welfare Division of Program Statistics and Analysis. June 1964. *Characteristics of Recipients of Aid to the Permanently and Totally Disabled. Findings of the 1962 Survey*. Washington, D.C.: U.S. Department of Health, Education, and Welfare. Mimeographed.

U.S. Department of Health, Education, and Welfare National Center for Social Statistics. 1972. *Findings of the 1970 APTD Study*, pts. 1 & 2. DHEW Pub. no. (SRS) 73-63853. Washington, D.C.: Social Rehabilitation Service, U.S. Department of Health, Education, and Welfare.

U.S. Department of Health, Education, and Welfare. 1973. Office of Youth Development. *Strategies for Restructuring the State Department of Youth Services*. (SRS) 73-26034. Washington, D.C.: U.S. Government Printing Office.

————. August 1977. *Comments of the Department of Health, Education, and Welfare on the General Accounting Office Final Report Entitled "Returning the Mentally Disabled to the Community: Government Needs to Do More."* Washington, D.C.: Office of the Secretary. Mimeographed.

————. October 1977. Memo. *Establishment of Task Force on Deinstitutionalization of the Mentally Ill and Mentally Retarded*. Washington, D.C.: Office of the Secretary. Mimeographed.

————. November 1977. *Deinstitutionalization: Introduction and Statement of Major Policy Issues*. Washington, D.C.: Office of the Secretary. Mimeographed.

————. January 1978. *Options to Promote Community-Based Care of the Mentally Disabled*. Washington, D.C.: Office of the Secretary. Mimeographed.

————. March 1978. Department of Health, Education, and Welfare Task Force on the Deinstitutionalization of the Mentally Disabled. Washington, D.C.: Office of the Secretary. Mimeographed.

————. May 1978. Program Interpretation Regarding AFDC Foster Care: Federally Reimbursable Cost Items for AFDC-FC Children Placed by State IV-A Agencies in Private Non-Profit Child Care Situations. Action Transmittal, SSA-AT-78-21 (OFA). Washington, D.C. Mimeographed.

U.S. Federal Security Agency. 1936–40. *Annual Report of the Social Security Board*. 4th report. Washington, D.C.: U.S. Government Printing Office.

————. 1944. *Sheltered Care and Home Services for Public Assistance Recipients*. Public Assistance Report no. 5. Washington, D.C.: U.S. Government Printing Office.

U.S. General Accounting Office. April 1976. *More Can Be Learned and Done about the Well-Being of Children*. Washington, D.C.: General Accounting Office.

————. October 1976. *Greater Assurances Are Needed That Emotionally Disturbed and Handicapped Children Are Properly Cared For in Department of Defense Approved Facilities*. Washington, D.C.: General Accounting Office.

————. January 1977. *Returning the Mentally Disabled to the Community: Government Needs to Do More*. Washington, D.C.: General Accounting Office.

————. February 1977. *Children in Foster-Care Institutions*. Washington, D.C.: General Accounting Office.

————. April 1977. *The Well-Being of Older People in Cleveland, Ohio*. Washington, D.C.: General Accounting Office.

————. December 1977. *Home Health—The Need for a National Policy To Better Provide for the Elderly*. Washington, D.C.: General Accounting Office.

————. January 1979. *Problems in Auditing Medicaid Nursing Homes*. Washington, D.C.: General Accounting Office.

————. November 1979. *Entering a Nursing Home—Costly Implications for Medicaid and the Elderly*. Washington, D.C.: General Accounting Office.

————. June 1980. *Problems Remain in Reviews of Medicaid Financed Drug Therapy in Nursing Homes*. Washington, D.C.: General Accounting Office.

————. September 1980. *Evaluation of Alternatives for Financing Low and Moderate Income Rental Housing*. Washington, D.C.: General Accounting Office.

U.S. Health Care Financing Administration. 1979–80. *Health Care Financing Review*. Washington, D.C.: Office of Research, Demonstrations, and Statistics of HCFA, Department of Health, Education, and Welfare.

U.S. House of Representatives. 1962. *Compilation of the Social Security Laws*. House Document no. 616. Washington, D.C.: U.S. Government Printing Office.

————. 1973. *Compilation of the Social Security Laws*. House Document 93-117, vol. 1. Washington, D.C.: U.S. Government Printing Office.

U.S. Law Enforcement Assistance Administration. 1974. *Children in Custody, 1971*. Washington, D.C.: National Criminal Justice Information and Statistics Service.

————. March 1975. *Program Announcement: Deinstitutionalization of Status Offenders*, prepared by Juvenile Justice and Delinquency Prevention Operations Task Group. Washington, D.C.: National Criminal Justice Information and Statistics Service.

————. May 1975. *The Nation's Jails*. Washington, D.C.: National Criminal Justice Information and Statistics Service.

————. May 1975. *Children in Custody, 1972–73*. Washington, D.C.: National Criminal Justice Information and Statistics Service.

————. 1976. *Community-Based Alternatives to Juvenile Incarceration*. Series A, no. 7. Washington, D.C.: U.S. Government Printing Office.

————. February 1977. *Children in Custody, 1974*. Washington, D.C.: U.S. Government Printing Office.

————. August 1977. *Secure Detention of Juveniles and Alternatives to Its Use*. Prepared by T. M. Young and D. M. Pappenfort. Washington, D.C.: U.S. Government Printing Office.

U.S. Law Enforcement Assistance Administration, National Criminal Justice Information and Statistics Service. 1975. *Sourcebook of Criminal Justice Statistics—1974*. Washington, D.C.: U.S. Government Printing Office.

―――. 1977. *Sourcebook of Criminal Justice Statistics—1976*. Washington, D.C.: U.S. Government Printing Office.

―――. October 1977. *Children in Custody, 1975*. Washington, D.C.: U.S. Government Printing Office.

―――. 1978. *Sourcebook of Criminal Justice Statistics—1977*. Washington, D.C.: U.S. Government Printing Office.

U.S. Law Enforcement Assistance Administration, National Institute of Law Enforcement. August 1977. Series A, no. 18. Washington, D.C.: U.S. Government Printing Office.

U.S. Law Enforcement Assistance Administration, Office of Juvenile Justice and Delinquency Prevention. September 1975. *The First Analysis and Evaluation of Federal Juvenile Deliquency Programs*. 2 vols. Washington, D.C.: U.S. Government Printing Office.

―――. 1976. *Second Analysis and Evaluation of Federal Juvenile Delinquency Programs*. 2 vols. Washington, D.C.: U.S. Government Printing Office.

―――. 1977. *Juvenile Correctional Reform in Massachusetts: A Preliminary Report of the Center for Criminal Justice of the Harvard Law School*. Washington, D.C.: U.S. Government Printing Office.

U.S. Office of Federal Register. April 1978. *Code of Federal Register*, vol. 20, pts. 400–499. Washington, D.C.: U.S. Government Printing Office.

―――. August 1978. *Code of Federal Register*, vol. 43, pt. 159, pp. 36,402–10.

U.S. Senate Committee on Finance. April 1978. *The Social Security Act and Related Laws, April 1978 Edition*. Washington, D.C.: U.S. Government Printing Office.

U.S. Senate Committee on the Judiciary. May 1977. *Juvenile Justice and Delinquency Prevention Act of 1974, As Amended through October 3, 1977*. Washington, D.C.: U.S. Government Printing Office.

U.S. Senate Committee on Labor and Public Welfare, and U.S. House of Representatives Subcommittee on Select Education of the Committee on Education and Labor. December 1975. *Foster Care: Problems and Issues*. Joint Hearings, pt. 1. Washington, D.C.: U.S. Government Printing Office.

―――. September 1976. *Foster Care: Problems and Issues*. Joint Hearings, pt. 2. Washington, D.C.: U.S. Government Printing Office.

―――. October 1971. *Alternatives to Nursing Home Care: A Proposal*, prepared by staff specialists at the Levinson Gerontological Policy Institute, Brandeis University. Washington, D.C.: U.S. Government Printing Office.

U.S. Senate Special Committee on Aging. November 1971. *Mental Health Care and the Elderly: Shortcomings in Public Policy*. Report no. 92-433. Washington, D.C.: U.S. Government Printing Office.

―――. July 1973. *Home Health Services in the U.S.* Washington, D.C., U.S. Government Printing Office.

―――. November 1975. *Congregate Housing for Older Adults*. Report no. 94-478, prepared by Marie McGuire Thompson. Washington, D.C.: U.S. Government Printing Office.

―――. 1975. *Adult Day Facilities for Treatment, Health Care, and Related Services*, prepared by Brahna Trager, University of California. Washington, D.C.: U.S. Government Printing Office.

U.S. Senate Subcommittee on the Handicapped of the Commitee on Labor. August 1976.

Education of the Handicapped Act As Amended through December 31, 1975. Washington, D.C.: U.S. Government Printing Office.

U.S. Senate Subcommittee on Long-Term Care of the Special Committee on Aging. December 1974. *Nursing Home Care in the United States: Failure in Public Policy.* Report no. 93-1420. Washington, D.C.: U.S. Government Printing Office.

————. 1975–76. *Supporting Paper Nos. 1–9.* Washington, D.C.: U.S. Government Printing Office.

U.S. Senate Subcommittee on Long-Term Care of the Special Committee on Aging, and the U.S. House of Representatives Subcommittee on Health and Long-Term Care of the Select Committee on Aging. October 1975. *Proprietary Home Health Care.* Joint Hearing. Washington, D.C.: U.S. Government Printing Office.

U.S. Senate Subcommittee to Investigate Juvenile Delinquency. April 1975. *Ford Administration Stifles Juvenile Justice Program.* Hearings on Assessment of Implementation of the Juvenile Justice and Delinquency Prevention Act of 1974. Washington, D.C.: U.S. Government Printing Office.

U.S. Social Security Administration. 1933–80. *Social Security Bulletin.* Washington, D.C.: U.S. Government Printing Office.

————. 1966–73. *Social Security Programs in the United States.* Washington, D.C.: U.S. Government Printiing Office.

————. 1974. *1967 National Survey of Institutionalized Adult Residents of Long-Term Medical Care Institutions.* Research Report no. 46. Washington, D.C.: U.S. Government Printing Office.

————. 1974, 1976, 1980. *Social Security Bulletin: Annual Statistical Supplement.* Washington, D.C.: U.S. Government Printing Office.

————. 1976. *The Supplemental Security Income Program for the Aged, Blind, and Disabled: Selected Characteristics of State Supplementation Programs.* U.S. Department of Health, Education, and Welfare, Social Security Administration. Office of Research and Statistics. Prepared by Donald E. Rigby and Malcolm H. Morrison. HEW Pub. no. (SSA) 76-11975. Washington, D.C.: U.S. Government Printing Office.

————. 1977. *Program and Demographic Characteristics of Supplemental Beneficiaries, 1975 and 1976.* HEW Pub. nos. (SSA) 77–11977 and (SSA) 78–11977. Washington, D.C.: U.S. Government Printing Office.

U.S. Social Security Administration, Office of Research and Statistics. 1976–78. *Research and Statistics Note(s).* U.S. Department of Health, Education, and Welfare. Washington, D.C.

University of Massachusetts Institute for Governmental Services. 1977. *The Children's Puzzle: A Study of Services to Children in Massachusetts.* Boston: University of Massachusetts.

University of Minnesota Developmental Disabilities Project on Residential Services and Community Adjustment. 1978. *Project Overview,* Brief no. 1. Minneapolis: University of Minnesota.

————. 1978. *1977 Survey Completed. Community Residential Findings Summarized,* Brief no. 2. Minneapolis: University of Minnesota.

————. 1979. 1977 *National Summary between Public and Community Residential Findings,* Brief no. 3. Minneapolis: University of Minnesota.

Vinter, R.; Downs, G.; and Hall, J. 1975. *Juvenile Corrections in the States: Residential*

Programs and Deinstitutionalization. National Assessment of Juvenile Corrections. Ann Arbor: University of Michigan.

Vladeck, B. C. 1980. *Unloving Care: The Nursing Home Tragedy*. New York: Basic Books.

Warner, A. G. 1908. *American Charities*. New York: Russell and Russell. Revision of 1894 edition by M. R. Coolidge, and reissued in 1971 by Russell and Russell, a division of Atheneum Publishers.

Weisbrod, B.; Test, M.; and Stein, L. 1980. An Alternative to Mental Hospital Treatment: Economic Benefit-Cost Analysis. *Archives of General Psychiatry* (in press).

Windle, C., and Scully, D. 1976. Community Mental Health Centers and the Decreasing Use of State Mental Hospitals. *Community Mental Health Journal* 12, no. 3:239–43.

Wing, J. 1978. Planning and Evaluating Services for Chronically Handicapped Psychiatric Patients in the United Kingdom. In *Alternatives to Mental Hospital Treatment*, edited by L. Stein and M. Test. New York: Plenum.

Witkin, M. J. 1976. *State and County Mental Hospitals, United States, 1973–74*. In National Institute of Mental Health, *Mental Health Facility Reports*, Series A, no. 17. Washington, D.C.: U.S. Government Printing Office.

———. September 1980. Trends in Patient Care Episodes in Mental Health Facilities, 1955–77. National Institute of Mental Health, *Statistical Note*, no. 154. Washington, D.C.: U.S. Government Printing Office.

Wolfensberger, W. 1972. *The Principle of Normalization in Human Services*. Toronto: National Institute of Mental Retardation.

———. 1976. *The Origin and Nature of Our Institutional Models*. In President's Committee on Mental Retardation, *Changing Patterns in Residential Services for the Mentally Retarded*, pp. 35–83. Washington, D.C.: U.S. Government Printing Office.

Wolfensberger, W., and Glenn, L. 1975. *Pass 3* (Program Analysis of Service Systems Field Manual and Handbook). 3d ed. Toronto: National Institute of Mental Retardation.

Wolpert, J., and Wolpert, E. R. 1976. The Relocation of Released Mental Hospital Patients into Residential Communities. *Policy Sciences* 7:31–51.

Wyatt v. *Stickney*. 1972. 344 Federal Supplement 373 (Northern District, Alabama, 1972).

Index